DO
WHAT
YOU
WANT

DO WHAT YOU WANT

THE STORY OF BAD RELIGION

by

BAD RELIGION
with JIM RULAND

hachette
BOOKS
NEW YORK

Hachette Books
Hachette Book Group
1290 Avenue of the Americas
New York, NY 10104
HachetteBooks.com
Twitter.com/HachetteBooks
Instagram.com/HachetteBooks

First Edition: August 2020

Published by Hachette Books, an imprint of Perseus Books, LLC, a
subsidiary of Hachette Book Group, Inc. The Hachette Books name
and logo is a trademark of the Hachette Book Group.

The publisher is not responsible for websites (or their content) that are not
owned by the publisher.

The Hachette Speakers Bureau provides a wide range of authors for
speaking events. To find out more, go to www.hachettespeakersbureau.com
or call (866) 376-6591.

Print book interior design by Jeff Williams

Library of Congress Cataloging-in-Publication Data has been applied for.

ISBNs: 978-0-306-92222-0 (hardcover); 978-0-306-92473-6 (signed edition);
978-0-306-92472-9 (BN.com signed edition); 978-0-306-92224-4 (e-book)

LSC-C

10 9 8 7 6 5 4 3 2 1

FOR OUR FANS

CONTENTS

Introduction: A Dangerous Dissonance   ix

1   WELCOME TO THE HELL HOLE   1

2   I CAN DO THAT   14

3   LIVE FROM PURGATORY BEACH   21

4   LIFE ALONE IS SUCH A CURSE   33

5   SOMETHING BUT NOTHING   47

6   MUSIC FOR WEIRDOS   58

7   NEW LEAF   71

8   GO WEST   78

9   JERKING BACK AND FORTH   84

10   DO WHAT YOU WANT   92

11   SOMETHING MORE   104

12   SWIMMING UPSTREAM   117

13   ELEVEN WAYS OF LOOKING AT GOD   131

14	THE SWORD OF PROGRESS	141
15	A SUBTLE FUCK YOU	157
16	COLLAPSE	176
17	FASTEST DRIVER DRIVES THE CAR	186
18	A TANGLED WEB OF LOGIC AND PASSION	196
19	UNTETHERED FROM REALITY	207
20	PARADISE LOST	220
21	A SHITTY BAND LIKE YOURS	229
22	THE HURTING GROUND	240
23	SHOCK AND AWFUL	250
24	EVOLUTION OF REVOLUTION	260
25	HERE WE GO AGAIN	268
26	THE WORLD AND ELSEWHERE	279
27	THE END OF HISTORY	290
	Acknowledgments	305
	Discography	308
	Index	309

Introduction

A DANGEROUS DISSONANCE

"**T**HIS ISN'T ART, THIS IS SUICIDE!"
These words, snarled into a mic in a sweltering garage by Greg Graffin, Bad Religion's fifteen-year-old singer, were the first the band recorded. The song "Sensory Overload" was written by seventeen-year-old Brett Gurewitz while he and Greg were students at El Camino Real High School in Woodland Hills, California. The statement lands with the blunt force of a teenage manifesto but is layered with truths, taunts, and misconceptions.

The year was 1980 and there was nothing new about punk. The Damned had made their first appearance in L.A. three years before, and the Clash came not long after. The Sex Pistols had already walked off the stage forever at Winterland back in January of 1978. The Ramones were on the verge of releasing their *fifth* studio album, and English post-punk rockers Bauhaus, Siouxsie and the Banshees, and the Cure were staging their invasions of New York.

Yet, in Los Angeles, punk rock remained a vital force. Original L.A. punk bands like the Screamers, the Weirdos, the Bags, and the Plugz had to make room for hardcore upstarts like Black Flag and the Adolescents. Wary of the violent fans these bands were attracting, bookers and owners at many music venues banned hardcore punk bands from performing, and there were few places for groups just starting out to play. But that didn't stop new acts from forming. Fueled by fans farther from Hollywood's epicenter, surfers and skaters brought new levels of athleticism and aggression to shows.

The only thing that seemed to set Bad Religion apart from their Southern California contemporaries was that they were kids from Woodland Hills, a suburban community deep in the western reaches of the San Fernando Valley, a place maligned for its cookie-cutter homogeneity. If Hollywood was L.A.'s punk playground, its antithesis was the Valley. So how did four high school kids, two of whom would drop out of school, find a way to separate from the pack?

They weren't the first punk rockers from the Valley, nor were they the last. The sounds they made in their blast furnace of a garage were not particularly original, nor did the band's members ooze the kind of musical talent that signals a brilliant career. In fact, some of them were just becoming familiar with their gear. But they had one asset that made them stand out from the start: their intelligence.

In 1980, punk still had the power to provoke, and Bad Religion's evocative opening salvo suggested a shift from punk as artful expression to a philosophical imperative. While "Sensory Overload," like much of Bad Religion's early material, walks the line of nihilist negation, it stops well short of declarations of "Smash the state!" or "Fuck the LAPD!" that do nothing to advance an argument and are anathema to critical thinking.

Fusing the creativity of original L.A. punk bands like the Germs and X with the ferocity of their hardcore offspring, Bad Religion wrote songs that demanded its listeners think about the world around them and their place in it. This was a band with a unique worldview that had something to say. Their name and uncompromising logo—a white cross with a red slash through it, known today throughout the world as "the crossbuster"—signaled their rejection of the status quo at a time when Christian conservatism was bleeding into mainstream American culture.

Bad Religion arrived at just the right moment to say, "I think about what's true and what are lies." This outlook commanded the attention of millions of angry and increasingly disaffected youth—not just in the Valley or Los Angeles or even Southern California, but all over the world. Bad Religion's subversive spirit and thought-provoking lyrics made it okay to be rebellious *and* intellectual. The music is punk but the message is universal, and the lyrics in the band's impressive catalog of songs are more relevant now than ever. That's what makes Bad Religion's bold beginning so ironic. Its first recording wasn't "suicide," but the start of a forty-year career in rock and roll that continues to this day.

It wasn't easy. Along the way they broke up, drifted apart, and came back stronger than before. This is the story of how a group of teenagers from the Valley took L.A. by storm, lost everything, and worked their way back with a series of influential albums that changed the way America thinks about punk rock. But to understand how Bad Religion's unique sound paved the way for the mainstream success of punk rock bands that came after them, you have to go back to a blistering hot garage deep in the San Fernando Valley . . .

1

WELCOME TO THE HELL HOLE

THE STORY OF THE EARLY L.A. PUNK SCENE TAKES place in Hollywood, but many of the scene's prime movers were from the San Fernando Valley. One of the first L.A. bands to make its mark—the Dickies—was from the Valley. When Lee Ving started Fear he was living in Van Nuys. John and Dix Denney of the Weirdos, a band whose image helped put the L.A. punk scene on the map, hailed from North Hollywood, a short hop over the Hollywood Hills.

L.A. has always played fast and loose with its geography. The city's many film and television studios have made use of its abundant sunshine to create the impression that downtown L.A. was a car chase away from the beach with stops in Hollywood and Beverly Hills along the way. But the reality is more nuanced, and always has been. The boys from Black Flag, for instance, grew up closer to the surf and the sand than the Beach Boys. Although Frank Zappa's 1982 song "Valley Girl" suggests the Valley is a Hollywood-adjacent neighborhood that locates the Sherman Oaks Galleria as its cultural center, the Valley is actually a region of over 250 square miles and home to 1.77 million people.

The part of the Valley that Bad Religion came from was closer to the Ventura County Line than to Hollywood's city limits. It was as suburban as suburban gets, and El Camino Real High School was a typical suburban school. It had a large open campus, a renowned football team and cheerleading squad, and a decent track record of sending kids to college so they could become productive members of society.

Improbably, El Camino Real was also the birthplace of one of the most influential punk rock bands in America. When classes started up in the fall of 1979, Greg Graffin showed up for his sophomore year with dyed black hair and a Black Flag T-shirt. Jay Bentley had cut his hair short and came to class with a T-shirt that declared "VIRGIN." "I guess we're it," Jay said of the virtually non-existent punk scene at the school.

The two sophomores had both gone to Hale Junior High, so they were familiar with each other. They had many mutual friends but bonded over their love of music. There weren't any other punks at El Camino Real, but that would soon change.

Brett Gurewitz and Jay Ziskrout were both juniors and had already been in two bands together. The first, the Omega Band, never made it out of Ziskrout's parents' living room. They had a bit more success with their second attempt, the Quarks. They were a Beatles-esque group that leaned toward New Wave. Brett wrote songs, played guitar, and sang. Ziskrout played drums. Their one live gig was the afternoon talent show at El Camino Real.

Brett's best friend, Tom Clement, knew Greg, who'd bragged to Tom that he was a really good singer. Tom had "gone punk" and was encouraging Brett to do the same by starting a band with Greg. "Tom was smart enough to see that his two friends would make a good team when he introduced me to Brett," Greg said. "We were both nerdy intellectual types. Even though we were young kids, it was a meeting of the minds."

Brett, however, was reluctant to take the plunge into punk rock. "I had long hair like Ric Ocasek or Joey Ramone," Brett said. "I was getting ready to go punk. Tom had already gone all the way. I had a homemade T-shirt that said, 'FUCK YOU, I'M A LONGHAIR PUNK!' I was afraid to cut my hair. It was a big deal back then."

Tom introduced Greg to Brett at El Camino Real. Brett knew Greg's older brother, Grant, but had never met Greg. From the very beginning Greg was drawn to Brett's experience. "I would always tell Tom, 'I want to be in a band so bad!' but in my brain there was just no way because I didn't know anything. How do you make a band? So, when Brett and I got together, I looked up to Brett because he had all of the equipment. He had knowledge that I didn't have about how to make this thing work. He had the know-how."

Or, as Brett put it, "I had a PA."

Despite the fact that Greg used to tease Brett about his long hair, their desire to make music together solidified that spring when they went to the Hollywood Palladium together to see the Ramones. Brett was so inspired by the show that he wanted to start a band right away. "I know this is a bit of a cliché," Brett said, "and the Ramones are considered the Johnny Appleseeds of punk, but in my case it's truly what happened. Before the Ramones all my musical heroes were either virtuosos or rock stars. But when I found the Ramones I instantly thought, *This is something I can do.*"

The three teenagers agreed to meet at Jay Ziskrout's house for a rehearsal. Brett brought a song he'd written called "Sensory Overload." Greg had written a song on his mother's spinet piano called "Politics." They taught each other the songs and practiced them in the living room. When they had the songs down cold they made a tape recording.

They couldn't have known it then, but this rehearsal established a precedent for how the band would make music together for the next forty years. Brett and Greg would each write songs and bring them to rehearsal. They weren't riffs or melodies or bits of music, but complete songs with lyrics and titles. Then, when the band got together, the songs would evolve as the various musicians provided feedback. The manner in which Brett and Greg share their songs has changed over the years with the development of new technology, but the methodology has stayed the same: the songs are written independently and brought to the group for refinement.

Brett was impressed with Greg's talent and determination. "That very first rehearsal when we didn't have a bass player," Brett recalled, "I brought a song and Greg brought a song. Greg taught me his song on guitar. I taught him how to sing my song. We played them and they went well together."

Although everyone was happy with how the rehearsal went, they wanted to know what they sounded like with a bass guitar in the mix. The following Monday at school, Greg enlisted Jay Bentley, who remembered the conversation like this:

GREG: You're going to play in our band.
JAY: Okay. I have a guitar.
GREG: We already have a guitar player. You're going to play bass.
JAY: Okay. I don't have a bass.
GREG: Here are some songs we wrote. Can you find a bass?
JAY: Oh, fuck. Okay.

This, too, established a pattern for how they recruited band members from their immediate circle of friends. This speaks to how small the L.A. punk scene was even in 1980. According to Jay, "There was no one else to ask. I was already there."

Jay pleaded with his parents to buy him a bass guitar. "There was a lot of bargaining. 'I'll mow the lawn three times! I'll take the trash out forever!' My stepdad was a big Sears guy. So we went to Sears and bought a bass. It was a three-quarter jazz bass, a kid's bass. I didn't know shit about anything. So I got a three-quarter jazz bass and rented an amp from the guitar shop down the street."

Being new to the bass, Jay didn't know how to play, so he mimicked what Brett did during rehearsal. He quickly figured out the notes that corresponded with the barre chords and followed along.

Jay felt intimidated during that first rehearsal because he was a total neophyte and Brett and Ziskrout were older and had been in bands. "These guys aren't fucking around!" Jay said. "It was go time. I think we only had three songs so we played them a hundred times. I wasn't any good but it was fun."

But what Jay lacked in experience he made up for with an abundance of enthusiasm. Even though Jay didn't know how to play his instrument, Greg liked what he heard. "When [Bentley] came to our next rehearsal to play in [Ziskrout's] living room, it sounded so great with a bass."

After rehearsal they immediately discussed when they were going to do it again. But first they had to come up with a name.

"We were sitting in my mom's living room," Ziskrout recalled, "wondering what to call the band. We threw out all kinds of crazy names. I think it was Brett who said, 'How about Bad Religion?' We all loved it because the name went well beyond just religion. It was a reaction against adopting a system of thought. Here's what you're supposed to think, here's what you're supposed to believe. Our ethos was in opposition to walking through life like sheep."

The name resonated with Greg even though he had very little exposure to organized religion. "I was raised in a household that was devoid of any religious training because my mom was scarred by it. I didn't get any influence from religion. I didn't know the stories of the Bible. But I would say I was spiritual because when my teacher assigned Herman Hesse, I really enjoyed it. When my teacher assigned Thoreau, I loved it. I found myself driven to study nature and Buddhist philosophy. That was far more interesting to me. At those early rehearsals we didn't have a name, but when we became Bad Religion it made sense to me."

Brett felt an immediate kinship with his younger classmate, Greg. "We were quite lucky that we found each other," Brett said. "I would say that I was agnostic at a very, very young age, even though I had some religious training from my parents, which was really just for traditional purposes so I could have my bar mitzvah. I found myself to be profoundly skeptical of it. I came out of that not as an atheist, because I was always very interested in philosophy, but as an agnostic and possibly a pantheist. Most kids read *Siddhartha* in junior high and don't like it. I was really engaged by that kind of thing and Greg was too. I was into Western philosophy and the philosophy of the East and was skeptical of the religious training that I was exposed to."

Brett's attempts to synthesize what he was learning and seek answers to life's bigger questions set him apart from other students. To Ziskrout's way of thinking, the band was an extension of those interests. "Brett was a philosopher before most kids started thinking along those lines," Ziskrout said. "He was always giving me books to read."

The name Bad Religion provided a framework for the kind of band they wanted to be. It established an organizing principle and immediately made their position clear on a number of social issues. For Greg, the name "Bad Religion gave us a point of view," he said. "We were angry young men, there was no question about it, and as punks we needed to be against something. Whether we had a legitimate right to be angry as white kids in America in 1980, I'll leave that for others to decide, but we were. It's easy to do a post hoc analysis as to why we called it that, but it turned out to be very fruitful for us, in more ways than one. The name really allowed us a wide breadth of themes."

"If your name is Wasted Youth," Brett added, "it's tough to stay on message when you're fifty-five."

Even more eye-catching than their name was their logo: A cross with a slash through it. Brett came to rehearsal at Jay Ziskrout's living room with the drawing on a piece of cardboard, exclaiming, "I got it!"

Greg immediately realized they had something special. "I knew right then that was the one."

When Brett fleshed the logo out, he intentionally used red, white, and black, colors associated with the swastika, the symbol of the Nazi Party. "It wasn't uncommon to see people wearing swastikas in the early punk scene," Brett said. "I thought kids were probably wearing it for shock value, but I wasn't comfortable with that, and I could never wear one. The red, white, and black crossbuster is a strong, shocking icon. As a young Jewish kid, it was something I could wear that was equally shocking as a swastika."

In a relatively short period of time they'd settled on a name and a logo, but they also talked at length about how they wanted to present their ideas and how they wanted the band to be perceived.

They agreed to keep practicing, but the intensity of their rehearsals made it difficult to stay in one place for long. They went from Ziskrout's living room to Brett's garage, but the neighbors complained. They tried Jay's house and someone called the cops on them almost immediately. "We finally settled on Graffin's garage," Jay said, "because that seemed to be the only place that we couldn't get kicked out of."

That had as much to do with Greg's mother, Marcella, as it did their neighbors in Canoga Park. Marcella trusted her sons and didn't put down a lot of rules. "I didn't judge that way," she said. "They were just kids. When they transitioned into the band it seemed like it happened overnight. I had to move all my stuff to one side of the garage. I didn't ask too many questions. I would rather they be there than someplace else."

Despite having been raised in a religious family, Marcella wasn't offended by the band's name. "I loved it," Marcella said. "I really did. When the kids were asked why they named the band Bad Religion, they would say different things. What Greg said to me and to others was that anything could be a Bad Religion. If you give up your sense of independent thought and you're not thinking for yourself, then that's a Bad Religion. Well, of course, that appealed to me. I didn't have negative feelings about the name at all."

That said, there was one incident involving Jay Ziskrout that left a sour taste in her mouth. "I didn't care if they were in the house. For the most part they were not destructive. But one of Greg's friends was making himself at home. Not only was he going to the refrigerator and getting milk to drink, he was drinking straight out of the carton!"

There were also complaints about the noise. The boys tried to appease the neighbors by dampening the sound with egg cartons and foam—with limited success. "I was always impressed by the things they were doing," Marcella recalled. "Not necessarily by the level of noise, although the noise never really bothered me."

Brett christened their practice space by spray-painting "WEL-COME TO THE HELL HOLE" on the wall inside the garage. "The Hell Hole was the name that made sense," Jay said. "I don't think it had a whole lot of meaning. It was the fucking Valley. It was a million degrees in the garage but we didn't care. We would take off our shirts and sweat for hours and hours and hours until it got dark."

They continued to write songs and experiment with their sound. "It just kept going," Brett said. "At our next rehearsal, Greg brought another song. And I brought another song. That's how we did it."

Greg added "World War III" and "Slaves" and Brett wrote "Drastic Actions," which was his tribute to the Germs' song "Shut Down." Brett also wrote the iconic "Bad Religion," which the band refers to as their theme song, but back then it served as a mission statement that outlined their core principles and explained the meaning of the band. Consider these lyrics from the first verse:

Spiritual era is gone, it ain't coming back
Bad Religion, a copout that is all that's left

This is a direct commentary, not so much on the decline of spirituality in America, but on the rise of the Moral Majority and TV evangelists like Jimmy Swaggart, Jerry Falwell, and Jim and Tammy Faye Bakker shaking down believers for cash donations.

But if the first verse is a condemnation of the role of religion in society, the second verse makes it personal:

Don't you know the place you live's a piece of shit
Don't you know blind faith through lies won't conquer it
Don't you know responsibility is yours
I don't care a thing about eternal fires . . .
Listen this time it's more than a rhyme
It's your indecision
Your indecision is your
Bad Religion . . .

The shift to direct address at the end of the verse leading into the chorus is nothing less than a call to action for the listener to take responsibility for their beliefs. It's both a challenge to think for yourself and a warning of the perils of "blind faith." The line "Listen this time it's more than a rhyme" is postmodern in its self-awareness, which reinforces the urgency of the message: we're not in peril from the "eternal fires" of hell or even the lies of false prophets, but our own lazy thinking. Rather than railing against organized religion, the song rallies listeners to clarify what they believe. Figure it out for yourself, the song urges, "it's not too late."

Although the band was in its songwriting infancy and its members were all teenagers at the time, the song has a level of sophistication that was rare for hardcore bands of this era. While the music is relentless in its drive to make the listener *feel* something, the lyrics encourage the audience to not just think, but think critically.

As the band became more proficient, the Hell Hole became a hangout for the band's punk friends in the Valley. Sometimes kids would drive out from Hollywood to watch them rehearse as word about Bad Religion spread through punk circles. But it wasn't a party scene. Kids would come by after school and leave before dinnertime, when Greg's mom returned from her job at UCLA.

Interestingly, it didn't occur to the band to look for a place where they could play in front of a live audience. They only had six songs and, due to their habit of recording their garage sessions, were keenly aware they had approximately ten minutes worth of material.

"We used a boom box," Jay recalled. "We just recorded it like that. It wasn't very good but in all honesty it gave us a sense of how long we could play for."

Even with banter between songs their set would be no longer than fifteen minutes, which wasn't enough. Instead, they recorded a demo.

They went to Studio 9, which was located in the Hollywood & Western Building, and had seen better days. While businesses on the ground floor continued to operate, many of the units on the second, third, and fourth floors had been abandoned. Rooms without doors. Windows without glass. Several Hollywood punk squatters called it home and the walls were covered with graffiti.

Amidst this chaos was Studio 9, a one-room recording studio with a low-end eight-track. It cost $15 an hour to record and that came with an engineer. Greg remembered it was a wild-looking place. "There was graffiti everywhere," Greg said. "Not just the studio, but everywhere. There were all these empty rooms with graffiti on the walls."

The walls were adorned with the names of bands that had passed through or were squatting there. So Bad Religion decided to follow suit and leave their mark. "We got some spray paint and started spray-painting Bad Religion all over the place," Brett said. "Which was pretty stupid."

Jay also participated. "We went into one of the empty rooms and painted Bad Religion on the wall. I guess it's not smart to paint Bad Religion on the wall when the name of your band is Bad Religion."

The session didn't take long. They only recorded a few songs, but it was the first time they'd been somewhat professionally recorded, which proved to be an exhilarating experience. When they were sitting in the mixing room listening to the playback,

Brett got so excited that he jumped out of his seat, and his foot accidentally struck the glass surface of the coffee table, shattering it.

"Sorry," Jay said. "We'll totally pay for that."

As exciting as the session was, for Jay it was something of a revelation. "Oh my god! I'm terrible! I was missing notes everywhere and I couldn't play that fast. It was the first time I heard how bad I was."

Nevertheless, they walked out with a demo tape. But later that night Brett received a phone call from the studio manager.

MANAGER: Hey, you sprayed graffiti all over the place, didn't you?

BRETT: Yeah.

MANAGER: Well, you can't do that. That's vandalism. You gotta come out here and clean it up.

BRETT: Really? Because there was already graffiti everywhere.

MANAGER: Well, we don't know who did that, but your name wasn't up all over the place before you got here.

"I'm sure we didn't have to do this," Brett said, "but being stupid kids, we went back to Hollywood and covered up our graffiti."

The experience motivated the band to go back to the Hell Hole and write new material. Now that they'd had a taste of recording, they wanted to make a proper record—just not at Studio 9. They'd made a punk tape in a punk studio, but now they were interested in making something that actually sounded good. This desire to make music that was hard and fast but enjoyable to listen to set Bad Religion apart from its peers. Over the course of their career, their quest to make a perfect-sounding record would seesaw between an aesthetic and an obsession.

Through Ziskrout's drum teacher, they found a modest studio in the garage of the producer's house in Thousand Oaks to record their six-song EP.

For Brett, the experience was occasionally baffling. "We had no idea what we were doing," he confessed. "We had no idea how to make a record. We just had songs and we wanted to record them. Other punk bands made seven-inch records. We knew it was possible to do it. It never occurred to us to maybe get thirty minutes worth of music and play a show first."

Jay was still learning how to use his equipment—and how not to use it. "My little three-quarter jazz bass was a sunburst bass. Black, orange, yellow. I decided I wanted it to be all black because black was way cooler than sunburst. I went to the garage and all I could find was a can of flat black. I sprayed the back of the bass and it looked like rubber. Fucking cool. So I sprayed the front of it. I sprayed the fret board and the strings and the headstock. I didn't realize what I was doing!"

"He did it right before we went to the studio," Greg added. "That's how we got our unique sound on our first EP."

They brought the recording to Gold Star Studios in Hollywood, an iconic independent recording studio at Santa Monica and Vine, to have it mastered. This was a big step up from Studio 9. Phil Spector had learned the art of recording at Gold Star and used its unique acoustics to create his legendary Wall of Sound. The Ramones' *End of the Century*, released earlier that year, had been recorded by Spector at Gold Star.

When they arrived at the studio with their recording, they were greeted by Johnette Napolitano, who was working the reception desk. Johnette was helpful and encouraging and offered all kinds of advice. It didn't hurt that she had purple hair and an affinity for punk.

Once she heard the record, Jay recalled that she was even more forthcoming. "'You know, when you guys do your LP, instead of hiring an engineer that comes with the studio you should have my boyfriend produce it.'" Johnette's boyfriend was her bandmate Jim Mankey, who, along with his brother Earle, was one of the founding members of Sparks. Johnette and Jim were in a band together called Dream 6 and they would go on to form Concrete Blonde.

Johnette's enthusiasm gave the band a boost, but for Brett, being in a professional studio was a transforming experience. "The first time I saw a real studio, I was in love. That set the path for me. Not everyone has this reaction, but when I saw those rows of buttons and lights, I went nuts. I loved it. I thought to myself, *This is for me, I have to learn how to do this!*" He was eager to learn from more experienced musicians, especially those who didn't look down their noses at punk.

Once the songs were mastered, the next step was to get the EP made into an actual record. Brett looked in the phone book and found a record pressing plant. With a loan from his father, Brett got the record made, but it was going to take some time. It was the fall of 1980 and the EP wouldn't be ready to be released until early the next year.

Since they were putting out a record, they needed a name for their label. Greg and Brett came up with the name Epitaph based on the King Crimson song of the same name. The chorus of that song—"Confusion will be our epitaph"—suggests the label name was an offhand way of saying they didn't know what they were doing. Nevertheless, they'd made great strides as a band in a short period of time. They'd written some songs, recorded an EP, and made a demo. Instead of being offered these opportunities, they'd created them for themselves. Aside from rehearsals at the Hell Hole, the only thing Bad Religion hadn't done was perform in front of a live audience. It was time to play some shows.

2

I CAN DO THAT

ONE OF THE DEFINING FEATURES OF THE SAN
Fernando Valley was its overwhelming sameness.
The streets were laid out in a grid of long straight
boulevards, and these thoroughfares stretched for miles in all
directions. The Valley was hemmed in on all sides by mountain
ranges, and the poor air quality and thick smog had a disorienting
effect. To outsiders, one neighborhood varied little from the next.

Locals, of course, knew the difference and could proudly relate the history of each major intersection: first the farmland
was converted to orchards and then transformed by commercial
development into something unique to that particular time and
place. But the similarity of these suburban landscapes made it difficult for those who stood out to blend in. The members of Bad
Religion were acutely aware they didn't fit in, and starting a punk
band only exacerbated the issue. Like outsiders everywhere, they
were ostracized for being out of step.

Luckily, these smart, socially conscious kids found each other
through their passion for music. When they added punk rock to

the mix, they created something that would not only change the course of their lives, but would also have a lasting impact on the music they loved. Despite this bond, each musician took a very different path to becoming a member of Bad Religion.

For Greg it began in Wisconsin and Indiana, the homelands of his parents. In a sense, it started much earlier with his great-grandfather on his mother's side, Edward M. Zerr, a preacher and teacher who traveled the country leading courses in Bible study. During the span of his sixty-year career he delivered more that eight thousand sermons. According to Greg, "He was the first touring act in this family."

Zerr wrote a six-volume commentary on the Bible. He adhered to a strict interpretation of the Old Testament and as such he believed the earth was six thousand years old. Studying the Bible and sharing his findings was his mission, his calling, and his life's work. The conservative church Zerr belonged to prohibited dancing, playing music, and other frivolous pursuits. Even the hymns, which he also wrote, had to be sung without accompaniment.

Zerr's daughter—Greg's grandmother—was very pious and straightlaced, but she was a bit more open-minded than her father. She inherited one surprisingly progressive ideal from him: the value of a good education. She went to college at a time when very few women had the opportunity to pursue an education, and she raised her children to think for themselves. After Greg's mother, Marcella, had graduated from college and had children of her own, she decided not to teach her boys anything about the Bible, but she didn't try to shield her sons from religious music, which she always enjoyed.

After his parents split up, Greg and his older brother Grant divided their time between the family home in Racine, Wisconsin, where his father lived, and his mother's house in the Milwaukee suburbs. Greg grew up playing sports—baseball in the spring and ice hockey in the winter—and excelled at them, but from a very young age, he displayed an aptitude for music.

Greg attended Lake Bluff Elementary in an affluent northern suburb of Milwaukee where Jayne Perkins was in charge of the music department. She taught her students by encouraging them to sing along to popular music of the day. Perkins accompanied the choir on piano and directed them to sing choral arrangements of contemporary classics like "American Pie," "You've Got a Friend," "Age of Aquarius," and "Locomotion."

Greg enjoyed this so much that he joined the choir, where he learned how to harmonize with others. He was often selected as a soloist for concerts that were staged throughout the school year. This led to Greg receiving scholarships to attend summer music camps in Madison, Wisconsin. These experiences gave Greg confidence when he transitioned to punk and smoothed out some of the rougher edges of his vocal delivery.

"I have a very natural delivery," Greg said. "I hear melodies but in my head I'm singing the harmony already. That was the sensibility I brought to Bad Religion. Not the other way around. That comes from my tradition."

In 1976, Greg's mother moved to L.A. to take a job at UCLA. She settled in the San Fernando Valley, where the boys went to school. They spent their summers with their father, Walter, back in Racine. Marcella brought her spinet piano to California and that's where it reclaimed Greg's attention.

"Greg was always pounding on the piano," Marcella said. "He was making music all the time. Every time he passed the piano he would pound out a few chords."

The piano was a source of comfort as Greg navigated the strangeness of being a teenager in Southern California. Kids either conformed by seeking status, conferred by accruing cool clothes and toys, or rebelled by smoking weed and slowly burning out in a haze of rock and roll. Although he knew it meant a slide down the chute of social status, Greg rejected the crushing conformity of high school and pursued his own interests no matter how uncool they were, and there were few things less cool than punk.

Greg's punk rock baptism occurred at the age of fourteen when his girlfriend, who was a year older, dumped him. "I thought I was going to marry this girl. Then she dumped me for a guy who was seventeen. She was kind of preppy and I wanted to be the opposite of what she was. I distinctly remember showing up at school with a buzzed haircut dyed black and shabby clothes."

Greg took advantage of his mother being out of town to make his punk rock transformation. Marcella had invited a friend from Milwaukee to watch the boys while she was away. When Marcella came home her friend was sick with worry because Greg had dyed his hair. She was certain that Marcella would be furious, but instead Greg's mother found the whole incident amusing. "That was Greg's first punk action: to take his hair two shades darker."

Cutting and dyeing his hair and stenciling letters on his T-shirts made Greg the target of ridicule from students and teachers alike. Greg was shocked adults would find his refusal to fit in so upsetting. Some students tried to intimidate him with threats of violence, which only emboldened his commitment to break from the status quo. His transformation into a punk was a reflection of how he felt inside, and not an attempt to draw attention to himself by riling up his peers. Turning punk taught Greg that questioning norms, rejecting dogma, and seeking better answers would invite scorn, which he learned to handle at an early age. Embracing this nonconformist streak set him apart as both a thinker and a singer.

Brett Gurewitz, Greg's songwriting collaborator, couldn't remember a time when he wasn't playing and making music. "My grandmother in New York had a little piano that I used to bang on and she would dance around and hum to me," Brett recalled. "That's one of my earliest memories."

At a young age Brett took accordion lessons and learned to play a few songs. His first record, *Yellow Submarine* by the Beatles, which his parents gave him, ignited a passion for listening to records in his room and then trying to play along with them on his guitar. "I never thought I'd be in a band because all of the bands I loved were so amazing," Brett said. "The Beatles, Cat Stevens, Joe

Cocker, Stevie Wonder, Led Zeppelin, David Bowie. They seemed so unreachable."

The gap began to close after Brett was exposed to punk in 1977. "The Ramones were the first punk record I bought, and when I heard that debut Ramones record, something went off. Not only did I love it—and I really loved it, I was jumping on my bed—but I was instantly playing the songs. *Oh, yeah, there it is. 1-4-5. Wow, that's all you need?* It unlocked every rock and roll song from the fifties for me. It cracked the code of rock and roll. I found it was easier to make up songs than it was to learn them. So I started writing my own songs."

Brett didn't need a reason to write songs. He was a voracious reader, the kind of person who was always searching for answers to big questions. Songwriting gave him a new outlet for expressing his ideas. When the opportunity to join a band presented itself, he was ready. "I was always a creative kid," Brett said, "so I had songs before I joined a band. Like when I did the Quarks. I'm not sure how it happened but I already had songs."

Like Brett, Jay Bentley played guitar and, like Greg's parents, his mother and father had split up, which broadened his experience of Southern California. After the divorce, both of his parents remarried and relocated. Jay moved from Saugus (now called Canyon Country) to Woodland Hills with his mother and stepdad. His father settled down in Manhattan Beach and Jay spent his summers there. This suited Jay fine. "My mom remarried an executive of Textron, a suit-wearing guy. We never saw eye to eye. I felt bad for my mom. She married this guy and brought me along. That's a tough chew for a guy in a suit." Jay's father was the complete opposite: "a pot-smoking ex-Marine hippie dude who lived at the beach."

Jay got his first skateboard when he was eight and was thrilled to be so close to Reseda Skatercross, which was featured in *Skateboard* the movie as well as an episode of *CHiPs*. "I saw the Dogtown guys there. I was very into the skate culture."

He started hanging out at the beach and spent all his free time surfing and skating with friends whose older brothers had started the music zine *Raw Power*. They had access to music that Jay never would have found on his own. "They would take me to see the weirdest shit!" Jay said.

The heavy metal band Quiet Riot performed at El Camino Real, and seeing Randy Rhoads play guitar ignited Jay's desire to be in a band. He bugged his mom to take him to the Starwood to go see his new idol Randy Rhoads. "I knew he was the fucking guy and I'd never be that good. It was like dreaming of being an astronaut and realizing it's not that easy. It was the first time I recognized this idea I had in my head might not be possible."

Punk changed that. After going to a handful of punk rock shows, the dream of being a musician became a possibility for Jay. "I thought, *I can do that. I can play one note really fast!*"

As strange as it sounds, Jay started jamming with a future member of Bad Religion before Bad Religion even existed. "I had been playing guitar with a soon-to-be-drummer of Bad Religion, Davy Goldman. He lived down the street from me. We played Black Sabbath's 'Iron Man.' It was bad. We were no good, but he had a drum kit and I had a guitar and a little amp. We learned that we could plug a microphone into my amp as well as my guitar. So we would sing, 'I am Iron Man!' That was the beginning of playing music."

Jay Ziskrout, the final member of the foursome, grew up in North Hollywood but his parents moved out to Woodlands Hills, and that's where he met Brett. At Hale Junior High the two became fast friends. They were both into hiking and camping and ran track.

Ziskrout's musical education started in the seventh grade. "I took this beginning brass and percussion class," he said, "and as soon as I walked into the room I thought, *I want to play drums*. It was a very spur-of-the-moment decision about what I wanted to do in music. I started playing the snare drum. From there I got my first little Gretsch brown-sparkle three-piece jazz drum kit. I was off and running."

By the end of junior high, Ziskrout started playing with Brett in various bands, and he was on his way.

Together, the founding members of Bad Religion created something unique in the punk rock scene. Whether it was their name, their worldview, their style of music, or a combination of all of these elements, they went about learning how to be a band with a seriousness that belied their age. Each member brought different things to the band, but their passion translated to an added layer of intensity. Though they may have been at a loss to say what exactly they were trying to accomplish, there was nothing frivolous about the way they set out to do it. After just a handful of practices they reached an unspoken understanding that there was no turning back.

3

LIVE FROM PURGATORY BEACH

ONE OF THE PROBLEMS WITH BEING AN L.A. PUNK band in 1980 was there were very few places to play. Part of this was due to bias. If you weren't a known commodity, it was hard to get people to take you seriously. For instance, Keith Morris literally begged bookers and promoters to let Black Flag play. When his band was finally invited to perform at the venerable Masque, the show was shut down and the venue closed its doors for good. Many of the older punk scenesters from the seventies looked down at hardcore bands and their fans for the negativity they brought to their scene. They were too violent, too reactionary, or just didn't get it. To their minds, bands like Bad Religion embodied everything that was wrong with the punk scene.

Hardcore bands had to get creative. They realized that by supporting each other they could make their own scene within the scene. One of Bad Religion's first live shows was with a relatively unknown band from Fullerton called Social Distortion, who invited Bad Religion to play with them at a party in Santa Ana.

"I think our first show was at a warehouse," Brett recalled, "which was fairly common back then because there weren't that many venues that would book hardcore punk bands."

On the day of the gig, Jay was so anxious he threw up before the show. Steve Soto, a Fullerton native and bass player for the Adolescents, gave Jay a bit of friendly advice.

STEVE SOTO: You're really nervous.
JAY: I know. I get so nervous before we play.
STEVE SOTO: You should always drink at least a six-pack before you play.
JAY: Okay, I didn't know.

Greg remembered the audience being particularly hostile because the promise of free beer had not materialized, but they made it through their set unscathed. When they got off the stage, Brett received a boost from a familiar face who'd made the journey from Woodland Hills to Orange County to see them play. "After the show," Brett recalled, "my friend Tom Clement said to me with great seriousness, 'Brett, no matter what else you do, just don't break up. If you guys don't break up you're going to be huge—seriously. You guys are really good.'"

Another early show was even stranger: a frat party opening up for the Circle Jerks, the band Keith Morris started after leaving Black Flag, and one of the most popular L.A. punk acts of the early eighties. A Greek organization at the University of Southern California was having a punk-themed party and naively decided to invite actual punks to perform. Once the gig was confirmed, members of Bad Religion and the Circle Jerks invited their friends and distributed flyers like they would for any other show. The frat boys dressed like punks and the punks behaved like, well, punks.

For Lucky Lehrer, the drummer for the Circle Jerks, "it was a typical funny, bizarre, tragic night I'd come to expect with Greg Hetson, Roger Rogerson, and Keith Morris. At the end of the party, Roger got drunk off several free-flowing beer kegs and tried to fight half of the USC football team's offensive line. They beat the shit out of him." Apparently, Roger had it coming because Brett recalled watching him attack the jocks with a pair of nunchucks while blackout drunk.

Despite the hijinks, it was an important gig for Bad Religion. Punk photographer Gary Leonard documented the show, and the band made a favorable impression on Lucky. "I connected with Bad Religion a little because as we were loading all our gear back into cars and mini-trucks I sensed these 'kids from the Valley,' as I called them, were a little less insane than the Circle Jerks."

Lucky wasn't being condescending. They were teenagers who despite their intelligence and ambition had very little experience in the ways of the world. "That was the first time I ever witnessed a beer bong," Ziskrout said of the party.

Keith Morris also had fond memories of the show. When the beer ran out at the punk-themed party, Keith went searching for more, and discovered he wasn't the only one on a reconnaissance mission.

"My favorite part of the night wasn't playing with the Circle Jerks or watching Bad Religion," Keith said. "My favorite part of the night was scamming on as much keg beer as I could possibly glug down. We played fraternity or sorority row and every house had some kind of thing raging. Directly across the street was a party with a country theme. They had all these bales of hay stacked randomly in the front yard. I went to go check it out and there's this big, tall, blond-haired surfer dude in a USC frat jacket who turned out to be Ricky Nelson's son hanging out with Darby Crash."

The presence of Darby Crash and Pat Smear of the Germs did not escape Brett's attention. Brett, who idolized Darby, was astonished. "The first hardcore band that I ever saw and fell in love with was the Germs. It was distinctly separate from the punk I had been listening to. It was not the Buzzcocks or the Sex Pistols or the Ramones, who had this very accessible power pop sound, almost like it came from the fifties. The Germs were dark and felt more dangerous."

As a self-taught student of philosophy, Brett recognized what Darby was doing in his lyrics. His words were both poetic and philosophical, an attempt to synthesize the things he was reading and thinking about and then express those ideas in his songs. This made a lasting impression on the young songwriter.

"He was trying to figure out what it means to be human," Brett said. "Songs like 'Lexicon Devil,' 'Manimal,' 'What We Do Is Secret' are powerful, potent songs. They were really influential for me when I started getting into the Germs as a teenager."

While Darby's lyrics could be mysterious, his antics onstage were even more baffling to Brett. The Germs' live shows were infamous for what charitably could be called their lack of structure. For instance, during his performance in the film *The Decline of Western Civilization,* Darby was so impaired that he neglected to sing into the microphone. At shows that Brett attended, Darby didn't even attempt to sing the lyrics: he screamed and wailed and made animal sounds.

"He just didn't sing any words at all!" Brett said. "I loved him for his lyrics. I had every word and every nuance of his phrasing memorized. I would sing along with it in my car. Then I would see the Germs live and Darby would hardly sing any of the words. He was just making noise up there!"

While the Germs' music wasn't accessible, their enigmatic singer was. Brett would go to shows and see him in the crowd or in the parking lot afterward, an experience that he imagined was like seeing Jim Morrison at the Whisky a Go Go on the Sunset Strip in the sixties.

"He was like a demigod to me," Brett said. "He wasn't that much older. He might have been in his early twenties and I was seventeen, which is an unbridgeable gulf when you're that age."

That night at the frat party, Brett worked up the courage to talk to Darby after the show.

BRETT: Hey, Darby.
DARBY: Hey.

BRETT: Can I ask you a question?
DARBY: Sure.
BRETT: When you play live, why don't you sing the words?
DARBY: Because I can't remember them.

Brett's brush with greatness may have been a bit of a disappointment, but the fact that Darby had come to their show meant a great deal to the teenager. It was a reminder that what they did mattered—even at a ridiculous frat party. Sadly, just a few weeks later, Darby died from an intentional drug overdose, an event that was overshadowed by the assassination of John Lennon on the next day.

The show signaled the start of a long association between Bad Religion and the Circle Jerks, with Bad Religion being one of what Keith Morris referred to as "baby brother bands."

"The scenario with Bad Religion and the Circle Jerks," Keith explained, "was that we appreciated each other's music. There weren't any assholes in the group. There were no dicks. Everybody was cool. We wanted to go to the party and bust the punk rock piñata. The situation was because of our friendship with Bad Religion they started playing shows with us."

But that night at USC, Bad Religion learned that the Circle Jerks were going to be interviewed live on KROQ during Rodney Bingenheimer's show, *Rodney on the ROQ*. Rodney was one of the few L.A. scenesters who was connected to the music business and understood the importance of punk rock. (Greg Shaw of Bomp! Records was another.) He was an eclectic figure who'd had his own nightclub in the early seventies called Rodney Bingenheimer's English Disco. He ate lunch at the same Denny's in Hollywood every day. People in the music industry would drop off records, and musicians would try to get an audience with the "Mayor of Sunset Strip."

During his show he would often play music by local punk bands. For early enthusiasts it was the best way to find out about the latest music in the scene. Kids would record Rodney's show and exchange the tapes with other punks at school. As strange as it sounds in today's era of corporate commercial radio, in 1980 you could turn on *Rodney on the ROQ* and hear the Adolescents, the Circle Jerks, and the Germs. In fact, the Adolescents' song "Amoeba" broke through into KROQ's regular rotation and became an underground hit.

Brett understood Rodney's importance to the scene. "He was a guy who prided himself on knowing who the cool new bands were because he went to shows. Rodney had a radio show that started at midnight. He'd play imports from England that we couldn't get and local bands that were hard to find, but the bands would give him their tapes to play on the radio."

Rodney's show made Greg's dream of making music seem more attainable. The music Rodney played on his show included crude demos. This sparked the realization that you didn't have to be signed to a major label to get on the radio. All you had to do was do it.

For Ziskrout, Rodney's radio show was a crucial link to the Hollywood punk scene. "In those days KROQ had a really weak signal. We were out in West San Fernando Valley and we couldn't get KROQ at my house most of the time. I used to go to Brett's house because he lived up on a hill. There were times when someone would have to hold up a wire so the signal would come in clearly."

The Circle Jerks brought Bad Religion's demo tape to the radio station. (Both Hetson and Lucky have taken credit for delivering the tape.) Keith introduced the band and Rodney played the song "Politics" on the radio. Even though Ziskrout was aware that it might happen, he wasn't prepared for how he'd feel when it did. "The thrill of hearing yourself on the radio for the first time can't be put into words. There's nothing else like it."

Rodney's listeners were enthusiastic about the new band from the San Fernando Valley. They wanted more, and Rodney gave it to them. "That was really the start of the band getting popular in L.A.," Brett said. "Rodney really championed us. He liked the song. He felt we were good. That got us known because kids would tape the show. It was a way people could hear our songs before they were even on a record."

Bad Religion also appeared on *New Wave Theatre,* a cable TV show featuring live performances by underground bands. Over the course of the show's relatively short run, Bad Religion played twice. The first time was toward the end of 1980, when they played three songs: "Bad Religion," "Slaves," and "Oligarchy." The show was hosted by Peter Ivers, who was always costumed in cutting-edge New Wave fashion even though he was quite a bit older than the kids in the scene.

Bad Religion's appearance was memorable for what happened at the beginning and end of the show. Ivers, who liked to keep things loose and spontaneous, introduced Bad Religion as "high-speed tough guys from Purgatory Beach." He surely knew he was dealing with a bunch of kids who'd never been on television before, but by introducing the band as "tough guys," he was pandering to his audience in his portrayal of punk as brutal and violent, more sport than art.

After the show, Ivers would again play the role of provocateur during a short, videotaped interview with the band. It's a fascinating exchange that reveals their youthful energy and charm, as well as their intellectual rigor. Greg was restless and unable to stand still throughout the interview, but he was all smiles despite Ivers's confrontational tone. In the middle of the interview, Jay accidentally shocked Greg with his bass, which threw off Greg's concentration. Ivers asked Greg about "Slaves," and he replied that it was "a very inspirational song."

But Ivers wasn't done with Greg, and he urged him to explain himself. Unsure of what to say, Greg responded, "I just write the words." For a moment it seemed as if the band had stumbled into a trap. Sensing that Ivers was out to make them look foolish, Brett, wearing a T-shirt with the words SMUT MONGER scrawled down the front, jumped in.

BRETT: First of all, any organized system of thought is a bad religion. Any government is a bad religion. Any predetermined idea of how to act is a bad religion . . . Actually, we named ourselves Bad Religion to express the ideas that we have. We didn't call ourselves Good Religion. We call ourselves Bad Religion because we feel that religion is bad and basically any organized system of thought is a religion.

IVERS: You present yourself in a very primitive, almost animalistic way, but what you're talking about is really sophisticated.

BRETT: I don't think you should judge people by the way they act. I don't think it has any effect on what's inside their head.

GREG: Yeah, look at you.

Despite the band's snarling bravado onstage, the tape from the show reveals how awkward and shy they were off of it. They were the last generation of kids to grow up without a camera stuck in their faces 24/7, and their discomfort at being videotaped is equal parts charming and goofy. Greg's childish taunt of "Yeah, look at you" stands in stark contrast to his thought-provoking lyrics and the type of dialogue he would later encourage as an academic.

Jay is less circumspect about the show. "We were super nervous. We were so fucking weird!"

An appearance on a local cable TV show was hardly the big time, but it was an auspicious finish to an impressive year. They'd made a popular demo, played some shows, and recorded an EP. They'd accomplished more in their first year than many bands manage in their entire careers. That two of their earliest shows were with Social Distortion and the Circle Jerks and attended by people like Darby Crash suggested they were well connected.

They weren't. While punk was more popular than ever in L.A., there were very few places to play, so people would come out from all over greater Los Angeles and beyond to attend backyard parties and warehouse shows. On the flip side, punk bands were always looking for like-minded bands that were hungry to play and could be counted on to show up—even if it meant hauling their gear to someone's house or a rented hall in Oxnard, East L.A., or San Pedro. That was Bad Religion.

"The scene was fairly small," Jay said, "so you kept seeing the same people over and over again. You'd go to a show and watch a band play. You'd go to a show and you'd be the band playing."

In those days, a punk kid who'd never set foot in Hollywood could go to a show and stand alongside one of his heroes. Of course, the feeling of admiration wasn't always mutual. Jay's first interaction with John Doe of X was when the bass guitar player gruffly said, "Move, kid."

"He was probably twenty-one," Jay recalled, "and I was fifteen. He probably thought I was ruining his scene, and he was right."

One of the things about Bad Religion's early shows that stood out to the band members was how many kids knew the words to their songs—and their EP hadn't even been released yet. When people in the audience sang along with the band at their shows, it made them realize that this weird thing they did together after school in Greg's mom's garage had made an impact beyond their immediate circle of friends. It also reinforced the idea that what they were doing was important and had value. The realization slowly took hold that perhaps these kids memorized their lyrics because they had something meaningful to say.

With an audience made up of their heroes and peers, Jay found it hard not to be critical of his performance. "I remember always thinking, *That was a good song. That was a good one. Oh, that one sucked.*"

Jay wasn't the only one who struggled with nerves. Brett also admitted to feeling uneasy onstage but credits Greg's charisma for winning over the crowd. "I feel like Greg was a real performer from the get-go, and I think that was a big part of Bad Religion's success. A charismatic singer is very important to a punk band, and Greg was always a great performer while I didn't feel like I was until many years later."

Greg may have appeared confident, but inside he was just as nervous as everyone else. "It was really nerve-wracking but I had a lot of confidence in the music. My view was, *We're all in this together, so I'll do my part,* but if I'd been up there alone I'd be shitting bricks. And I've felt that every concert since. A big part of my confidence comes from the guys behind me."

It also didn't hurt that the three performers standing at the front of the stage were all well over six feet tall. With his dyed hair, motorcycle boots, and leather jacket Greg looked the part of a punk rock front man. Brett stayed out of the spotlight but exuded a don't-fuck-with-me aura. While Jay, the tallest member of the group at six foot four, focused on his guitar, his face a mask of intense concentration.

Brett, who was always a self-described "nerdy kid," was surprised to learn that simply being in a band deterred people from starting trouble with him. "I remember when we were starting to get popular, more than once tough punk kids would be very menacing to me. Then someone would say, 'Aren't you in Bad Religion?'" When Brett told the aggressor he was, that usually ended it.

The subculture distrusted outsiders and protected its own, even nerdy punks like Bad Religion. Going to a show where you didn't know anyone and they didn't know you could be dangerous. For Brett, encounters like these were part of his punk initiation. "What attracted me to the punk scene was it felt like a tribe of outsiders. I felt like a person who chronically didn't fit in. So, joining the punk scene was a way of making that a choice rather than having it inflicted on me."

Each of the members of Bad Religion had attended punk rock shows and had witnessed things that were difficult to understand or even explain. That's how the media was able to hijack punk and advertise it as a violent free-for-all that attracted people who were drawn to such behavior. It *was* violent, at times shamefully so.

At the first punk rock show that Jay attended, Black Flag and the Circle Jerks at the Hideaway, someone crashed a car into the warehouse where the show was being held and drove through the gate. Brett recalled a show attended by Jack Grisham of T.S.O.L., who brought a friend whom Jack kept on the end of a leash. Jack would introduce his friend to strangers and tell them they had to fight his "dog." If they declined, they had to fight Jack, who stood six foot five and reveled in violence. For Jay, the early Bad Religion shows were "exciting and terrifying and cathartic." Punk bands whipped the crowd into a frenzy, and when the audience gave that energy back, unpredictable things happened. Bad Religion tapped into that energy in places that were unsanctioned, unsupervised, and unsafe.

Many if not most punk rockers used drugs and alcohol to rise to the occasion and/or deal with the emotions the experience generated. For some punk bands, like the Circle Jerks, the party was their whole reason for being. But Bad Religion wasn't a party band, nor where they interested in writing confrontational lyrics for the sake of being obnoxious. They had a higher purpose in mind.

"There's a reason we called ourselves Bad Religion," Brett explained. "Greg and I were attempting to be intellectuals. On our debut EP I wrote a song called 'Oligarchy' and Greg wrote a song called 'Politics.' We weren't writing joke punk or funny punk. We were teenagers, still naive and quite immature, but we were trying."

For all their intelligence, there was no getting around the fact that they were suburban kids who didn't know what they were doing or what they were getting into. As fans, they were outsiders, but participating as performers didn't make things any less baffling.

"I felt like we were in an adult world that we didn't understand," Jay explained. "There were other people dealing with the business side of things that I didn't want to know about. I just wanted to play and leave. It wasn't business and it wasn't a party.

There was this feeling that this was important without knowing why. Maybe that was just youth and not having a grasp on things, but the party thing wasn't really for me. I think part of that was from our discussions in Greg's garage: 'What do we want to be as a band? What do we want to say? How do we want to present ourselves?' I don't know what other bands talk about when they're forming. I just know that we had that discussion. We didn't want to just be up there screaming, 'Fuck the cops!' or 'I hate my parents!' There had to be something more meaningful than that. That was how we felt about the band. It wasn't a vehicle for drugs. It wasn't a vehicle for money. It was a vehicle for us to say the things that we felt. That was more important than anything else."

4

LIFE ALONE IS SUCH A CURSE

FOR A BAND WITH A REPUTATION AS INTELLECTUALS, in the early days of Bad Religion its members harbored a cavalier attitude toward formal education. Greg did not distinguish himself in school after moving to California and Brett was more focused on his music than his studies. While Brett was trying to get projects for Bad Religion and Epitaph Records going, he would occasionally borrow money from his father. According to Richard, he loaned his son "$1,500 or $1,700" to make Bad Religion's first EP.

Perhaps more important than how much money Brett borrowed to finance Bad Religion's first release was *when* he borrowed it. At the end of 1980, Brett was essentially done with El Camino Real. "I wasn't doing well in school and I was sort of floundering. I took the GED in eleventh grade and never finished high school."

That Brett's father would lend money to his son so he could make a punk record after dropping out of school reveals one of two things: either he shared Brett's vision or he believed in the value of learning lessons the hard way.

"He wasn't a bad kid," Richard said. "I knew he was really working it. I could see he was passionate about it." Brett was more sanguine about his father's support.

"My dad is an entrepreneur," Brett said. "His dad was an entrepreneur. My mom's dad was an entrepreneur. It just sort of runs in my family. I think my dad was like, *Really? You want to try and do something entrepreneurial?*"

Nevertheless, funding Bad Religion's debut proved to be a smart business move, despite the band's offensive name and controversial logo. The EP also came with a mysterious message. Etched on one side were the words, "We're not Bad Religion . . . " and the flip side declared, "UR!" (i.e., "you are"). Unlike names such as "the Ramones," "the Sex Pistols" or "the Weirdos," "Bad Religion" wasn't a declaration of identity, but an observation about the world. Those looking to Bad Religion for answers would find their own reflections in the mirror the band held up to society. "Our name," Brett explained, "no less than our songwriting, was always meant to provoke and make people think."

But if any organized system of thought could be a bad religion, the band itself was extremely disorganized. Case in point, when the EP came out in early 1981, no one in the band knew what to do with it. Jay Ziskrout sent out copies to punk zines and college radio stations, but that was the extent of their marketing efforts. They didn't run any ads or plan any special events.

Brett took a more do-it-yourself approach to getting the record into fans' hands. "I would take a box of records," Brett recalled, "and bring them to Middle Earth Records in Downey, Moby Disc Records in Van Nuys, Zed's Records in Long Beach, and Poobah Records in Pasadena. I'd talk to the buyer and leave fifteen copies in their store. Then I would call around and say, 'Hey, do you need any more?' and lo and behold, they were burning through them and wanted more. So I would drive out there again. That was the extent of the business. It was pretty small-time, but that's how we did it."

Despite the modest sales generated this way, the connections Brett made would pay big dividends down the road. Slowly but surely, the EP made its way into the world. They went through their initial run of five hundred copies in a fairly short period of time. They used re-pressing the record as an opportunity to correct a problem with the recording that caused the record to skip, expanding to 1,500 copies.

That spring and summer the band only played about a half dozen shows, but they were memorable. On March 3, they performed with the Cheifs and China White at the Vex, a legendary venue in East L.A. that was an offshoot of Self Help Graphics. Photos taken by Gary Leonard show Jay Bentley and Jay Ziskrout with very short hair, and Brett appears to be growing out of a Mohawk. They played the Vex again on April 30 with T.S.O.L. and a third time on May 29 with the Adolescents, Social Distortion, and Saccharine Trust. This show represented something of a milestone: it marked the first time Bad Religion played two consecutive nights, and the previous night's gig was the band's first in front of a local crowd at Valley West in Tarzana.

In May, they piled into Brett's Volkswagen Vanagon with all of their gear and drove up to San Francisco for a Sunday night show at the Mabuhay Gardens, booked by the notorious "Pope of Punk," Dirk Dirksen. During the trip, Ziskrout came down with the flu and all he could do was lie in the back of the van and try not to get sick on the equipment. Pete Finestone, a San Fernando Valley punk who was a fan of the band and unofficial roadie, had to set up Ziskrout's equipment and break it down after the show, but the show did go on.

In the beginning of the summer, the punk rock community suffered a blow when the legendary Starwood closed its doors for good on June 13, 1981. The Starwood, located on Santa Monica Boulevard at Crescent Heights, was an important venue for L.A. punk bands and out-of-town acts like Blondie, the Damned, Devo, and the Jam. The Germs famously played their final show there on December 3, 1980, and Darby Crash overdosed four days later.

Greg and Jay hitched rides to the Starwood from Pete. "I had a car," Pete explained. "Every Tuesday and Wednesday when there were shows at the Starwood, I would drive across the Valley, pick up Greg—sometimes Jay, but mostly Greg—and we would drive to shows. That led to me being their roadie."

The closing of the Starwood was a big deal because the parking lot was as much a scene as the club itself. It was a place where punks hung out before the show, and then afterward they headed over to Oki-Dog, which was nearby and open late, long after the clubs had all closed down. Typically, punk shows were held on weeknights, and when the Starwood shut its doors that summer, it left a huge void in the scene.

On the Fourth of July, Bad Religion played its first show at a Hollywood club: the legendary Whisky a Go Go with the Alley Cats and the Dickies. The band had expanded the set list to include a number of new songs, including "Fuck Armageddon . . . This Is Hell," "We're Only Gonna Die," "Part III," "Latch Key Kids," and "New Leaf." The show was particularly memorable for Greg.

"We were playing 'Only Gonna Die' and I'll never forget it because my mom came to that show and brought her friends," Greg said. "Someone came up onstage to do a stage dive and ran into me and I cut my lip on the microphone. I was so mad that I took the mic stand and I clocked the guy in the front row with the base of the stand. It landed right on his skull! After the set, our roadie said, 'Greg, that was the wrong guy! You fucking hit the wrong guy!' I felt so terrible. And even if it was the right guy I would have felt bad. I said, 'Please go get that guy. I want to talk to him and apologize.' The roadie found him and the guy was like, 'It's cool man. Tell Greg no problem!' He was having such a good time he assumed it was par for the course to get hit by the mic stand. He didn't even care!"

One of the reasons they played so few shows was that Greg returned to Wisconsin for the summer. While Greg was away the band started to get letters from places like Amsterdam, Copenhagen, Munich, and Rome. Brett didn't think much of it at the time. "I'd go to the P.O. box and get all this fan mail. I thought, *European kids must write a lot more than American kids.*"

Some of the letters would include reviews of their EP from newspapers and zines that had been published in Europe. They couldn't read the clips, and they assumed their listeners overseas didn't understand the lyrics, but the logo was a different story. Brett's father recalled a music magazine from Italy put the crossbuster on its front cover.

"Even more than the name," Brett said, "the logo helped get us known. We were just trying to be punk, but that logo was like a shot heard around the world. It spread like wildfire in L.A. because you could spray-paint it. But when the EP made it to Italy, Germany, and Spain, our logo caught their attention."

It's probably no coincidence that the letters came from fans living in places where Catholicism's influence was particularly strong. While lyrics are open to interpretation, an effective logo communicates its message on a psychological level. The crossbuster's meaning is universal; its message unequivocal. If Bad Religion hadn't invented it, someone else probably would have.

"It's not just that it was extreme," Brett said of the logo. "I think it has a profundity that hits people in a deeply psychological way. They see it and they remember it. It's not just simple and graphic. It's like a wake-up call."

That fall Greg started his senior year of high school. Ziskrout had already graduated but Brett and Jay were no longer attending classes at El Camino Real. Jay was asked to leave and, like Brett, opted to take the GED. While formal education wasn't a priority for most members of the band, they remained curious about the world and its complex mysteries. "I always tell people I dropped out of school and got all my education in Bad Religion," Jay said. "I learned a lot from these guys. The discussions that we would have—about everything from geology to astrophysics—were phenomenal for a sixteen-year-old. I learned way more from this band than I ever would have learned sitting in a classroom."

The band had written enough material for a full-length record and many of the songs were battle tested. Plus, they were making money from the sales of their EP and occasionally from live shows. Brett estimated that he had enough to pay for the recording and then he'd figure out how to finance the pressing. Around this time he got a call from Bob Say, who was one of the buyers for the Moby Disc record store in Woodland Hills. Bob explained that he had moved on to Jem Records, an indie distributor and importer in the Valley. He invited Brett to come down to his office for a meeting, which Brett recalled went like this:

BOB: Your EP sold well at Moby Disc. Are you doing an LP?
BRETT: Yeah.
BOB: Okay, then I'll take three thousand.
BRETT: Three thousand?
BOB: Yeah, I'll take three thousand.
BRETT: Where am I gonna get the money to make three thousand?
BOB: Well, if you let Jem be the exclusive distributor, I will advance you the money so you can press it.
BRETT: All right. How much would that be?
BOB: We'll pay you five dollars a record.
BRETT: You'll give me fifteen thousand dollars?
BOB: Yeah.

Bad Religion was officially in business. However, Jem was only willing to put up the money to make the record as long as there was a record to make. With the money they'd made from the sale of the EP, Brett calculated they could afford to go to a professional studio. "My parents have always been super supportive. I can't promise that I didn't go back to my dad and ask for a little more money. If I did it wouldn't have been much."

Next, Brett reached out to Jim Mankey, who secured a place for them to make the album in Hollywood near Paramount film studios called Track Record. They were able to get a discount rate by booking the late shift from 10 p.m. to 8 a.m. It was an eye-opening experience for Brett—in more ways than one.

"When I refer to Hollywood, it's not the Hollywood we know today, and it's not the Hollywood of the glory days of the Sunset Strip in the sixties. I think people who aren't from L.A. conflate Hollywood and Beverly Hills. So when they think of Hollywood they think of palm trees and mansions. In the late seventies and early eighties, Hollywood was a seedy, crime-ridden area. It was very rough. There were a lot of hookers and junkies and crime. Strip bars, liquor stores, and dilapidated venues. Basically, it was a playground for punk rockers. But if you left a guitar in your car, it was broken into. The glass was smashed and the guitar was stolen. I had two or three guitars stolen that way."

With Mankey at the helm, they went to work, recording and mixing as they went. They recorded half of the record, including "Voice of God Is Government," "We're Only Gonna Die," and "Fuck Armageddon . . . This Is Hell," which Greg played on the studio piano. "I didn't know we were actually recording," Greg said, "but I'm glad [Mankey] had already put a mic on the piano. I listened through the headphones and it was the first time I heard myself play piano. It was surprising and very motivating. We were so inexperienced back then that it didn't occur to us to try piano on the album. But I was a big fan of Sham 69 and they'd put out an album around that time called *The Adventures of Hersham Boys* that had piano on it. So that was enough motivation for me to go ahead and play punk piano on our own album."

The recording session took longer than expected and they ran out of money. Jay recalled telling Mankey, "We gotta play some more shows, make some more money, and then we'll be back." They booked a number of gigs that winter so that they could finish the record. But then a bizarre series of events unfolded.

They'd hired Edward Colver to do a photo shoot in Hollywood and around Los Angeles. Colver was the man behind the camera for numerous photos that appeared on the covers and sleeves for many Southern California punk bands, including Black Flag, Circle Jerks, China White, Suicidal Tendencies, and T.S.O.L. If you were an L.A. punk band with a record in the eighties, chances were Colver shot the cover. Colver took Bad Religion to the Hollywood Cross, a thirty-foot-high Christian cross that overlooks the Hollywood Bowl and the Hollywood Freeway, for the photo shoot.

During the break in the recording, Colver's proofs arrived at Brett's house. Jay and Greg happened to be there when the package was delivered. They looked at the proofs and picked out the ones they liked. They were very happy with the shoot. In fact, they would eventually use the shot of downtown L.A. for the cover of their debut full-length album, *How Could Hell Be Any Worse?*

When Jay got home, he got a call from Ziskrout.

ZISKROUT: I heard you looked at pictures without me.
JAY: Yeah, so what?
ZISKROUT: Fuck you guys, I quit!

Apparently, Ziskrout was under the impression that he had been deliberately excluded from the meeting. Jay was baffled. "He quit because we looked at pictures without him. I'm not joking. He called me and quit because we looked at pictures without him."

It's not a moment Ziskrout is particularly proud of. "For some reason the guys got together to look at pictures and for whatever reason I wasn't there. I got really pissed off and I quit. It was really very silly. Instead of just mentioning that I was unhappy I stormed off in a huff. It was very childish. It's actually one of the things in my life that I regret. I regret it for a couple of reasons. That's not the way to move on from something and certainly not the way to respond to something that you're unhappy about. And also I wish I could have played with Bad Religion for longer, if not still to this day."

Bad Religion was now without a drummer. This put the band in a serious bind. Not only were they in the middle of recording an album, they'd booked a number of shows in the hopes of earning enough money to finish the record. They were in dire need of a drummer.

Greg recruited their friend from the Valley, Pete Finestone, who was one of Bad Religion's roadies and Ziskrout's drum tech— though those titles were a bit overstated. "There was an age-old thing that punk rockers did," Jay explained. "If you showed up at the club and carried a guitar case or a cable inside, you'd get in for free." That's what constituted a "roadie" in the L.A. punk scene circa 1981. To Jay, Pete was more than a guy who could be counted on to carry a case into the club—he was a friend. Asking him to play in Bad Religion was a no-brainer.

"Pete was always around and was a good friend to all of us," Jay said. "It never occurred to anyone to do anything different. There's Pete. He's got a drum kit in his car and he knows the songs. He's *standing right there*."

Pete may have known the songs, but he didn't know how to play them. Also, he didn't own a complete set of drums and had never taken any lessons, but he knew how to set up a drum kit and break it down. It would be comparable to hiring the sound guy to sing because he knew how to set up the microphone. But to Pete's credit he was ready, willing, and able to learn, which were the three requirements that mattered most.

Pete was from the San Fernando Valley and both of his parents worked at California State University, Northridge. In fact, Pete's parents knew Greg's parents from academic circles long before their sons got acquainted.

Pete had a slight speech impediment and felt ostracized from other kids. He would get into fights and had to change schools. "I was a kid who was very uncomfortable in his skin. I didn't have a lot of friends. I had a brother who was a jock. I was a very lonely kid. Very self-aware of my loneliness and being different."

A friend who'd been to London tried to get Pete interested in punk rock by playing the Sex Pistols for him, but he didn't like it. "'This shit sounds terrible! What is this garbage?' I thought it was really silly."

Pete had his punk rock awakening in the summer of 1978. He had tickets to go see Jethro Tull during the Bursting Out tour at the Long Beach Arena, but his friend urged him to go see the Clash, who were playing at Santa Monica Civic.

"I went back and forth," Pete said. "Finally, I decided to go see the Clash. I think it was their first or second time through the United States, and that changed everything. *What is this? This is talking right to me!*"

Punk rock introduced Pete to a new community of outsiders. He didn't go to El Camino Real, but he knew Arnel Celestial, Bad Religion's first fan. Arnel introduced Pete to Greg in Hollywood on the day the band recorded its demo at Studio 9, and Pete had been part of Bad Religion's circle of friends ever since.

None of this changed the fact that Pete didn't know how to play. Greg, however, was steadfast in his support. "You're our friend," Pete recalled Greg telling him, "it will work out fine."

Pete talked his mother into buying a drum kit. "We didn't have much money. She had some saved up and we went to Pro Drum and I bought this little drum set. I took it home and I tried to learn all their songs by playing along with the cassette, but I didn't really know what I was doing. I didn't really know how to play. I was flying blind, trying to learn the drum parts without knowing how to play."

The next few weeks were a roller coaster of emotions for Pete. He was excited to be a part of the band he loved, but the pressure was intense. The low point was his first practice in the Hell Hole. "I set up my drums and started to play. I've never been so nervous in my fucking life. Everyone was looking around. I think Brett and Jay were probably thinking, *This isn't working out.* But Greg told me

42

it sounded great and to keep practicing. We had a show coming up at Godzilla's with Fear and China White in a month or so, and somehow they were patient with my playing. Again, I didn't know how to fucking play!"

Not only was the show scheduled, it was for the grand opening of Godzilla's, a club operated by Mark, Adam, and Shawn Stern of Youth Brigade on the east end of the San Fernando Valley. Godzilla's was big, which meant that everyone Pete had ever known could come and watch his debut with Bad Religion.

"I'd never played a show in my life," Pete said, "and I'm playing a show with Fear in front of a thousand kids. Everyone seemed to have a great time. I was on cloud nine. Girls were talking to me for the first time. I'd never had girls talk to me. Even in the punk rock scene you still had a pecking order and I was accepted for playing in this band that people liked."

There was no time for Pete to rest on his laurels as he went out of the frying pan of a live performance and into the fire of the recording studio.

When Bad Religion returned to Track Record with their new drummer in early 1982, they had already recorded and mixed eight of the fourteen songs that would appear on their first full-length album, which they'd decided to call *How Could Hell Be Any Worse?* The album title is a lyric from the song "Fuck Armageddon . . . This Is Hell," which Greg composed on his mother's piano.

The song begins with a bass line that's so muted and subdued, you barely know it's there. Against this backdrop a single guitar—solemn and somber-sounding—pierces the air like the horns that herald the end of days. The tempo ratchets up, the drums kick in, and we're back on the familiar footing of a Bad Religion song. The contrast between the slow introduction and the headlong thrust of the lyrics lends "Fuck Armageddon" an epic quality.

> *There's people out there that say I'm no good*
> *Because I don't believe in things that I should*
> *In the end the good will go to heaven up above*

The bad will perish in the depths of hell
How could hell be any worse, when life alone is such a curse?
Fuck Armageddon . . . this is hell!

These lyrics introduce a Bad Religion trademark: irony, especially when it comes to religious themes. Greg, who wrote the song, most certainly didn't believe "the good will go to heaven up above." But the lyric goes along with the accepted truth of this received knowledge for the purpose of puncturing it with sarcastic wit.

Since the narrator isn't part of the crowd that will "go to heaven up above" he will be left behind with the damned. But with countries constantly at war with another and corporations poisoning the earth, life on earth is no picnic. Forget about the afterlife, the song argues, we're already in hell.

The irony and sarcasm are a roundabout way of getting at an interesting philosophical question: in a world without moral restraints, what's the use of being good? The last line of the chorus, which is also the song title, answers the clarion call of the solitary guitar at the opening: forget about the afterlife, look at the hell we've made of this world. Here, at last, the singer is deadly serious, urging us to get our heads out of the clouds and into reality. For all its talk of the end, the song isn't nihilistic. "Fuck the world" is nihilistic. "Fuck Armageddon" is a wake-up call.

Jay was still playing his hand-painted Jazzmaster bass during the first recording session with Ziskrout but it was stolen after a show. "I don't remember what the venue was, but I remember seeing the guitar and then it was gone. That I remember like it was yesterday." It was a blessing in disguise because that prompted him to purchase a Rickenbacker—again with help from his parents.

"We were in the middle of making a record. It was obvious to my parents that I wasn't fucking around now. I was going to do this whether they liked it or not. That was when I got them to agree to buy me a real bass." (Many years later, Jack Grisham of T.S.O.L. would tell Jay that he had stolen his bass and thrown it off the roof of the venue.) Brett also bought a new guitar and they went back into the studio with new gear and a new drummer.

They had six more songs to record, including "Part III," which was one of two songs on the record that Jay wrote. (The other was "Voice of God Is Government.") "Part III" is about War World III, but since they already had a song called "World War III" they settled on a synonym that stresses how these cataclysmic conflicts are part of an ongoing saga. Jay wanted a second guitarist to play against Brett to complement the theme of warfare. Jay invited Greg Hetson of the Circle Jerks to play on the album. This marked Hetson's unofficial beginning as a contributor to the band, a relationship that would continue for over thirty years.

Pete had never recorded in a studio before and felt the band should try to find someone else to play the last remaining songs for the album, but once again Greg was adamant in his support. For better or worse, the job fell to Pete. "If you look back at that record," Pete said, "you can really hear Ziskrout's parts versus the songs I played. Ziskrout played 'Fuck Armageddon . . . This Is Hell,' which is probably the most popular song on the record. I played 'Oligarchy.' There's a distinctive difference between Jay's jazz-influenced style of punk rock and my playing, which is atrocious."

In addition to having two different drummers, the album reflects the band's unorthodox approach in other ways. "We're Only Gonna Die," "Damned to Be Free," and "Fuck Armageddon . . . This Is Hell" all feature piano, which was unusual for a punk band. "We're Only Gonna Die" also has some acoustic guitar. Interestingly, Greg wrote four of the first five songs on the album, while Brett wrote four of the final six, yet the album is cohesive in terms of the band's vision and sound.

How Could Hell Be Any Worse? is full of images of death and destruction. Despite the record's apocalyptic feel, the mayhem stems from mankind, not from a divine agency. The album opens with "We're Only Gonna Die," which is listed on the liner notes as "We're Only Gonna Die from Our Own Arrogance," a parable of modern man done in by primitive urges. The keyword is "arrogance." Humankind has the knowledge and the power to avoid catastrophe, but our monstrous hubris and warlike urges lead us down the path of destruction again and again. Incidentally, this song was later recorded by the legendary Orange County band Sublime.

Both "Faith in God" and "Pity" drip with scorn for the ignorant masses, with the former offering advice not to "be feeble like all of them." Meanwhile, "Damned to Be Free" revisits the themes laid out in "Fuck Armageddon . . . This Is Hell" in which the singer rejects religion's dogmatic oppression. When it comes to choosing eternal damnation or freedom, the only choice is freedom. But "Damned to Be Free" isn't a song about living for today; rather, it emphasizes the responsibility that comes with freedom.

The band wrapped up recording *How Could Hell Be Any Worse?* in a single weekend. The artwork was ready to go. With a distribution deal in place, they were able to get the records pressed and shipped. At the time, the number one song in the U.S. was "Centerfold" by the J. Geils Band. *On Golden Pond* occupied the top spot at the box office, and Ronald Reagan was in the second year of his first term as president of the United States. Bad Religion had just released its first full-length record. Would anyone care?

5

SOMETHING BUT NOTHING

IN EARLY 1982, THE L.A. PUNK SCENE WAS ON LIFE support. To all but its most stalwart supporters the once vital movement had taken a nosedive into obscurity. The Starwood had shut down, kids were falling out of the scene, and musicians were growing out their hair. The Sunset Strip now featured metal bands that borrowed from punk fashion and glam theatricality. But Bad Religion's debut, *How Could Hell Be Any Worse?*, proved punk still had a pulse.

The month after Bad Religion released its first full-length album, the Circle Jerks came out with *Wild in the Streets*, its follow-up to *Group Sex*. Down in Orange County, Goth rockers Christian Death with guitarist Rikk Agnew, formerly of Social Distortion and the Adolescents, debuted *Only Theatre of Pain*. Punk was moving in new and interesting directions: the hardcore front pushed the music into "loud and fast" territory while other bands experimented with slower tempos and synthesizers to sustain an atmosphere of discontent. To put it another way, hardcore lashed out ("Fuck you!") while Goth, death rock, and post-punk looked inward ("We're fucked!").

Bad Religion received enthusiastic support from the hardcore crowd. Although the band's popularity was growing with fans and promoters, other bands looked down at them. Once again, it came down to geography and their age. "We were something, but we were nothing," Jay explained. "We were just some dickheads from the Valley. That was the way people would write us off. 'You guys are from the Valley,' as if only real punk came from Hollywood. I think we only got away with it because we were kids."

Class also played a role in the punk hierarchy. Hollywood kids presumed their peers in the Valley came from money. While Hollywood was chaotic and dangerous, the Valley represented stability and safety. For the members of Bad Religion, the truth resided somewhere in the middle. Greg was a latchkey kid in a single-parent home for much of middle school and high school. After his parents divorced, Jay shuttled between the Valley and the beach. Brett's father worked out of his garage when Brett was young, but managed to carve out a comfortable, middle-class existence for his family. "There was a bit of a class thing going on," Brett said. "Valley kids versus city kids. In the punk world, we were thought of as second-class citizens, even though we weren't rich white kids."

Although the members of Bad Religion were far from rich, their parents supported the band's efforts and provided them with instruments, a place to play, and the opportunity to pursue their passion—privileges that many kids simply didn't have. For instance, Brett's family employed a Salvadoran housekeeper a few days a week. When Greg or Jay called Brett and the housekeeper answered the phone, she would call for "Mr. Brett" to pick up the phone. Of course, Brett's bandmates teased him about this, but rather than run from the nickname, Brett embraced it.

"That became sort of like my stage name," Brett explained. "Part of the reason I didn't mind it was I felt like there was some anti-Semitism in the scene and it made me reluctant to use my Jewish-sounding last name. At first the scene was just a bunch of freaks hanging out. There was a lot of experimentation and insanity that felt transgressive and even revolutionary. Back then, society wasn't as aware of gender and identity issues as it is today, but in the early eighties punks were the ones challenging societal norms and that's something I'm proud of. Even so, what had started out as a revolutionary and radical expression, slowly morphed into something more uniform and dogmatic. When homophobia and racism crept into the hardcore scene, it felt sinister. To be honest, I didn't feel particularly safe. That's why I started going by Mr. Brett on our records and the nickname stuck."

While the first L.A. punks came from diverse backgrounds from all over the county, new fans from the beach communities and the suburbs were mostly white and male. Many came from surf and skate culture and were drawn to punk for the violence of the live performances. Some of these recent converts were extremely aggressive and hostile to anyone who wasn't like them. Instead of championing punk's nonconformist worldview they traveled in packs and espoused a gang mentality of "us against you."

"The embryonic punk scene was revolutionary," Brett said, "and when I say revolutionary, I mean it was open, it was idealistic. There were philosophers like Tim Yohannan from *Maximum Rocknroll* and Darby Crash of the Germs, who were interesting and well-read and forward thinking. And then there was the mirror image of that, the other side of the coin, the darker side, which were punks who were racist, close-minded, and violent. It was all mixed together and I think what people found in the punk scene is what they brought to it."

The split between the "original" Hollywood punks and some of the other scenes was becoming increasingly apparent. "In the early eighties when you went to Hollywood," Jay said, "you could tell the difference. Hollywood punks were generally a little older and more of an art crowd. When you got down to Long Beach and beyond it was tough fucking kids."

The Fleetwood in Redondo Beach, an important venue in the beach punk scene, served as a prime example of the excessive violence that plagued punk shows during this period. Greg had not-so-fond memories of the club, which was located a few klicks down Harbor Drive from Hermosa Beach, the birthplace of Black Flag. "All you had to do was go to the Fleetwood," Greg recalled, "the famous punk club where those guys would hang out, and slam dancing was vicious. They took their slam dancing onto the streets and the fists would fly. Then they'd join in when someone was down and start kicking them."

But the violence wasn't confined to certain clubs or neighborhoods—though some were more dangerous than others. It infected the whole scene. Jay described it as a violent, dangerous time. "The places where we were playing were not safe. There seemed to be a lot of people coming to shows that just wanted to hurt people. They paid their five bucks to come in and beat the shit out of somebody. You used to see a lot of guys get stabbed. There were no body searches. No metal detectors. A lot of crazy shit."

Through all of the changes in the punk scene, one place remained an oasis of consistency: Oki-Dog, a fast-food establishment whose house specialty is two hot dogs smothered in chili and fried pastrami and wrapped in a flour tortilla. Located on Santa Monica Boulevard in West Hollywood,[1] Oki-Dog stayed open late, served cheap food with generous portions, and had a large parking lot. These factors made it attractive to West Hollywood hustlers, teen runaways, and punks—young people at the margins of society seeking safety in numbers. Oki-Dog's owners famously turned a blind eye to some of their patrons' unhealthy habits and occasionally helped out those who were in dire straights.

Even after the Starwood closed, Greg remembered Oki-Dog as the place where punks gathered. "It was where everyone converged after the club," Greg said. "When the gig was over you went to Oki-Dog."

---

1. The original Oki-Dog is long gone but the infamous culinary creation lives on at two locations: one on North Fairfax Avenue and another on West Pico Boulevard. Caveat emptor.

While many were there to see and be seen by punk rock royalty, for teenagers from the Valley it was one of the few places they could hang out with like-minded kids. It was a place where the distinction between performers and fans, which was tenuous at best, completely melted away. Greg credited Oki-Dog for the friendships he formed with bands at all ends of the spectrum, from the Circle Jerks, who were practically famous, to Mad Society, whose members were even younger than Bad Religion's. Most of all, Greg enjoyed going to Oki-Dog because it was a place where he could kill time while hanging out with his friends. "It was an excuse not to go home," Greg said. "Not that my home life was bad, but it was boring to me. I loved hanging out and being where the people were."

Because Oki-Dog had a reputation in punk circles as a hangout, and had even been written about in songs, it continued to attract new fans, but some of the more narrow-minded hardcore kids found themselves at odds with Oki-Dog's West Hollywood clientele. In 1980, a group of Nazi punks viciously attacked a gay fourteen-year-old runaway and left him for dead. (The victim survived and, in a remarkable twist, reunited with one of his attackers twenty-five years later while volunteering at the Museum of Tolerance.) Even members of the LAPD would use homophobic taunts when rousting punks from the popular late-night eatery.

Sadly, confrontations like this were all too common at Oki-Dog and other places along Santa Monica Boulevard, where homophobes would prey on punks, hustlers, and young gay men— anyone who didn't conform to their view of masculinity. One such incident sent shockwaves throughout the punk community.

The night started in unusual fashion with a punk rock party in Bad Religion's neighborhood, a rarity in those days. A student at El Camino Real threw a party at her house on Woodlake Avenue in Woodland Hills while her parents were out of town. Greg knew the neighborhood. "It was almost halfway between my house and Jay's house. It was my walking route to school every day. So we knew that house pretty well and I believe we knew the girl who lived there. I don't know how we even heard about the party."

Greg, Jay, and Pete went to the party and were surprised to see Mike Muir of Suicidal Tendencies there with several members of the Dogtown skateboarding crew, including Jay Adams, Dennis "Polar Bear" Agnew, and other skate punks from Venice Beach. Jay knew the Dogtown boys from his years of skating and they, of course, knew about Bad Religion.

A group of high school football players were having a party next door. Jay sensed trouble brewing from the beginning. "The unfortunate reality was the next-door neighbor was a jock kid who was having a football party and they were from El Camino Real. So these were people that Greg and I knew."

A young punk was accosted by a group of football players. When he arrived at the party, bruised and bloodied, he explained that some guys from the house next door had jumped him. The Dogtown boys promptly went to the jock's house to confront them. The football players miscalculated the situation and emerged from the house with baseball bats, thinking this would intimidate the punks. The skaters from Venice Beach were not the punks the jocks from El Camino Real were accustomed to dealing with. These punks were every bit as athletic and aggressive as they were, if not more so, and to say they had a predilection for street violence would be an understatement.

For Greg it was like a scene out of a movie. "The dumb football players came outside with baseball bats. The beach punks just walked right up to them and took the bats out of their hands because these football players weren't used to being stood up to. They grabbed their bats and chased the football players away."

When the football players fled, the beach punks went into the house and trashed it with the weapons the jocks had threatened them with. "They tore apart that house," Greg recalled. "Just dismantled it," Jay added.

None of the boys from Bad Religion took part in the vandalism at the party, but they all recognized it was time to go. Pete left with his girlfriend, and Greg and Jay headed to Hollywood with members of the Dogtown contingent.

Jay drove his old Toyota Corona, which he affectionately called "the green turd." "I was following Dennis Agnew and Jay Adams because I remember on the freeway Adams opened the door and was hanging out the door peeing. I remember thinking, *That guy's fucking nuts!*"

At Oki-Dog, the various factions split up to hang out with their friends. A fight broke out after Adams taunted a gay couple, one of whom was African-American, with racist and homophobic epithets. The black man, Dan Bradbury, confronted Adams, and a fight broke out. In the ensuing melee Bradbury fell and struck his head, and everyone scattered.

For the second time that night, Jay left in a hurry. "I got in my car. Greg got in my car. And a guy named Tommy Hawk got in my car and we drove away." As they were leaving, a vehicle pulled up alongside Jay's car and the woman behind the wheel shouted at them through the open windows. "I remember taking off with Jay," Greg said. "But some lady in the car next to us screamed, 'I saw you! I saw you!'"

Jay sped away, dropped off his friends, and went home; but he was in for a rude awakening. At three o'clock in the morning, he received a visit from the West Hollywood sheriffs. "They pounded on the door and my mom let them in," Jay recalled. "They just burst into the house and came into my bedroom with their guns drawn. I can't imagine what my parents were thinking. *What the fuck have you done now?*"

Dressed in a pair of swim trunks and nothing else, Jay was cuffed and stuffed into the back of a police car. They drove him back to West Hollywood, where he learned that Dan Bradbury, the African-American man who had been assaulted at Oki-Dog, had died. To make matters worse, the police accused Jay of being the one who attacked Bradbury, and they said they had witnesses who had placed him at the scene. "After I finally got them to tell me what was going on, they said I was the guy that knocked

[Bradbury] down. I said, 'It wasn't me.' They said, 'It was you. We have eyewitnesses who saw you do it.' So I spent two nights at the West Hollywood Sheriff's Station."

Jay figured the lady who had screamed at them as they were leaving Oki-Dog had recorded his license plate number, but they had the wrong man. "I kept telling them I didn't have anything to do with this," Jay said. But that didn't matter. He was a high school dropout in a punk band who could be placed at the scene. That was enough for them.

Finally, an eyewitness came forward and informed the police that the man who'd started the brawl was much shorter. In other words, they had the wrong Jay.

For Greg, his troubles started when he returned to school on Monday. Word of the incident at Oki-Dog had spread throughout the punk community and made its way to El Camino Real. The severity of the violence overshadowed the vandalism on Woodlake Avenue, but the jocks didn't see it that way, and Greg was concerned they would take their revenge out on him.

"I'm dead, man," he'd said to Muir the previous evening. "Those guys are going to kill me." Muir told Greg not to worry. If the jocks gave him any more trouble, Muir would put a pipe bomb in their mailbox. This wasn't exactly reassuring.

The jocks threatened Greg as soon as he arrived at school that morning but somehow restrained themselves. While he was in class there was a knock at the door. The principal wanted to talk to Greg, but there was a surprise waiting for him outside the classroom.

"It wasn't just the principal but the police," Greg said. "They paraded me down the hall. Everyone in my school saw me being taken away by the police."

Greg, along with the rest of the student body, assumed he was in trouble for what went down at Oki-Dog. He wasn't. These cops wanted to talk to Greg about the party on Woodlake. Greg explained he didn't have anything to do with the vandalism at the house party, nor did he have anything to do with the punks who'd trashed the place. When the police realized they didn't have anything on Greg, they gave him a stern talking to.

"'This is a community up here. You're getting mixed up with the wrong people. Those guys from Hollywood are bad news.' They must have thought I was a good student or something," Greg said.

Although Greg and Jay were quickly cleared of any wrongdoing, the effects of the incident at Oki-Dog lingered. Adams pled guilty to felony assault and was sent to jail, but he maintained his innocence after he got out. He claimed that Bradbury died after getting kicked while he was down. Muir held a grudge against Jay. It didn't sit right with him that Jay had been released while his friend went to jail. He confronted Jay at Godzilla's, where Bad Religion was opening for the Damned. Pete remembered that things escalated very quickly. "Muir attacked but Jay fought back and held his own." Eventually, Jay and Muir were separated and that seemed to settle the matter between them. "It wasn't a big deal," Jay said.

Jay had experienced his own brush with gruesome violence a few months earlier. Jay had been a roadie for the Adolescents at a show in Arizona. The stage was in an actual boxing ring. The security staff was hostile to the band, and one of the bouncers got into it with one of the Adolescents' guitar players and put him in a headlock. Jay told the bouncer to let go, and when he didn't, Jay punched him in the face, which was a mistake. The bouncers were all kickboxers, and they beat him up and put him in the hospital.

For the punk rock community, the Oki-Dog incident was a sign that things had changed and not for the better. Indeed, the worst was yet to come with the rise of punk rock gangs and escalating police violence; it made attending punk rock shows a dangerous proposition and deterred many fans of the music from attending.

For Greg, it was all the evidence he needed to know that the scene was dissipating. What had been wasn't coming back and what had replaced it wasn't very much fun. "Nobody wanted to be a part of that," Greg said. It was also a reminder that the world of punk rock wasn't a bubble, that what happened at a party or a show could impact his life or even his future.

While Greg wasn't the best student, he was trying to change that. He was planning on going to college in Wisconsin after he graduated from high school. Unlike many in the punk community, he was looking beyond the horizon of the next show and he didn't like what he saw. In his mind, Bad Religion was different from other bands, but in the minds of the police, the press, and their parents, there was no difference. They were all a bunch of violent troublemakers. What was the point of being in a so-called "smart" punk band if it meant getting lumped in with violent racists and homophobes who were slowly taking over the scene?

The incident also had a negative effect on Jay's home life. He'd dropped out of school, and because he was a still a juvenile, he had dragged his parents into Bradbury's horrifying death. "It changed how my parents looked at me," Jay said, "because now I was just the worst guy ever."

Jay's relationship with his parents was already strained. As Bad Religion became more popular, he was required to play shows farther from home and he would often be out late. A typical exchange about where he was going and when he would be home would often end in an argument.

JAY: I'm driving down to Riverside to go play this show.
PARENTS: You have to be home by ten p.m.
JAY: I'm not gonna be home at ten p.m.
PARENTS: You're not gonna get your allowance.
JAY: Well, let's see, I'm probably going to make a hundred dollars and my allowance is twelve. I'm okay not making my allowance. Fucking ground me.

When Jay was in his early teens, he was hit by a car. He was on his bike in a crosswalk when another teenager in a station wagon plowed into him. Jay jumped up on his bike seat and went up and over the windshield. As a result of the accident, both of his legs were dislocated. A family friend who was a lawyer sued on his be-half and Jay received a settlement that he would be able to access when he turned eighteen.

"I wasn't crazy enough to think, *Dude, I'm never gonna have to work again.* It was only about fifteen grand, and I had to give half of it to the lawyer." All the same, Jay knew that money was coming on his eighteenth birthday and it colored his thinking about the fu-ture, which was frequently at odds with his parents' expectations. Now they saw him as a violent person. This was frustrating to Jay because that's not who he was or how he behaved in the punk community. "I was never a 'destroy' guy," Jay explained. "I was al-ways a 'we can do better' guy."

Unfortunately, things were about to go from bad to worse for the band.

6

MUSIC FOR WEIRDOS

IN HIGH SCHOOL GREG BECAME PASSIONATE ABOUT something even less cool than punk: paleontology. He was always a curious kid, but as he got older the questions he had about the world and what it was like thousands of years before he was born intensified instead of diminished. While he was a senior at El Camino Real, he volunteered in the paleontology department's fossil-preparation laboratory at the Natural History Museum of Los Angeles County. His job was to take rocks that the museum's staff had collected and chip away at them with a variety of arcane tools until the fossil inside was revealed.

The work was grindingly dull, and Greg had to take a long bus ride to the museum for a job he wasn't even being paid for. Sometimes he'd work for hours on a simple tooth or bone fragment. When he finished, the fossil was sent to another lab, never to be seen again, leaving Greg with questions about how the pieces fit together and what it all meant. Many of these searching questions found their way into Bad Religion's lyrics.

The work sparked a desire in Greg to know more about the fossils he helped excavate. Where had they come from? What had happened to them? But he didn't just want to know the who and the what, i.e., the taxonomy of these fossils, he wanted to know the how and the why. In short, he wanted to know their *story*, which was also the story of our planet's geological record.

These experiences at the Natural History Museum led Greg, whose great grandfather believed the earth was only six thousand years old, to pursue a course of study in geology. However, Greg's grades at El Camino Real weren't good enough to get him into the University of Wisconsin, where he could have taken advantage of free tuition because his father was a tenured faculty member in the English department. Instead, he enrolled in California State University, Northridge, in the fall and took classes in geology and biology. For the first time in his life, Greg felt motivated to excel at school.

Bad Religion continued to play shows, including a gig with Bad Brains at the Ukrainian Culture Center in L.A., and took the occasional trip to San Francisco, but they rarely played more than two or three times a month. Nevertheless, the band was encouraged by how well *How Could Hell Be Any Worse?* was doing. Throughout the year Brett kept re-pressing the album to meet demand, and by the end of 1982, they'd sold ten thousand copies, a number that surpassed everyone's expectations. "It was kind of a big deal in the punk scene back then," Brett explained.

They were also now part of the regular rotation on Rodney Bingenheimer's show and had the ear of L.A.'s ragtag punk rock scene. Bad Religion was even invited back to *New Wave Theatre*,[2] which somehow Greg Hetson found out about. On the day the show was taped, he showed up at the studio wearing a hat and trench coat and played "Part III" with the band. Whenever Hetson attended a Bad Religion show, he would come onstage to play

_____

2. Sadly, Peter Ivers, the show's host, was bludgeoned to death in his apartment in March 1983, and his murder was never solved.

"Part III," a practice that would continue until he became, for all intents and purposes, a de facto member of the band.

Things were going so well for Bad Religion that Brett bought a Roland Juno-6 synthesizer. When Greg wrote songs, he often used his mother's hopelessly out-of-tune piano. The new keyboard came with a multitude of effects and was portable. It was a handy tool to have, but its presence would have severe repercussions on the band.

By 1982, the use of synthesizers in pop music was so pervasive you couldn't turn on the radio without hearing them. Most punk bands eschewed the use of synthesizers for aesthetic reasons. They rejected them *because* they were so popular in mainstream music.

Brett knew exactly what he was getting into when he bought the Roland Juno-6. "At the time," he recalled, "even though synths were anathema, a lot of our peers in the hardcore scene were moving toward a post-punk sound influenced by English bands like Joy Division and Public Image Limited. I knew it was a risk, but I thought it might be fun to experiment."

Then T.S.O.L. released *Beneath the Shadows* on Alternative Tentacles, which featured Greg Kuehn on keyboards and even had an instrumental song. In its second full-length album, T.S.O.L. had pushed its death rock sound in the gloomy direction hinted at in the EP *Weathered Statues,* which came out in between the band's first two albums. In Brett's eyes, *Beneath the Shadows* marked a major shift in the musical landscape.

"Particularly influential, at least to me, was T.S.O.L, who were one of my favorite bands in the L.A. hardcore scene. They had just made their album *Beneath the Shadows,* which had synth on it, and it was a real change. It signaled a move from a very aggressive hardcore sound to an almost postmodern sound."

Was punk over or had it entered a new, experimental phase? Some bands discouraged violent hardcore fans from wreaking havoc at their shows by writing music those fans would hate. Other bands softened their approach in order to play at venues where punk had been banned. For Greg, controlled violence was part of the punk rock experience. "I was athletic and I loved to slam dance. I found it exhilarating." Brett held similar views. "The violence of the punk scene was never central to anything Greg or I were doing," Brett said. "But I always enjoyed the violent dancing. It was cathartic. The pit, with its chaos of reckless swirling bodies, was a way to lose yourself and connect to others, if only for a few minutes. It was good clean violent fun."

Until it wasn't. Their size and their status helped insulate them from confrontations with violent punks at shows. While the members of Bad Religion weren't as big or as rowdy as T.S.O.L., they physically towered over bands like the Circle Jerks. But there was no getting around the fact the landscape had changed. When Brett and Greg began writing material for the new record, it wasn't the same scene that produced the Screamers, the Weirdos, and X. Greg wrote a song and brought it to rehearsal. To Brett's surprise, the song featured the Roland Juno-6. Greg didn't just use the synthesizer to compose the song, it was one of the featured instruments. Brett took notice of the new approach.

"He was using the synth but not the way T.S.O.L. used it," Brett said, "which was kind of a Joy Division thing. This was different." Up to this point synthesizers were used on the margins of punk rock to create an atmosphere of doom and gloom. But Greg's song, "It's Only Over When . . . ," was upbeat, relentlessly so, like the opening sequence to an eighties movie.

"The Roland synth I bought for the band might not have been the best instrument for the job in that it was monophonic. But Greg brought a song in and it was a prog song. Instead of going, 'Oh, that's lame!' I said, 'I'll write one, too!'"

For the next rehearsal, Brett brought in, "The Dichotomy," a song he thought would complement Greg's song. "That song is my attempt at writing 'Dogs' by Pink Floyd sideways." The writing process for the new record continued in a similar fashion, with Greg and Brett producing material that would go well with the other songwriter's work.

Brett's song "Billy Gnosis" is an allusion to Billy Pilgrim, the central character in the Kurt Vonnegut novel *Slaughterhouse Five*. But the song that really stuck out from the rest was Greg's "Time and Disregard" because it was broken into four parts and was seven minutes long. "Greg loves Jethro Tull," Brett explained. "I grew up on Jethro Tull, too, but Greg likes them more than I do."

It was clear to Brett what they were doing: this wasn't a punk album; they were writing a prog record. "Greg and I share an affinity for prog and I don't think that's the case for anyone else in the band," Brett admitted. "Before we went punk we both listened to a lot of prog: Yes; Emerson, Lake & Palmer; King Crimson. It wasn't mainstream rock. In the seventies, other kids were listening to Peter Frampton, Led Zeppelin, Black Sabbath or whatever. Prog was the avant-garde music of the time. It was music for us weirdos."

Despite the differences in their age and upbringing, Greg and Brett shared a passion for several prog rock bands. One of the unwritten rules of going punk was rejecting the music you used to like. You had to throw away the records that weren't considered cool anymore. The pain of parting with a favorite uncool record was better than having your punk friends finding it in your collection. But like so many other trends, Bad Religion bucked this one, too.

"That's probably where Greg and I really hit it off," Jay said, "because we are both fans of music. Not just punk rock. There would be guys who would come over to our area at school and they'd talk punk rock with us and we'd go, 'Uh-huh.' Then we'd go back to talking about ELP." They didn't reject the music of their youth. They embraced it. Though some of the members embraced it more than others.

For instance, although Jay wasn't a fan of prog—"I was in the KISS Army"—he was keenly aware that everyone in the band was influenced by different things. He was interested in the places where those musical influences intersected. "We had wild influences from all over the place. Brett came in with the Ramones and

Greg came in with the Dead Boys and I came in with the Jam. We all had our own sort of idea of what we were going to be, so that's how we molded into the band that we became. We never said we're going to be like Black Flag or the Germs. We didn't have that in us. I realized that the artist that I had in common with Brett was Elton John and the artist that I had in common with Greg was Discharge and the artist that we all had in common was Elvis Costello. Maybe Greg listened to Jethro Tull more than the rest of us, but we all had Genesis records."

While their musical interests were diverse, there's no disputing the influence of local bands. What made Bad Religion so appealing to its fans was that it was a synthesis of the best of Southern California punk: they had the energy and intensity of hardcore bands from the beach cities, like Black Flag and the Circle Jerks; intelligent lyrics that could hold their own with Hollywood's best, like X and the Germs; and melodic sensibilities of Orange County bands like the Adolescents with harmonies and background vocals. Bad Religion had a quintessential L.A. sound, but with their new material they were turning away from that.

At first, Jay wasn't too concerned with labeling what they were doing. "We'd been learning the songs and sort of working on them and they made sense to me." The times had changed and so had punk. Brett loved David Bowie, who seemingly reinvented himself on every record, and Bowie's influence can be heard on the opening riff of his song "Chasing the Wild Goose." Greg believed this played a part in Brett's decision to pursue a project that was more prog than punk. "For Brett, changing your identity on an album wasn't a big deal. I think Brett thought, *I'm an artist, man. This is what you do.*" Besides, T.S.O.L. had already done it.

When Bad Religion had enough material for a record, they reached out to Thom Wilson, a respected punk rock producer in Southern California. Thom had produced a number of records by their friends, including the Adolescents' self-titled debut and Christian Death's *Only Theatre of Pain*. He'd also worked extensively with T.S.O.L. and had produced both *Dance with Me* and

Beneath the Shadows. This was someone who seemed to have his finger on the erratic pulse of punk rock and that made him attractive to Brett. "I always thought the records he did were the best sounding, so we hired him."

They went to a studio that Thom liked to work out of called Perspective Sound in Sun Valley. The problems started almost immediately after they began working on the first song, "It's Only Over When . . . " After laying down tracks, Jay was ready to move on to the next song, but instead they spent hours on overdubs, tinkering with the synthesizer and its many effects. "I just didn't understand it," Jay said. "When we got into the studio things started to loom into absurdity. We have to put this *pffft* thing here . . . We need to do this reverb there . . . What are we doing? You could hear it becoming this carcass."

Pete recalled that Jay was very upset: "'This is terrible! I fucking hate this! This isn't what Bad Religion is about!'"

Jay argued that they were a punk band with a following and that their fans weren't going to like what they were doing. Brett and Greg countered that it was more punk to do what you want than to do what was popular. Be that as it may, Jay wanted no part of it. He walked out of the studio and didn't come back.

The band decided to continue without Jay, but then they made another change. Brett informed Pete that Thom thought the new material was too complicated for Pete and didn't want him to play on the record.

Pete was devastated. To get up to speed on the drums, he'd been taking lessons from Lucky Lehrer, but the new songs were more complex than the punk songs he'd been playing. "I was practicing my ass off," Pete said, but it wasn't enough. "I was heartbroken."

To fill out the rhythm section, Greg turned to Paul Dedona, a bass player, and Davy Goldman, the jazz drummer who'd jammed with Jay before Bad Religion had formed. It didn't take long to record the rest of *Into the Unknown* as it only had eight songs, but they were longer than the songs the band had previously recorded. Once they were finished, they took the record to Gold

Star to have it mastered, and Brett prepared to ship Bad Religion's new release.

Throughout 1983, the band played material from *Into the Unknown* during their live shows—sans synthesizer. In March, they played three songs from the album at the Starlite in Long Beach, and the flyer for their show in August at the Vex in East L.A. touted *Into the Unknown*. Davy wasn't able to play that show, so they turned to Pete, who hadn't been fired per se, but put on hiatus. Pete agreed to play, but the night before the gig he got in a drunken bar fight and sustained injuries that required plastic surgery. The show went on without him.

That fall, while Brett got the new record ready, Greg returned to Wisconsin, this time as a full-time student when he transferred from California State University, Northridge, to the University of Wisconsin.[3] One of the things that made returning to Wisconsin so appealing to Greg was the opportunity to study with John Talbot Robinson, the renowned South African paleontologist who taught in the anthropology department. Greg did an independent study with Robinson and took a seminar with him on taxonomy.

Back in L.A., Bad Religion soldiered on without Greg and *Into the Unknown* was released on November 30, 1983. The album featured artwork of a scene from deep space. "I bought that painting at an art fair in Phoenix," Brett said. "There was an artist who did airbrush on glass. It looked really cool." It did not look like a punk record. Even the title, *Into the Unknown,* signaled a shift.

Ten thousand copies of the new record went out the door on day one. Keep in mind that it took several pressings and the better part of a year to reach those numbers with *How Could Hell Be Any Worse?* As Brett prepared for the release, he thought, "*Oh wow, this one is going to be huge!*"

---

3. It's also where Milo Aukerman of the Descendents studied after he earned his degree in biochemistry from the University of California, San Diego, but Milo's time at the University of Wisconsin didn't overlap with Greg's.

It wasn't. In fact, the record flopped. It didn't take long for Brett to realize that people weren't buying the album. Then the returns started coming in. Brett would later joke that people hated the record so much that "we shipped 10,000 copies and received 10,001 returns."

Word of mouth about the new record was intensely unfavorable. Fans decried the album's new direction and complained that it was too soft. This review that appeared in *Maximum Rocknroll* was typical of the vitriol: "Basically, this new Bad Religion album totally sucks, unless you like slickly-produced early '70s wimp rock. After playing it, I hurled it out the window, into the unknown."

Everyone was aware that punk was changing, and die-hard fans were quick to castigate bands that turned their back on the scene. By any measure, *Into the Unknown* lacks the intensity of Bad Religion's previous recorded material, and they did it without warning. For example, before releasing *Beneath the Shadows,* T.S.O.L. put out an EP that showcased their gloomy new sound. However, T.S.O.L. included songs on the record that were loud and fast. If they chose to do so, they could play songs from the new album in a live set that blended in with their old material.[4] The same was also true of Bad Religion—as long as they left the synthesizer at home.

So, what happened? Was Bad Religion ahead of their time or did they make a bad record?

Jay thought the success of *How Could Hell Be Any Worse?* prevented Brett and Greg from being able to think critically about what they were doing. "We are great! People love us! All we have to do is fart into a microphone and people will buy it."

That's a harsh assessment, but one Brett believed wasn't far off the mark. As Epitaph expanded over the years, he had the opportunity to work with scores of young musicians who had experienced success for the first time with their first album and were figuring out what to do next. Most young bands, in his opinion,

---

4. It's worth noting T.S.O.L.'s fans weren't happy with *Beneath the Shadows* either.

lacked the maturity to see that a successful record was the product of many factors that came together at the right time, of which the band was just a single part—an important part, but a part nonetheless.

"It's not that they want to reinvent themselves," Brett explained. "They don't realize they've been invented. When a bunch of talented teenagers make their first record and it's phenomenal they're likely to think, *Oh, cool. That was easy. I just write anything I'm feeling and it's automatically great.* But they don't realize it was something about *that* particular thing in *that* particular moment. It's very hard to take a step back, to look at what you've made, and say, 'Wow, how the hell did that happen? And what's significant about it?'"

One explanation for the failure of *Into the Unknown* is that Bad Religion didn't recognize how passionate people were about their music. Pete subscribed to this view. "I think Greg and Brett honestly felt in their hearts that people would think, *All right, this is a little bit different for Bad Religion, but it's cool . . .* I don't think they were prepared for the antipathy toward the record by their fans. There was so much hate."

When Bad Religion played songs from *Into the Unknown* at shows, they played them without the Roland Juno-6, and that made all the difference. When fans heard the synthesizer on the record, they freaked out. Jay, who was very much aware of their fan base, agreed with this sentiment. "In all honesty, I would say that fifty percent of the problem with *Into the Unknown* was not really understanding that you've built a fan base around the band. When you've put out a record that people like, you just can't say, 'Oh, we've reinvented ourselves, and now we're this' and keep people happy. That just doesn't work. The other fifty percent was drugs."

Throughout high school Brett had experimented with psychedelic drugs. He has suggested in interviews that his LSD use was partly responsible for *Into the Unknown* being so out there. "I liked psychedelic drugs and I liked psychedelic music as a kid,"

Brett explained, "and those things go together. That is part of my personality."

Nevertheless, the inspiration for the album didn't come from some psychic dimension, but Brett's own bandmate. "When Greg said, 'Here's my new song,' I thought I should write a song that would go with his. So I brought a song to the studio that was a proggy song. It's not his fault that I went along with it, but he started it. I should have thought twice about that. I never thought to stop and say, 'Why are we doing this?' Back in the eighties every punk band eventually made their synth-y disco album, even the Clash did it. And there was Public Image Limited. But no punk band had ever made a prog album—except us!"

At the time, Brett believed the thing that made Bad Religion stand out from other local bands was they had made a record, not that the record was good. In his mind, *anyone* could get modestly popular simply by making a record and putting it out into the world. "It just didn't seem plausible that we were exceptional in any way," Brett said. "I didn't understand how rare it is for an un-signed band to make a record and have people like it. I had no idea that we, to quote Steve Jobs, had put a dent in the universe."

In other words, they'd underestimated how much their music meant to their fans who cared deeply about the band and its music. "I was only like eighteen or nineteen years old," Greg said, "so I didn't pay attention to that stuff. It wasn't punk to be aware of your fans. You were supposed to be one *with* your fans, open and tolerant of each other's quirks and choices."

Bad Religion had devoted a great deal of time and energy to being the best punk band they could be. While still in their teens they'd become seasoned veterans of the scene. They'd learned how to play and developed a large following. They'd spent count-less hours rehearsing, playing, and recording in subpar spaces under less than ideal conditions. They'd paid their dues as a punk band. As a prog band they had not.

"There wasn't a whole lot of tact involved in what we did," Jay said. "There wasn't a lot of thought. We were entering into a realm that we knew very little about. Much like it was my dream as a youngster to be an astronaut, it wouldn't be wise of me to get into one of those space rockets and shoot myself into the sun and go, 'I'm an astronaut!' There's a little more to it than that. I think there was a lot of ambition, there was a lot of ego, and in a sense maybe it was good to get pounded down a notch."

Brett has been brutally honest about *Into the Unknown*'s failings but insisted that it wasn't a calculated decision to push the band in a new direction.

"We went into it completely naively," Brett said. "Honestly, it was a bad choice and if we'd had any foresight or wisdom of any kind we wouldn't have done it."

Even Brett's father miscalculated the album's potential. "I probably gave him bad advice," Richard recalled. "I thought he'd be more successful with *Into the Unknown*. I thought that was a better way to go [than punk]. I think I had some influence on that and it was the wrong direction."

Today, *Into the Unknown* has its fair share of fans, the majority of whom seek out the record as a curiosity. This raises an interesting point: would *Into the Unknown* be considered a good album if anyone other than Bad Religion had put it out?

Brett didn't think so. During the recording he recognized that the album had problems. "It started becoming this proggy, unfocused, inconsistent patchwork of a record."

Jay's opinion of the record has softened somewhat over the years. "I think that it was an okay album that was poorly put together," he said. "The songs aren't terrible. My feeling is if you're going to be a prog rock band, be a prog rock band."

In retrospect, transferring to Wisconsin had been a prudent move for Greg as he wasn't in L.A. when *Into the Unknown* was released and he was spared the intense backlash the record generated. As a student at the University of Wisconsin, Greg was insulated from the album's failure. "I had no idea how angry people were," he said. Greg played the record for his friends, who had little or no frame of reference for what Bad Religion was all about, and they liked it. At the time, Greg was focusing on his studies, which he felt as passionately about as he did music. He had other things going on in his life besides Bad Religion.

That wasn't the case for Brett. He was Epitaph's only employee and the fate of the album fell squarely on his shoulders. This intensified the loss all the more. He'd gambled and lost.

"The failure of *Into the Unknown* affected Brett more than it did Greg," Jay said. "Greg had nothing to lose. For Brett, it was both a creative and a commercial failure, so it hit both sides of his psyche. It was a knife in his side and watching him bleed out was tough."

The least Brett could do was cut his losses. "I took all the returns and had a ritual burning. I burned boxes of vinyl in my driveway. After a couple of boxes I realized what a toxic death fire I was creating. Terrible, noxious smoke rising up out of the driveway."

Brett was unapologetic about his desire to "Stalinize" the record, i.e., make it disappear and forget it ever existed. But he didn't get all of them. An unspecified number of boxes made their way to Bomp! Records, along with the original artwork for the album. There was nothing left to do but pick up the pieces and move on, except there were no pieces to pick up. Even worse than poor sales and a damaged reputation, their journey into the unknown had broken up the band.

7

NEW LEAF

WHEN THE CALENDAR FLIPPED TO 1984, BAD
Religion was more or less defunct. Their latest
album had tanked, and the musicians who'd
recorded *How Could Hell Be Any Worse?* were all following different
paths through life. Bad Religion's prospects were bleaker than
they'd ever been. The band might have stayed dormant and
eventually dissolved if not for the efforts of a guitar player who
wasn't even a member of the band: Greg Hetson.

Hetson was the ultimate L.A. punk rock scenester. He was a
founding member of the influential band Red Cross (which later
became Redd Kross); was currently in the Circle Jerks, one of the
most popular punk bands in L.A.; and he seemed to know everyone who was anyone in Hollywood. He went out virtually every
night and knew all the bartenders, bookers, and bouncers. He
knew the up-and-coming bands and which bands were looking for
a drummer or a roadie. If a band canceled a show or there was an
opening at a club, Hetson knew about it. When he learned that

Greg Graffin was back in town, he called him up to find out when Bad Religion would be playing again.

Greg had hoped that his father's status as an English professor at the University of Wisconsin would exempt him from out-of-state tuition, but in the university's eyes Greg was a California resident. After a semester in Madison, he was unable to afford the tuition and transferred to UCLA to continue his studies. He wanted to take classes in geology and biology each quarter, but neither major would permit him to do that. Greg settled on majoring in anthropology because it gave him the freedom to enroll in the classes he wanted to take. This proved to be a fortuitous decision because in a history class he met Greta Maurer, an undergraduate from Del Mar, a seaside town north of San Diego, and they eventually moved in together as a couple.

David Markey of the fanzine *We Got Power* was getting ready to release *Desperate Teenage Lovedolls,* a campy, low-budget film about two women whose passion for rock and roll is stymied by rival bands, dangerous gangs, and a creepy manager played by Steve McDonald of Redd Kross. Markey asked Hetson to contribute a song to the soundtrack, and Hetson teamed up with Bad Religion's front man on "Runnin' Fast," a simple song that was more straightforward than the tunes on *Into the Unknown* but was not going to spark rumors of a Bad Religion comeback. On the soundtrack, they were listed as Greg Greg.[5]

But a comeback was in the works. Greg had kept writing songs while he was in Wisconsin, and with Hetson's encouragement, Greg warmed to the idea of playing Bad Religion gigs again.

"Hetson was the guy we all looked up to as a success," Greg said. "He was the first guy that came home from a national punk tour with thousands of dollars in the bank. He was older than me so I looked up to him as being smarter than me and better at the business of music, if there was such a thing."

---

5. When the soundtrack was reissued they appeared as Greg Graffin and Greg Hetson.

The two were an odd pair. While Hetson was earning his reputation as a barfly every night, Greg never drank and was genuinely
passionate about science. But Greg bonded with the guitarist over
their shared sense of humor. "Even though I looked up to him we
were on the same level, cracking jokes with each other. Hetson
and I were always joking. Our whole life was just sharing jokes with
each other."

Greg reached out to Pete Finestone to see if he'd be interested
in playing the old Bad Religion songs.

"Fuck yeah!" was Pete's reply.

But who would play bass? Hetson had some ideas. He re-
cruited his old friend Tim Gallegos, who'd played with Lucky
Lehrer's brother, Chett, in Wasted Youth in the early eighties.
In fact, Tim had replaced Jay Bentley when he left that band
too. Hetson met Tim at Hawthorne High School, where Tim
took music lessons from the same teacher who taught the Beach
Boys how to play their instruments when they were his students.
Tim's father was a Hollywood stuntman who worked with Bruce
Lee and Elvis Presley, and from a very young age Tim worked as
an extra in movies, including Cheech and Chong's *Up in Smoke,*
which famously concluded with a battle of the bands emceed by
Rodney Bingenheimer. The Germs, the Dils, and Geza X all recorded songs for the movie that day but none of them made it
onto the final cut. Nevertheless, Darby Crash and Pat Smear appear in the movie as extras.

"We went to the same school and knew the same people," Tim
said of his future bandmate. "Greg [Hetson] was into punk, I was
into rock. I always had long hair. When I went to the gigs, I had long
hair and a big long earring. Punks never gave me shit. I thought, *I
like these people, I'm going to cut my hair and be a punk, too!*"

Tim was a regular in the South Bay scene and would go to
shows at the Fleetwood in Redondo Beach, the Barn in Torrance,
and Dancing Waters in San Pedro. He was at the infamous Black
Flag show at Polliwog Park in Manhattan Beach in 1979 when

angry attendees threw food and beer at the band. (Hetson and Jay were also in attendance.)

Greg, Hetson, and Pete welcomed Tim to the band and started rehearsing. They worked on a mix of old Bad Religion songs, plus some new numbers that Greg and Hetson had written. Eventually, Greg approached Brett about recording the new material. Eager to release a record that was comparable to Bad Religion's old sound, Brett agreed.

The EP has just five songs and each one is distinct. It opens with "Yesterday," a ruminative song with an apocalyptic feel. Many of Greg's songs from this period deal with a past that reveals things about the present if we really look and see what's there. This is also a good description of the job of the geologist.

Hetson's influence is strongest on "Frogger": the loud, abrasive song features Hetson's slash-and-smash style of guitar playing and would not be out of place on a Circle Jerks album. Although the lyrics appear to reference L.A. traffic, Greg wrote the song with a friend from Racine named Wrye Martin while they were in school at Wisconsin. He and his dorm mates had to dash across a busy street to get to the campus cafeteria. The reference to the popular video game gives the song a tongue-in-cheek feel that struck just the right note for their follow-up to *Into the Unknown,* as if they were encouraging their fans not to take any of this too seriously. The song remains a classic example of punk colliding with pop culture, though the band rarely plays it at shows.

A new version of "Bad Religion" serves as the record's centerpiece, a reminder that, despite the band's ups and downs, they could still deliver the goods. It's Brett's sole creative contribution to the EP, although he didn't play on the record.

The EP also features the band's first anthem: "Along the Way." With its martial beat and slower tempo, the song struck a somber-sounding note that was new for Bad Religion. The song's final verse begins,

Like Tommy you are free and you will not follow me
Until we see each other once more on the path along the way.

This is not a reference to Tom Clement, Greg's high school classmate who died in a car crash and would be immortalized in a future Bad Religion song, but a childhood friend of Greg's from Wisconsin named Tommy George. Tommy and Greg were part of a tight-knit group of friends who grew up together in Racine. Tommy lived in a house behind Greg's father's place, and he and Greg played ball together every summer. Greg wrote the song after learning of Tommy's death, and said that its intimation of an afterlife was "as close as I ever got to being religious."

"New Leaf," the final song on the EP, signals a return to broader themes, but it strikes a personal chord in its desire to "turn over a new leaf." Obviously, both Greg and Brett were eager to move on from the disaster of *Into the Unknown,* but Greg's disappointing departure from Wisconsin and the death of his friend communicated his recognition that an important chapter in his life had come to a close.

The EP was recorded in a single night in April at Pacifica Studios in Culver City and, like their first EP, was sent off to the Alberti record pressing plant. Hetson jokingly suggested "Back from into the Unknown" as a title, which Greg shortened to *Back to the Known.* The cover features the band's name and the crossbuster logo with a set of green frog footprints across the bottom. Instead of putting two songs on one side of the album and three on the other, the band decided to put all five songs on one side and leave the other blank so that listeners wouldn't have to flip the record over.[6] *Back to the Known* was the first record that Brett engineered and mixed—but it wouldn't be the last.

---

6. Many years later, in an interview with Jack Rabid of *The Big Takeover,* Greg joked that Brett knew that CDs were coming so they were ahead of the curve in releasing a record with only one side.

Bad Religion played its first post–*Into the Unknown* show in the spring of 1984 at Cathay de Grande. The lineup consisted of Greg, Pete, Hetson, and Tim. Brett and Jay attended the show and had a good time double-decker slam dancing with Jay riding on Brett's shoulders. Later that month, Bad Religion played a show at Lazaro's Ballroom. The flyer for the show billed Bad Religion as a "special guest . . . after 1½ yrs," as if *Into the Unknown* had never happened. The whitewashing had begun.

On June 1, Bad Religion played the Grand Olympic Auditorium with the Exploited, D.O.A., Kraut, and Love Canal. They played a spirited set that included their old material, some new songs, and a cover of REO Speedwagon's "Ridin' the Storm Out." They continued to play shows that summer, but in the fall, Pete announced he was leaving the band to attend school in London. His last show before departing for England was at Club Lingerie, where Brendan Mullen, formerly of the Masque, was the booker. It was not the send-off Pete had hoped for. "That last show at the Lingerie was Greg, Tim on bass, Hetson, and me," Pete said. "And there were like five people there. It was so depressing. *Oh, god, no one cares about Bad Religion. No one.*"

Bad Religion had enjoyed some success playing in front of large crowds with other hardcore bands, but could they draw a crowd on their own? Had *Into the Unknown* done permanent damage to their reputation?

Before they could answer that question, they would need to find a new drummer. Hetson knew a musician from Claremont named John Albert who was one of the founding members of Christian Death. Hetson gave him a call. "'You play drums, right? Do you want to be in Bad Religion?'"

Although John associated with punks in the Orange County scene, he wasn't a stranger to Bad Religion. He got to know Jay Bentley through the Adolescents and was at the infamous show at the boxing arena the night Jay got beat up by the bouncers. When the fight broke out, John and Steve Soto locked themselves in the dressing room and then climbed out the back window with all of the beer and a deli platter. While Jay was in the hospital, they went back to their hotel and drank beer and ate sandwiches.

John had a drum kit, but he was primarily a guitar player, not a drummer. They rehearsed in a studio in North Hollywood. "Weird way to become a drummer," John said, "but the songs were pretty basic. It wasn't complex."

Like Pete's parents, both of John's parents were college professors, so John got along well with Greg. Greg was unlike anyone else John had met in the scene. While John knew other punk rockers who went on to college, he'd never known anyone who had his own collection of fossils. Greg struck John as his own person who wasn't all that interested in punk rock music.

"We were driving to San Francisco and I had to listen to hours of Jethro Tull," John said. "He never listened to punk rock. He would wear a Yes shirt onstage and people would think he was making an ironic statement. He wasn't."

In 1985, the band stayed close to home with gigs around L.A., Long Beach, and the Inland Empire, as well as an occasional trip to Arizona or San Diego. But Bad Religion's drummer had a not-so-secret secret: John Albert was a heroin addict. Although he tried to hold it together and be discreet, he was a drummer with track marks. His situation couldn't have been any more obvious. Also, he was intermittently wasted. On December 14, 1985, John decided he'd finally had enough. He left the band to check himself into a rehab facility, and didn't come out for a year. His time in Bad Religion was over and the band, once again, needed a drummer.

8

GO WEST

WHILE GREG WAS PURSUING HIS COLLEGE DE-gree, Brett was getting an entirely different kind of education. As a smart, bookish kid, Brett thought he'd eventually end up on a path similar to Greg's, but it didn't work out that way. Although he didn't graduate from El Camino Real High School and had gotten his GED, Brett didn't see himself as a dropout. "I wasn't really quitting school in my mind. I thought, *I'll go to junior college and I'll take classes that I'm interested in and I'll get enough units to go to a regular college. That will be my path.*"

Brett enrolled in Pierce College, a community college in the San Fernando Valley, and took music and philosophy classes, but he didn't really apply himself. "I just couldn't conform to the academic program, so I always failed. I failed classes and started ditching and became a pretty heavy drug user." Brett tried art school next and took classes in painting and color theory at Otis-Parsons in downtown L.A., but the results were the same.

"I didn't really have the discipline to show up for that either," Brett said. "The big thing for me was I was just very dissipated and didn't have good work habits and was pretty wild. A lot of recreational drug use and going to shows."

Brett's parents, though supportive, were exasperated by their son's failure to thrive. If he wasn't working or enrolled in school, he needed to find someplace else to live. This seemed reasonable to Brett, who was now dating Suzy Shaw, who'd been married to Greg Shaw of Bomp! Records and essentially ran the label. Suzy was twelve years older than Brett, so living at home was seriously cramping his style. With Suzy's help he got a job at Sounds Good Imports and moved out of his parents' house. Brett found an upstairs apartment overlooking a gas station at the intersection of Moorpark Street and Tujunga Avenue in North Hollywood.

But the move that changed the course of Brett's life was his decision to enroll in night school at the University of Sound Arts in Hollywood to learn how to record music. This was the missing link in his education. While everything else he was doing made sense to Brett, the skills he learned at the University of Sound Arts gave him a sense of purpose. He was learning the ins and outs of running a label from Suzy, gaining an understanding of the business side of things from his job at Sounds Good Imports, and acquiring skills as a recording engineer at school. Brett was essentially getting a crash course in the music industry. "I was a heat-seeking missile for this kind of information," he said. The icing on the cake was that it all benefitted Epitaph Records.

At University of Sound Arts he became friends with John Gerdler, a musician from San Juan Capistrano who shared Brett's passion for music and recreational drugs. They became roommates and, eventually, business partners. They had a strong desire to make records, but no clients. So when Greg approached Brett about recording the *Back to the Known* EP, Brett jumped at the opportunity to do it.

"I can't say whose idea it was. I don't want to take credit for that, but it was something to cut my teeth on because I was going to recording school, the University of Sound Arts, and I very much wanted to record something real. I will say I'm not proud of that recording at all. I had no idea what I was doing. I wasn't really ready to do a recording. I'm always a little overeager. I jumped right into it. We made a lot of really terrible-sounding recordings in those days. Punk records were not known for sounding good. So it was fine compared to what else was out there, but it wasn't a Thom Wilson production."

On a personal level, Brett was eager to connect with Greg, with whom he felt he was losing touch. When Brett wasn't at work or school, he immersed himself in the underground club scene—a scene that was as foreign to Greg as the rigors of academia were to Brett.

"The L.A. scene was exploding with new sounds," Brett explained. "The kids from the punk scene were channeling beatniks, growing their hair out, taking MDMA, coke, and heroin. It was around that time that I discovered narcotics. It was quite the opposite of what my dear friend Greg was doing, which was going to UCLA. He was very centered and focused."

Brett's roommate, John, learned that an extremely wealthy distant relative had died and left him a small part of his fortune. With that money, and another loan from Richard Gurewitz, they decided to open their own recording studio. When Brett was recording *Back to the Known* with Bad Religion at Pacifica Studios, he noticed they had a little room in the back that they weren't using. Brett approached Pacifica about the space and they agreed to rent it to him. He moved in his equipment and Westbeach Recorders was open for business.

Why Westbeach? "We were fuck-ups," Brett said. "I had blue hair and John had track marks and we were always getting loaded. We weren't people that could go into a bank and get a loan. We didn't want to name it Snot Recording Studios. We wanted to name it something that would sound legit so that if we invoiced somebody they would actually pay us. At the time there was a studio called Westlake Recorders. Westlake was one of the biggest studios in L.A. Michael Jackson recorded there. We could never dream of ever being in a studio like that, or even affording an hour there. I said to John, 'Well, Westbeach kinda sounds like Westlake . . . ' The idea being, if I met somebody at a recording equipment store, I could say, *I'm with Westbeach Recorders.* It might ring a bell because it sounds like Westlake and give us credit."

The designer who created their logo won an award for his work. So Brett and John would refer to their business as "the award-winning Westbeach Recorders." For Brett, "it was an inside joke. It had nothing to do with our sound."

Westbeach Recorders was located on a little street called La Cienega Place where La Cienega and Venice Boulevards came together. The building had once been a domestic residence, so Westbeach was literally in a closet in the back of Pacifica Studios.

They had a studio, they had equipment, and they had a little know-how. There was just one problem: Brett was broke. "I didn't have any money, but I knew what bands could be good to sign." Brett approached his bosses at Sounds Good Imports about doing a pressing and distribution deal—what's known in the music business as a P&D deal. He would sign the bands and Sounds Good would advance the money to manufacture the records and provide distribution. Best of all, Brett already had a record he could start with: Bad Religion's *How Could Hell Be Any Worse?* Because Bad Religion's debut was now out of print, it seemed like the perfect situation.

Sounds Good agreed to this arrangement and started paying Brett $3,000 for every band that he signed. It was a bit of a Faustian bargain because, while the band's recording fees went toward paying Westbeach's rent, the bands also expected to be paid. This would have been difficult to manage even without the chaos of his growing appetite for drugs, which was becoming increasingly unmanageable.

"To give you an idea of what my existence was like back in those days," Brett said, "I would get my paycheck, go down to the check cashing place, get cash for it at lunch, go buy cocaine from my connection, come back to work before the end of my lunch break and my paycheck would be blown before that day's work was done. Then I would go into my weekend going, *Fuck! What am I gonna do?*"

Brett started spending all his free time at Westbeach. Like Studio 9, he charged $15 an hour, which included the services of the studio's engineer: him. "I was working two jobs and only making enough to pay my rent at home and in the studio and get high. I had no other money."

Bomp! was putting out a lot of psychedelic garage bands at the time and Suzy steered some of those bands Brett's way. He recorded the Morlocks, the Primates, and the Things. One of the stranger psychedelic acts he recorded was Sky Saxon of the Seeds. Greg Shaw of Bomp! knew him from Haight-Ashbury and the Sunset Strip. Saxon had gone underground after his involvement with the Source Family, which was a cult-like commune in the Hollywood Hills, but he came out of hiding to do a month of recording at Westbeach. Brett had to pick him up from the motel where he was living, drive him to the studio, record all day, and then drive him back before heading home to his own apartment in North Hollywood.

Brett remembered it as an interesting time: "Sky Saxon was a beautiful soul, a beautiful guy, I think his real name was Richard, but he was a real acid casualty. He had long hair and this silver lamé cape. Ten watches on each arm with each one set to a different time like he was a time traveler. He claimed he could look in your eyes and discover your true universe name. So he did that with me and it was Starbolt."

Keith Morris got wind of the nickname and made sure that it stuck—not that Brett was opposed to it. When Brett performed multiple roles on an Epitaph record, he would sometimes ascribe the engineering duties in the liner notes to "The Legendary Starbolt," as he did on the Bad Religion albums *Suffer, No Control, Against the Grain,* and *Generator.*

Brett also worked on projects with his friends in the wider punk community. He recorded Thelonious Monster's *Baby . . . You're Bummin' My Life out in a Supreme Fashion,* a veritable who's who of what Brett referred to as "the luminaries of the Hollywood freak scene." K. K. Barrett from the Screamers, Dix Denney of the Weirdos, Keith Morris of the Circle Jerks, Angelo Moore of Fishbone, and many more all made guest appearances on the record, and that doesn't include the guest producers. "I was in that mix," Brett said. "That was my world. We were partying together."

All-nighters were not uncommon at Westbeach. On one occasion Brett did a seventy-two-hour session with Stiv Bators, formerly of the Dead Boys. "He brought in this thing called a Fairlight CMI," Brett recalled, "which was a state-of-the-art digital synthesizer from the eighties that had thousands of string sounds. He was doing post-punk in the Lords of the New Church. He was into speed and I was into coke. We were just listening to these string sounds, trying to pick the best one, but when you're gacked out of your mind and you're on the seventy-fifth one, at some point it just spirals into sheer insanity. You can't even tell what you're hearing anymore."

Sheer insanity was quickly becoming Brett's modus operandi, but this was getting to be a problem because just about the only person who didn't know about Brett's drug use was his girlfriend, Suzy. Although they shared a number of interests, drugs weren't one of them. To maintain his relationship with Suzy, he had to keep his behavior a secret. Westbeach gave him a place where he could do his drugs without Suzy finding out about it, but it was getting harder and harder to keep his life as an addict a secret.

9

JERKING BACK
AND FORTH

AFTER JAY BENTLEY QUIT BAD RELIGION IN 1983, he was so fed up with the scene that he sold all his gear and stopped playing music. At the time, he was also playing in Wasted Youth and T.S.O.L., but the life of a punk rock musician was no longer for him. He went to a party one night and bumped into a pretty girl named Marie. They hit it off and they ended up dating for the next three years. Prior to that, Marie had briefly dated his old bandmate Greg, but Jay's relationship with Marie lasted considerably longer, and he eventually went to work for her dad as a machinist in Alondra Park. His time in Bad Religion faded into a distant memory.

But then Jay's old life came creeping back. He started hanging out with a party crowd, which Marie didn't like as he was fairly settled at that point. When Greg Hetson asked Jay to play a gig with the Circle Jerks at the Music Machine in Santa Monica, Jay accepted the invitation.

He bought some cheap equipment and got ready to play, but Jay became so inebriated during the show that he threw his bass guitar up in the air and, much to his chagrin, it didn't come down. The venue had a drop ceiling and Jay's bass had somehow gotten stuck in the ceiling tiles. Jay thought this was hilarious, but it was the end of his career as a Circle Jerk. "I played one show and they kicked me out because I was super drunk," he said. Keith and Hetson wanted to give Jay another shot, but they were vetoed by the Circle Jerks' drummer, Keith Clark, aka "Adolph," who had the unenviable job of being the only adult in the band.

"The Circle Jerks, were experiencing some technical difficulties in the bass player department," Keith recalled, "and we had guys like Jay Bentley and Tim Gallegos playing with us. I think Tim only played a show with us, and I remember Jay Bentley playing with us at the Music Machine. I was probably just as drunk as Jay was. Maybe we were splitting the case of beer. I remember at the Music Machine the guarantees were next to nothing, but there was always a bunch of beer in the back."

After his short stint with the Circle Jerks, Jay did spot duty for a couple of other bands. He did a gig with T.S.O.L. and he played in another Jack Grisham project called Cathedral of Tears. During this period Jay would occasionally bump into Brett in Hollywood. They didn't run with the same people, but they all knew each other. Jay was more of a drinker and Brett was experimenting with drugs. Still, they remained friends. Jay helped Brett move in and out of his North Hollywood apartment because he had a black pickup truck, which he'd bought with money from his injury settlement.

Once word got out that Jay was playing again, Greg Graffin gave him a call. Jay recalled the conversation went down in much the same way as his first introduction to the band.

GREG: Do you want to play some shows?
JAY: No.
GREG: We're only going to play the old stuff.
JAY: Okay.

Jay's first show back was at Fender's Ballroom in Long Beach with the Circle Jerks and Gang Green on May 1, 1986. He had long hair and wore a cowboy hat. Pete was back from London and also had been coaxed back into the fold. He was taking classes at California State University, Northridge, and living at home with his parents. He had nothing to do but play the drums all day and was all too happy to reunite with his former bandmates. They played songs from *How Could Hell Be Any Worse?* and both of their EPs. During the show, Greg announced to the crowd that they hadn't played some of the songs from the first EP in three years.

Jay discovered that Bad Religion had found a nice niche for itself. While they weren't a headliner, they had more than enough material to share the stage with anyone—if they could pull a lineup together.

The band had an opportunity to go on a short East Coast tour for the first time. Pete couldn't go because of his class schedule, and they were once again without a drummer. This time they called in a favor from a friend who'd been there from the very beginning.

Keith "Lucky" Lehrer left the Circle Jerks in 1982 at the height of the band's popularity. He took the bar exam and went into his family's business, but he remained active in the punk scene and would occasionally take on drum students, like he did with Pete Finestone. Regarded as one of the best punk rock drummers in L.A., Lucky could play a number of different styles and was frequently sought out as a fill-in or session drummer. So, in the winter of 1986, when Bad Religion needed a drummer for the East Coast tour that Hetson had arranged, they turned to Hetson's old bandmate, Lucky.

Their vehicle was an old Volkswagen microbus, which barely had enough room for the band and their equipment. Their driver was a gentleman named Dank whose religion, according to Lucky, forbade him from showering. Jay and Lucky rode in the back with the gear, separating them from the rest of the band so that their view was a wall of amplifiers. To make matters worse, one of the side windows was missing so the vehicle was freezing cold, especially at night. "It was like being in a cave," Jay recalled.

Because of the broken window, someone had to spend the night in the bus with the gear to make sure it didn't get ripped off. To pass the time between gigs, Jay and Lucky would do mushrooms. Once, Jay got so high, he demanded they stop the vehicle. Jay got out and wandered around in the cold for a while before getting back in without explaining what had happened. It was a long ten days for the boys from Southern California.

The tour had stops in North Carolina, Washington, D.C., and Boston. One bright spot on the tour was at the Hung Jury Pub in Washington, D.C. On the flyer for the show, Bad Religion was the headliner but billed as "with 2 ex Circle Jerks." Jay and Lucky met a girl who agreed to drive them to Boston and give them a respite from the cold and malodorous Volkswagen.

Lucky did not have fond memories of the tour. "My relationship with Bad Religion was more about laughter and inside jokes than the performances. When we actually did play together, it was disastrous."

While Bad Religion was struggling along, Brett was expanding Westbeach's operations. However, his partner, John, was losing interest in the studio. John sold his half of the business to Donnell Cameron in what Brett characterized as an amicable split. Donnell was a music aficionado who was interested in learning how to record music. He was independently wealthy and shared Brett's enthusiasm for drug-fueled late-night sessions.

"It was a pretty toxic combination for me," Brett admitted, "because I liked to smoke cocaine, but I was broke, and Donnell was never broke."

Once again, with the help of Jay and his truck, Brett moved out of the closet on La Cienega Place to a bungalow on Vista del Mar in Hollywood between Cathay de Grande and Raji's. It was a 1,200-square-foot duplex with two bedrooms and a kitchen that had been built in the 1930s as part of the Hollywood studio system. Brett converted the front bedroom into an office. "That's where I started Epitaph for real," Brett said.

Brett quit his job at Sounds Good so he could work at Westbeach full time. He rented an apartment in Beachwood Canyon in Hollywood, which put him closer to the studio. While he waited for his P&D deal with Sounds Good to expire so that he could start signing bands to Epitaph, he put in eighty to ninety hours a week at Westbeach.

One of the first bands Brett recorded in the new location was the Little Kings, a popular rock and roll band with a guitar player named Gore Verbinksi. Brett wasn't choosy about his clients. He recorded lounge acts, underground art bands, even country-and-western bands. Steve Fishell, a country music producer and musician who was Emmylou Harris's pedal steel guitar player, discovered Westbeach and started sending musicians to record with Brett. "Steve Fishell knew all these country studio musicians," Brett said, "and he would bring them in because he couldn't believe how cheap it was."

Word was getting out about the little house in Hollywood with the engineer who knew how to get good sounds. "I was cutting my teeth and becoming a good recording engineer," Brett said. "I was living the life. Eating, sleeping, breathing music and recording. Not writing anything, but hearing what everyone else was doing. I was a music sponge. Music was everything. Every molecule. And a lot of drugs. I was very fucking high for a lot of it."

Brett's drug of choice was freebase cocaine. The high was intense, but didn't last long, and he needed more and more coke to sustain his high. To balance out the incredible amounts of cocaine Brett was taking into his system, he drank a quart of Jack Daniel's a day—without becoming impaired. Sometimes he'd take opiates to come down. This cocktail of drugs and alcohol was getting harder to manage, especially when the night bled into the day and he found himself wide awake as the sun came up. "I'd drive home in the early morning," Brett said, "and everything had a blue tint to it. That weird shadowy feeling of existence. That was my life."

That life, or that chapter of it, was coming to a close. One night he met up with a connection who had a home recording studio. They started to make music and mess around with the recording equipment. The night turned to day, as it so often did when he was in the studio, but then it was night again. Two nights turned into three. Then four. Brett's bender lasted a week.

When Brett came out of the darkness of those seven days, his friends and acquaintances who knew about his drug habit were of two minds: they assumed he was off on a run or that he'd died. Those who didn't know about how bad things had gotten were bewildered by his disappearance, with one exception: his girlfriend Suzy was furious.

Brett knew he had to do something about his problem. He'd tried rehab before, but it wasn't for him. He'd smuggle drugs into the facility or bug out before completing his treatment. After his weeklong bender, there was no question that his drug use was out of control. On April 14, 1987, Brett got clean and sober, and this time it stuck.

Greg was also going through a period of dramatic personal changes. In the winter of 1987, after five years and three schools, he finally graduated from UCLA with a degree in anthropology. But he wasn't done with his education. In fact, he was just getting started. He had applied and been accepted into UCLA's master's program to study with Peter Vaughn and Everett C. Olson, who were luminaries in the field of vertebrate paleontology. Part of Greg's duties as a master's candidate would be to teach undergraduate classes at UCLA. This would require that Greg trade in his microphone stand for a lectern. But before he started the coursework for his master's degree, Greg decided to take a quarter off so that he could travel to South America.

Greg had been hired by the Natural History Museum of Los Angeles County, where he'd volunteered as a high school student.

He was on the job for only a few weeks when he was offered the opportunity to travel with an expedition to the Amazon basin in northern Bolivia to collect specimens and help establish a protected conservation zone. Naturally, Greg jumped at the chance.

His title on the expedition was "Collector of Birds and Mammals," which meant he was responsible for shooting and killing just about anything that moved in the rain forest. Greg learned how to skin and flense small birds and animals with precision while documenting the specimen. After six weeks of training, he was ready.

The expedition flew from Los Angeles to Miami and then on to La Paz, Bolivia, where they spent several days waiting for their permits to the Amazon to be secured. La Paz sits at eleven thousand feet, and Greg was not prepared for the dramatic change in elevation. He succumbed to altitude sickness and spent several days vomiting in his hotel room. It took longer than expected to get the paperwork they needed, but after a week they were on their way to the Amazon basin, where they would explore a remote tributary of the Madre de Dios in the northern part of Bolivia. They flew from La Paz to Trinidad to Riberalta, a town on the banks of the Madre de Dios. The scientists boarded the fittingly named *El Tigre de Los Angeles,* which bore the Natural History Museum of Los Angeles County's logo: a saber-toothed cat.

Greg was thrilled that the expedition was finally underway, but after a week on the river, Greg felt lonely and homesick. The camaraderie and scientific discourse he'd anticipated never materialized. The farther they traveled into the jungle, the further the scientists retreated into their own minds.

Greg obsessively listened to his Walkman and pined for the company of his bandmates. No matter how hairy things got on the road, there was never a dull moment. They always shared the things they were reading and learning and thinking about with each other, and would talk for hours about everything from music to politics to the latest scientific discoveries. Greg didn't realize how much he missed these conversations with his bandmates until all he had for company were the sounds of the tropical rain forest.

In his book *Anarchy Evolution,* published in 2010, Greg recalls filling the lonely hours on the boat by listening to music, which he did with a new sense of urgency: "One of the recordings on my tapes was a three-song studio project that I had recorded with Bad Religion. The songs never made it onto any of our albums because we felt that they needed more refinement. I listened to those songs over and over again. I felt a great sense of comfort as I dreamed of ways to improve the band and my songwriting. Music got me through those dark, solitary nights in the forest. It reminded me that brighter times were waiting for me upon my return."

After three weeks on the boat, they returned to Riberalta to replenish their supplies. There, Greg was informed that the curator was leaving the expedition along with several other members, essentially putting Greg in charge. To make matters worse, they learned that while they were in the jungle, Bolivia had undergone a coup and its government had been overthrown. This meant the permits they'd been issued were no longer valid. In the eyes of the government, their scientific specimens were now contraband.

Greg didn't want to give up the expedition but was afraid that if they ran afoul of the Bolivian authorities, as the de facto leader he would be the one to take the fall. He prudently decided to leave the country as quickly as he could. Enlisting the help of an Indiana missionary who owned a Cessna airplane, Greg left the jeweled forests of the Amazon behind. He returned to L.A. disillusioned about the failed expedition, but with a renewed sense of hope for his band.

10

DO WHAT
YOU WANT

NO ONE REALIZED IT AT THE TIME, BUT A BIT OF bad news changed the course of Bad Religion's career and irrevocably altered the future of punk rock.

Bad Religion was getting ready to start 1988 with a show in Berkeley, California, at 924 Gilman Street, a relatively new punk club that had opened the year before. There was just one problem: the Circle Jerks were going on tour and Greg Hetson wasn't available to play. For the last four and a half years, Bad Religion had been playing gigs with a rotating cast of players in the rhythm section, but this was a new challenge. Who would replace Hetson on guitar?

Greg reached out to his old friend Brett to gauge his interest in playing the Gilman Street gig. Brett recalled the phone conversation went like this:

GREG: Hey, Brett, how are you doing?
BRETT: I'm doing really good.

GREG: That's great. You won't believe how big the band is
   now. We're bigger than we ever were.
BRETT: Really?
GREG: Yeah, we're playing shows at Fender's Ballroom and
   we get like a thousand people now.
BRETT: Really?
GREG: You should play with us. It's so fun.
BRETT: Nah, I don't do that anymore.
GREG: Well, we have a show at Gilman Street. Hetson can't play
   so we can't do the show unless someone plays it with us.
BRETT: Oh, I don't know.
GREG: Come on. Trust me. It will be fun.

Brett relented and agreed to play the show. He got his gear
together and practiced to the records. Prior to the show, Brett
joined the others to rehearse at Uncle Rehearsal Studio on Kester
Avenue in Van Nuys. The rehearsals went well and being back with
his former bandmates felt like old times. They drove up to San
Francisco, and to Brett's surprise and delight, Greg hadn't been
exaggerating about Bad Religion's popularity.

"I don't know what Gilman Street holds," Brett said. "But it
was packed and kids were going berserk for all of our old songs,
just going nuts, 'Fuck Armageddon . . . ' and 'Bad Religion' and
'We're Only Gonna Die.' It was really fun."

Reuniting with his old band proved to be crucial because the
experience got Brett thinking about the possibility of making another record with Bad Religion. He was clean, had his own studio,
and had improved his engineering skills since recording *Back to the
Known.* "I was twenty-five, I was getting my life together, and I had
a recording studio," Brett said. He'd also completed his pressing
and distribution deal with Sounds Good, which cleared the way
for him to sign new bands. In fact, he had just signed the band L7
to Epitaph. Nevertheless, he was apprehensive about approaching
his old bandmates about making a new record.

"I knew I could make us sound killer," Brett said, "but the guys didn't know what I'd been doing. They kind of thought of me as this fuck-up with a really bad drug problem. That's how Jay and Greg regarded me."

The apprehension went both ways. Playing a gig with Brett was one thing, but writing and recording a new album was something else. Greg recalled that around the time they were recording *Back to the Known,* Brett would call him up from time to time and tell him he had some royalties for him, but they were always cash payments, never a formal royalty statement. "I think Brett had a lot of guilt," Greg said. "*How Could Hell Be Any Worse?* was successful, but the bank account was in Brett's name and he didn't pay royalties. We were just kids and he really didn't know what he was doing."

But they weren't kids anymore. They had a come-to-Jesus meeting to talk about the band's future. Brett wanted them to know, Greg and Jay especially, that he was clean and sober now and was taking Epitaph seriously. He acknowledged the mistakes he'd made with *How Could Hell Be Any Worse?* If they made another record together, he assured them he'd do things the right way. Brett's word was enough. Greg and Jay put their misgivings aside and agreed to start working on a new record.

There was one question that remained: with Brett back in the fold, what did that mean for Hetson?

"When it came time to make *Suffer,*" Greg recalled, "Brett said, 'We should have two guitars.' The two-guitar attack sounded cool and Hetson liked that too. From *Suffer* on, he recorded with us and toured with us as well."

Shortly after the gig at Gilman Street, Brett went to visit Greg in his dorm room at UCLA. Greg was living with Greta, who was now his fiancée. Brett and Greg sat down with a couple of acoustic guitars and wrote a song. They took the chords from Neil Young's "Cowgirl in the Sand" as a jumping-off point and started playing around with them. A song came together very quickly. "We wrote the whole song," Brett recalled, "including the chords, changes, melodies, and lyrics right then and there. We really liked the way it came out."

That song was "Suffer."

Although the way they wrote the song together was very different from how they usually collaborated, it was the first time they'd written new Bad Religion material since *Into the Unknown*. "It was a nice reunion," Brett said of the session. "He and I needed to have a new starting point." But it was more than a clean slate. "Suffer" showed the way forward—for the rest of the record and beyond.

The band continued to meet at Uncle in Van Nuys to rehearse. Greg and Brett agreed they would each have a new song ready every time they got together to practice. "The first rehearsal," Brett said, "I brought a song called 'Give You Nothing.' That was the first one I brought in. I think Greg brought 'Land of Competition.' We each brought one song. It was pretty straightforward to teach the band the songs."

The process was a bit more involved for Brett because he had to teach Greg how to sing his songs, but it went very smoothly considering how long it had been since they'd worked together in a creative environment. "That sort of cemented the tradition of sharing the songwriting," Brett said.

But there was something different from the last time they'd all gotten together to make a record: Pete's playing had noticeably improved. Ever since he'd returned from London, Pete had been practicing and getting better. As a result, he was much more confident than he'd been when he was brought in to replace Jay Ziskrout.

Greg and Brett kept writing songs and bringing them to rehearsal. "My day job was working at Westbeach Recorders," Brett said. "I'd be working on a band, and whenever I was on a break, I'd have a guitar in the lounge and I'd write a Bad Religion song on the couch with a pen and pencil on the coffee table."

After seven or eight rehearsals they realized they'd written fifteen songs in approximately a month. That was enough for a new record. "It was amazing to see them write songs so quickly," Jay recalled. But were they any good?

Greg thought so. "I was starting graduate school and I didn't want to be putting out songs that didn't have some intellectual merit. I wanted it to have some meat. That started the tradition that most people came to know as Bad Religion. Mixing the style of music with themes of intellectual and philosophical inquiry defined the course of my life."

In other words, Greg didn't want to write songs like "Frogger" any more. He applied the same level of intellectual rigor to his songwriting that he brought to his studies. Greg wasn't chasing a piece of paper so he could get a cushy job in academia. His studies were fueled by a thirst for knowledge and a desire to understand how the world worked. Bad Religion provided Greg with an opportunity to shape that understanding and share what he'd learned in a meaningful way.

Brett was also optimistic about their collaboration, but he wasn't quite sure what they had. "I don't think I realized how good the songs were in the moment," Brett said, "but I did realize how easy they were flowing, which was fun."

That was the operative word. If it wasn't fun, it wasn't worth doing. After eight years of ups and downs, they recognized they didn't need to reinvent themselves; they needed to reclaim the passion they'd felt when the band was forming in the Hell Hole. They still didn't know what they were doing, but they had a better understanding of how to do it.

Despite their growing enthusiasm for the new material, their expectations for the record were modest. It was their first full-length album since *Into the Unknown,* and they knew their hardcore fans, if they had any left, would be stoked. Beyond that, they didn't know what to expect.

In April 1988, they started recording the new album at Westbeach. Brett wasted no time laying down the tracks on his cherished MCI JH24 two-inch 24-track tape machine. It only took a week to record the album. During Bad Religion's long layoff, Brett had been recording bands nonstop and knew how to make a record that sounded good. He also knew that no one was making music like this.

"When we recorded *Suffer*," Jay said, "the world had written Bad Religion off. We were a dead band. We recorded this album, the way I look at it, like mad scientists in a laboratory. We were doing this thing and the only people who knew what we were doing was us. We knew we were doing something that was kind of out in space."

But it wasn't just Bad Religion that had been written off. Punk rock was at a low water mark and had been in steady decline since the early eighties. The popularity of MTV had pushed punk deeper underground as young audiences turned to punk-influenced bands. In the mid-eighties, independent labels like SST had released records by Minutemen, Hüsker Dü, and Sonic Youth, but struggled with administrative issues (to put it mildly). Fewer bands were making punk records and those that did understood it wasn't a viable path to commercial success. But *Suffer* was about to change all of that in a big way.

"It felt like a demarcation line had been crossed," Pete said. "A new chapter was about to start."

The album opens with an address to the listener. The first track, "You Are the Government," begins with the words "Hey sit down and listen," like a storyteller beginning a tale. The opening lyric to the last song on the album, "Pessimistic Lines," is "So here we are again," framing everything in between the first song and the last as a conversation between the band and those who have stayed loyal to Bad Religion.

The songs weren't all that different from their early material, but they were faster, more melodic, and, in most cases, noticeably shorter. The addition of a second guitar ramped up the intensity, but thanks to Brett's skills in the studio, the overall sound was much improved. This sound showcased all of Bad Religion's talents, from Greg's singing to the faster rhythms to the harmonizing background vocals.

"The moment it dawned on me that we had something special," Brett said, "was when I was driving home from a show at Iguana's in Tijuana with Jay Bentley. I had the finished, mastered album of *Suffer* on cassette. I was in a late eighties Buick Century, which had the best GM Delco stereo. We were driving home, listening to *Suffer*. We'd listen to the whole album, then the tape would flip and we'd hear the whole album again. Then it would flip and we'd hear it again. We listened to it three or four times, and we just looked at each other like, *Holy fuck! Is this as good as I think it is?*"

Jay felt the same way. "I remember Brett and I kind of looking at each other and laughing. *Holy shit. Is this really happening?*"

That summer, Greg was working at a restaurant as a salad-bar host with a fellow student from UCLA named Jerry Mahoney. Jerry was an artist who was proficient in airbrushing. Greg told him the name of the album and Jerry came up with the image of a boy in a suburban setting wearing a T-shirt with the crossbuster logo, immersed in flames like a Buddhist monk. Whereas *How Could Hell Be Any Worse?* featured an apocalyptic vision of downtown Los Angeles, the image that Mahoney created feels more intimate set against the clean lines of suburban sprawl. The boy isn't being consumed by the flames, but instead seems to be generating them with the force of his defiance.

Suffer was intended to signal a fresh start for the band, and it sounds like it, but there are several links to the Bad Religion of old. The first is "Give You Nothing" with its primitive drumbeats and ferocious guitars. The band's high school friend Tom Clement, who brought Greg and Brett together and had died in a car accident under mysterious circumstances, inspired the song. The chorus, which repeats the line, "I give you me, I give you nothing," was something that Tom used to say. The song sometimes appears with "Tom Clement" in parentheses.

Another link to the early days of Bad Religion has created a great deal of confusion over the years. "Part II (The Numbers Game)" is the eleventh track on the album, and the penultimate song is called "Part IV (The Index Fossil)." But there isn't a song called Part I or Part III on *Suffer*. Bad Religion did write a song called "Part III," but it appears on *How Could Hell Be Any Worse?* and is about World War III. Because "The Numbers Game" is all about the buildup to war, Brett decided to call it "Part II." Following that logic, "Part IV" is about the aftermath of war and is presented from the perspective of a society in ruins after humankind has been wiped off the face of the earth. Needless to say, "Part IV (The Index Fossil)" was inspired by Greg's studies in geology. Taken together, the three parts tell the story of before, during, and after a cataclysmic war.

The song that pointed the way forward was "Do What You Want." On one hand, it's Brett's sly critique of the malignant philosophy of Friedrich Nietzsche. Indeed, the song's title is his interpretation of Nietzsche's will to power; in other words, what the philosopher posited is the driving force within all human beings. Nietzsche believed this will to power was neither good nor bad, but when it has been embraced by fascists and authoritarians, it conveniently ignores the fate of those who get trampled by those who seize power and seek more and more of it.

Ironically, "Do What You Want" is the ultimate "Go for it!" anthem, a song that has launched millions of skate sessions:

Say what you must
Do all you can, break all the fucking rules
And go to hell with Superman and die like
a champion
Ya-hey!

Its ferocious guitar licks and relentless rhythm power the song along. When all is said and done, "Do What You Want" clocks in at just over a minute. As for the compression of "Yeah!" and "Hey" into "Ya-hey!" Greg said he "copied it from Joey Shithead" of D.O.A.

Brett was very much aware that the skaters and surfers were Bad Religion's core audience. Epitaph advertised in *Thrasher*, and

Brett noticed the magazine frequently offered giveaways for new subscribers. This promotion was usually in the front of the magazine. That gave Brett an idea.

"I called the guy at *Thrasher* and said, 'Hey, I'll give you some records for the subscription promo so anyone who subscribes to *Thrasher* gets the new Bad Religion cassette.' They were like, 'Yeah, we'd love to do that!' It was like getting an ad and paying for it with records, and it was advertising to the exact right people. It was a really good thing."

Suffer was released September 8, 1988, but due to a miscommunication, copies of the record weren't ready when the band set out on its first nationwide tour. Joining them was L7, some of whose members played on *Suffer*. Jennifer Finch provided backup vocals on "Part II (The Numbers Game)" and Donita Sparks and Suzi Gardner played guitar on "Best for You." Jennifer was no stranger to Bad Religion. She was part of the crew during the Oki-Dog days and had even attended Bad Religion's first show, and was not particularly impressed.

Jennifer was also a close friend of Maggie Tuch, another punk from the Valley. "We knew them because they came to all of the shows," Keith Morris said. "They'd come to Circle Jerks shows. They'd come to Bad Religion shows. They'd come to shows that we were playing together. We ended up being their personal chauffeurs at one time. If Bad Religion was our younger brother band, along with Social Distortion and Wasted Youth, they were like our younger sisters."

The tour began in Houston, Texas, with dates throughout the Midwest before they headed to the East Coast. Bad Religion was such an unknown in the middle of the country that flyers advertising their shows read, "Bad Religion, featuring Greg Hetson of CIRCLE JERKS."

"On the Suffer Tour in the states," Jay said, "almost all of the Bad Religion billboards said 'featuring Greg Hetson.' It wasn't something we were trying to sell. It worked because he was bigger than us."

On the road, the band discovered that Hetson had another talent. Hetson had been to most of the cities on the Suffer Tour while traveling with the Circle Jerks, and he had an uncanny memory for finding venues, hotels, and restaurants that he'd been to before. Whenever they arrived at the city they were playing, the driver would turn the wheel over to Hetson, who would guide them to wherever they needed to go. This earned Hetson the nickname "Mr. Memory."

Copies of *Suffer* finally caught up with the band in New York, where Bad Religion played a sold-out show at CBGB. In places like New York and Chicago the kids lined up around the block to see the band, but outside of the major cities the crowds were modest.

"We played a lot of shows for less than ten people," Brett said. "I remember playing shows in the Midwest where there'd be no one in the club. We'd go out to the parking lot and there would be four cars out there. Kids would stay out in their cars and drink six-packs because the beer inside was too expensive. So we'd go outside to the parking lot to see if there were people loitering and we'd beg them to come inside. We'd tell the management, 'Don't worry, people are coming.' Then the show would start and we'd have twelve people."

"Fun is fun," Greg said, "but not if you don't have anybody in the audience."

Jennifer Finch echoed this sentiment. "L7 toured with Bad Religion throughout the country and we didn't do that great. There was a notorious show in St. Louis where there were just eight people. I have a great picture of these skinheads in Boston who sat in front of the stage with their backs to the band. It was a great experience but they weren't at a level where they were pulling people out to see them."

Bad Religion played approximately two dozen shows from coast to coast in less than a month, but most of them were sparsely attended, and when all was said and done the tour was in the red. The van they rented from the Circle Jerks cost money. So did the U-Haul. They also had to pay for gas, food, and lodging. "We didn't make any money," Jay said. "In fact, we each owed money."

Greg was the only one in the band with a credit card and he racked up a bunch of charges booking hotel rooms. He would pay for a hotel room and they would all sleep on the floor, five guys to a room. Greg came back from the tour with $3,000 of debt on his credit card, which put him in a difficult situation. Shortly before *Suffer* was released, Greg and Greta were married in a little wooden church by the sea in her hometown of Del Mar. As always, Greg was looking beyond the next show or the next album and was thinking about his future, but losing money on the road was neither sustainable nor a recipe for success. If the goal was to make money or break even, the tour was a failure.

"People look back on *Suffer* like it was some monumental milestone," Greg said, "but it didn't feel like that at the time."

As discouraging as the tour might have been, there was considerable reason for enthusiasm. By the end of the year, *Suffer* had sold ten thousand copies and more records were being pressed to meet demand. More importantly, it had been named the best album of the year by the only two publications in the country that were still paying attention to punk rock: *Flipside* and *Maximum Rocknroll.*

Suffer had also introduced a new term into the lexicon of punk. In the liner notes, the "oohs" and "aahs" of the background vocalists were transformed into "oozin' ahs." "It was just a cutesy way to describe the background vocals," Brett explained, but it would become a mainstay for Bad Religion. The "oozin' ahs" were a key component of their sound and set them apart from punk rock bands that came before them.

The word was out: Bad Religion was back and better than ever. *Suffer* was a game changer. The new songs were short, fast, and undeniably intense. But they were also catchy, melodic, and fun to sing along to. With *Suffer,* Bad Religion immediately slid into the pantheon of Southern California punk bands who made smart, sharp records that had something to say. The fuck-up with a drug problem, who had reluctantly agreed to fill in for the guy who had taken his spot in his old band, had produced the best punk record of the year, a record that would mark a seismic shift in the punk rock landscape whose aftershocks can still be felt today.

But in 1988 they had the field to themselves. Not to take away from *Suffer*'s excellence, but as Brett intuited when he was recording the album, no one was doing what Bad Religion was doing. That, too, would soon change.

11

SOMETHING MORE

THERE WAS NO QUESTION BAD RELIGION HAD created something extraordinary. With *Suffer*, not only had the band returned to form, they'd surpassed their own expectations, and reclaimed the attention of the punk rock community. Seven years is an eternity in pop music, but to punk rock enthusiasts who dutifully read their fanzines and ordered records and tapes through the mail, the return of Bad Religion was cause for celebration. While sales were slowed by *Suffer*'s delayed release, they picked up again after the accolades started rolling in. More proof that *Suffer* had "put a dent in the universe" came from the band's peers.

Brett learned there was a new demand for his services as a recording engineer. One of the first bands to come calling was NOFX. Fat Mike, NOFX's singer and bass player, loved the sound that Brett had captured on *Suffer* and wanted to make an album with him. Brett recorded *Liberal Animation* at Westbeach and offered to put it out on Epitaph, but the band opted to release it themselves. When NOFX eventually signed with Epitaph, it was rereleased after *S&M Airlines* and *Ribbed* as the third album of a three-record deal.

"I had a lot of energy back then," Brett said. "I was a kid. I was a workaholic. I would work all night long. I don't know where it came from but I was clean and sober and I was driven. I felt like I was on rocket fuel. *Suffer* did well. Westbeach was doing well. I kept signing bands, each one doing better than the last. I was working nonstop, seven days a week. I would work sixteen- to eighteen-hour days."

The rest of the band shared Brett's enthusiasm and they had a strong desire to do it again. "With *Suffer*, we knocked it out of the park," Brett said. "We needed to show that it wasn't a fluke. We'd done a good record once and lost our minds. Now we had to show that we were trustworthy."

While Brett was keeping busy at Westbeach, he and Greg continued to write new material. Though the songs weren't coming at quite the same pace as they had the previous year, it didn't take long before they had written enough material for a new album. Bad Religion played a few shows that spring, including a gig with NOFX at their old stomping grounds, the Reseda Country Club on Sherman Way.

The venue began as a drugstore in the fifties and then a rock venue in the seventies run by Steve Wolf and Jim Rissmiller. Everyone from Metallica to Tom Petty to U2 played there in the early stages of their careers. By the time Bad Religion was playing at the Reseda Country Club on a regular basis it was a shell of its former self. "They weren't high class," Jay said. "Everything was kind of run-down. The chairs were fucked up and the carpet was torn up and the lights didn't work. That seemed to be the kind of place that we'd end up. If we ended up in a nice place with chandeliers we'd think, *We don't belong here. This is too nice for us.*"

On April 29, 1989, Bad Religion played with Scream at a VFW hall in Phoenix. Pete remembered that Scream was due up on-stage but no one could find the drummer. "Everyone was like, 'Where's Grohl? Where's Dave Grohl?' I went out to find him. I didn't know who he was but me and their roadie found him in their van. He was passed out."

Pete roused Grohl and Scream played its set. Afterward, Pete had a conversation with the inebriated drummer that would prove prescient:

GROHL: You gotta go to Europe.
PETE: What are you talking about?
GROHL: Trust me. You'll be huge in Europe.
PETE: Who are you?

Little did Pete know that Bad Religion's booking agent, Doug Caron, had already pitched the idea to Brett. Doug believed there was demand for Bad Religion overseas and urged them to go. After their less than stellar experience on the road in the United States, they weren't in a hurry to do it again in Europe, where they didn't know anyone.

But Doug was persistent. He'd taken the Vandals to Europe and they'd had a good experience. Eventually, Bad Religion relented and decided to go. "He did a good job of managing our expectations," Brett explained. "Doug said, 'Don't expect anything big. You can tour, but don't expect to be huge.'"

While it's true they didn't know anyone in Europe, Bad Religion was far from an unknown quantity overseas. Epitaph's main distributor in Europe was a Dutch company called Semaphore. "I was shipping a lot of records overseas," Brett said. "I was exporting fifty percent of what we were producing. If we sold ten copies of a record here, we sold ten there. But I didn't know exactly what that meant. I didn't know if we were really big in one place, or if we were kind of big in a lot of different places. I really had no idea. It was hard to tell from the fan mail because it came from Spain, Italy, Germany, and all over Europe."

Before they set out to test the waters in Europe, they convened to record their new album. They started recording *No Control* in June 1989, less than ten months after they'd made *Suffer*. For the first time in their career, they were returning to the same studio with the same lineup. Brett was determined to show the world that *Into the Unknown* was the outlier, not *Suffer*. "I remember very clearly what I was thinking: We can't make the same mistake we made with *Into the Unknown*. We might have done that once, but we're not doing it again. *How Could Hell Be Any Worse?* was a great record, people loved it, and then we blew it with the follow-through. We came back and redeemed ourselves with *Suffer*. Now we needed to prove it wasn't a fluke. Now we needed to follow this record up with another one that was just as catchy, but even harder hitting. I wanted to show that we were a bona fide punk band."

They set out to make another record that did the three things they did well on their previous album: make it fast, make it aggressive, and make it catchy. "I realized you could buy a Ramones record and you knew what you were getting," Brett said. "That's what we needed to do. That's what we should have done after *How Could Hell Be Any Worse?* I think smarting from *Into the Unknown*, even though I was one hundred percent responsible for it, really helped because I was able to learn from the mistake."

Greg wrote the title track, and in it he returns to the familiar theme of the futility of humankind. Instead of warning the listener of the damage caused by our attempts to manipulate our environment, "No Control" takes the long view:

There's no vestige of a beginning, no prospect of an end.[7]
When we all disintegrate it will all happen again.

From the human perspective, "No Control" is awfully bleak, but if we adopt the point of view of the geologist, the song is oddly liberating because it reduces the sum of our struggles to a petty drama played out on the human stage. If time is the great equalizer, and the geological record of the planet tells us that it is, then

---

7. This line was taken from the eighteenth-century Scottish scientist James Hutton, the grandfather of modern geology.

everything from our search for meaning to consumer capitalism is equally pointless. We can choose to feel bad about this, but there's no point in that either.

These are heavy ideas for a song that's a little over a minute and forty-five seconds long, but if you paid no attention to the lyrics, you could be forgiven for thinking the song is upbeat. The rhythm is up-tempo, the vocal delivery is almost jaunty, and the chorus has the quality of a sing-along. It's a song that clamors for the listener's attention. It's tempting to view "No Control" through the lens of someone wrestling with big ideas about humankind's irrelevance while dealing with the very real deadlines and demands of graduate school.

The new album also features one of Brett's favorite songs, "Automatic Man." "The song is about valuing agency," he explained, "and noticing how in our daily routine there's often an unrecognized element of automaticity. One day I was driving somewhere, and I needlessly got off at the exit I'd always use to go to my recording studio and I thought, *I'm a fucking automatic man.* I was working so much I was totally lost in thought, and my body was doing the driving."

The album contains a number of songs that quickly became fan favorites, perhaps none more so than "I Want to Conquer the World." The song is another example of using satire to skewer your subject. For Brett, "it's an ironic critique of nationalism and the idea of male machismo and patriarchy." Obviously, he doesn't want to "give all the idiots a brand-new religion" or "expose the culprits and feed them to the children." The song takes shots at everyone from the high-and-mighty to the self-righteous and sanctimonious. But from the context of surf and skate culture, where the first hurdle is overcoming one's own fear, the idea of "conquering" has enormous appeal. Conquering societies? Not so good. Conquering waves or a skate park? Radical.

It would have been nothing short of miraculous if the recording had gone as smoothly as it had during *Suffer,* but there were a few hiccups. Pete had trouble with the song "Sanity." As he struggled to get the beat, the tension in the studio grew. He recalled Brett chiding him. "Aw, come on, Pete. The song's simple! Why can't you get the timing?" At one point Hetson became so frustrated he threw down his headphones and stormed out of the studio. Eventually, Pete ended up playing along to a click track, which was humiliating for him.

"There was a lot of pressure on me," he said. "I always felt insecure about my playing with Brett. I felt I was one mistake away from Brett saying, *You're not in the band anymore!*"

From anyone else in Bad Religion that would sound unrealistic, but it had happened to Pete before when he was asked to step away during the recording of *Into the Unknown*. In addition, after *Suffer,* band members openly talked about Pete's limitations as a drummer in interviews. Although his lack of training was usually characterized as an asset, Pete felt like the weak link in Bad Religion.

The problems with the new album continued after they finished recording. Brett wasn't happy with the way the record sounded, but it had nothing to with the band's performance. In his quest to produce the biggest sound, Brett had recorded *No Control* through an Aphex Compellor. A self-proclaimed gearhead, Brett was always looking for ways to make punk rock records sound better.

"Bill Stevenson of Black Flag and the Descendents was in my studio producing Chemical People," Brett said. "Westbeach was a widely used public studio at the time. He came in with a piece of gear by Aphex called the Compellor that controls the dynamics of sound. I thought it was cool. I had gear envy. So I bought one too."

The Aphex Compellor worked as a combination compressor, leveler, and limiter, hence the name, and was part of a wave of new digital equipment flooding the marketplace. That didn't necessarily mean the audio enhancer was a good fit for what Bad Religion was trying to do.

"By the early nineties you could make any sound out of anything," Jay said. "You had drum machines and pedals and computers. It was a cool time but a terrible time. People were throwing away analog desks that would now cost hundreds of thousands of dollars. You're being told, 'That's that old garbage. You need the new digital whatever.' Well, maybe that analog stuff was better."

When Brett ran the tracks through the Compellor, they sounded all right but when it came time to mix those tracks it was a different story. "After I was done, I thought, *Oooh, maybe I shouldn't have done that.* It sounded a little weird. There was an artifact of compression called "breathing" that I thought I was hearing everywhere. But I salvaged it in the mix by going back to my tried and true gear and everything turned out fine. But for better or worse, I think it contributed to the sound of *No Control.*"

Just as Brett was always experimenting in the studio, he was constantly searching for new and innovative ways to get his music in front of fans. But sometimes those opportunities came to him. He was sitting in his office at Westbeach one day when Kelly Slater called.

SLATER: Hey, is this Brett?

BRETT: Yeah.

SLATER: My name is Kelly Slater and I'm a professional surfer.

BRETT: I know who you are.

SLATER: I'm putting out a surf video that I'm going to sell at skate and surf shops. How much would it cost to put your music in it?

BRETT: It won't cost anything.

SLATER: Really?

BRETT: Put as much of my music in your video as you want for free. I would be stoked!

Slater wanted to make something comparable to the music videos that were airing on MTV but, instead of bands pretending to play music, it would have edited footage of Slater tearing up the waves. Brett figured that Slater had tried to get music from major labels that wanted an arm and a leg for it. Brett took the opposite approach and gave it away for nothing.

Slater became the most famous surfer of all time and his videos were no small part of his success. Brett recalled that after Slater's video came out, "all the surf and skate companies started calling me for our music because they knew they could use it for free. To me it was a no-brainer. Whether it was surfing, skating, or snowboarding, our music was a perfect fit."

The song from *No Control* that would reach the largest number of people was "You"—thanks to its inclusion in the video game *Tony Hawk's Pro Skater 2*. In the game, players pick which skater they want to be and run through a course pulling tricks and stunts. During the game, the soundtrack plays on a loop in the background. The first version of the game only had eight songs, but *Tony Hawk's Pro Skater 2* had three times as many, and Bad Religion's "You" was one of them. This exposed a lot of young skateboarding enthusiasts, who might not have discovered the band on their own, to Bad Religion. Gamers genuinely liked the song. Bad Religion's blend of hooks, hardcore, and harmonies was the perfect accompaniment to hours of virtual shredding.

"That was huge," Brett said, "because when you play the game you've got a finite number of songs and you're doing tricks over and over to the music. The music becomes the soundtrack to that period of your life." It was a new way to market music to potential fans and proved to be the right music for the right audience.

But in the summer of 1989, even with *No Control* in the can, the band was still in the odd position of promoting *Suffer*. They played a show at Raji's in Hollywood on June 20, and then they opened for their heroes the Ramones at the Warner Grand Theatre in San Pedro. They got the gig by volunteering their services to Gary Tovar of Goldenvoice for free. Although it was a great experience getting to share the stage with the legendary Ramones and playing in front of kids who had never heard of Bad Religion before, it was disappointing to see the Ramones play so poorly. "The Ramones were at the end of their run," Jay said of the show, "and they were terrible."

Except for a tune-up at the Reseda Country Club, the band didn't play any more shows that summer before its European tour.

On August 16, they flew into Amsterdam in the Netherlands. Greg recalled there were about 100 to 150 kids at their first show. Their tour manager kept harping on the fact that it takes time to build up a following. "You're not going to be the biggest band just because you're an American band." But when they got to Germany it was a different story.

"I remember it as if it was yesterday," Pete recollected. "Those clubs in Germany were run by punk kids and the government would help pay for it. It was like a youth center type of deal. I remember pulling up this dirt road and going over the hill and seeing thousands of fans lined up. *What the fuck? Really? Maybe we're on to something here . . .* "

There were so many people outside the club that they had a hard time believing they'd all come to see *them*. And these were the kids who couldn't get inside. There were another one thousand waiting inside for Bad Religion to take the stage.

"It was a pretty good-sized place," Brett recalled. "It had a capacity of five hundred or six hundred people. Maybe more. Some kind of a warehouse squat. I think it might have been a coal mine. I don't remember what the fuck it was. All I can tell you is there were three thousand punks. They squeezed a thousand punks into that space and there were two thousand in the street that couldn't get in. They knew every word to every song. They were singing so loud I couldn't hear Greg. It was just mental. And our booking agent was like, 'Wow, I had no idea!'"

"Talk about complete disbelief and appreciation," Greg said. "We came into Essen and people were wearing our shirts and singing our lyrics. *How do these people know this?* And they were all so earnest. We did so many fanzine interviews and these guys followed us around with a video crew. They just wanted to document one of the old-school punk bands, but it was a rebirth for us."

It didn't take long for their incredulity to become a desire to put on a great show. Here was an audience for whom *Into the Unknown* had never happened. Because of the language barrier and Brett and Greg's propensity for big words and big ideas, German fans had to work a little harder to understand the lyrics. They consulted their dictionaries and talked about what the songs meant with their friends. It's possible they felt the lyrics more intensely than their American counterparts because they had to earn their fandom.

"European fans had so many obstacles to overcome," Jay said. "They had to dissect every word to understand the meaning of the song. One fan confronted me after the show: 'I hate you because you are American but I love your music!'"

Bad Religion had stumbled upon the audience they'd always wanted and they intended to make the most of it. The show in Essen marked the first of many sold-out shows in Germany that summer. Not only were the venues filled to capacity, but there were many, many more people outside hoping to get in. It was clear to Brett that the shows were grossly underbooked and they could have played much larger halls.

"We were huge there," Brett recalled, "and there were cross-busters everywhere. That's when I realized the power of our logo. They got it immediately and it just spread. Maybe because Europe is hundreds of years ahead of the U.S. in terms of secularization and the moment was right for it. In any case our logo spread far and wide. It was a meme before there was a word for that."

The fans brought an incredible amount of energy to the shows and the band fed off of it night after night after night. Part of the reason for their success was that so few punk bands toured Western Europe in those days when the Berlin Wall was still standing. The Circle Jerks and Black Flag had played some gigs, but not a full tour. Bad Religion helped establish a network of venues, most of which were community centers with government funding but with professional sound and light systems.

"We were treated like kings, the people appreciated us, and we made money," Greg said. "We didn't come home broke. So we started a tradition of playing there. They're some of the best fans in the world."

For Jay, the European tour breathed new life into the band. It validated the work they'd done to get to that point and sustained their enthusiasm for doing it again. "It was everything," Jay said. "If we didn't go to Europe that summer, I just don't see us continuing on. If you want to boil it down to fucking brass tacks, it was the financial reward for everything that we'd been doing. We finally got paid. I'm not saying that we were in Learjets, I'm saying that someone was actually coming to see us play. That was happening in California, but not at that level. It was just so obvious that these people were coming to see *us*. It was one hundred percent affirmation. The kind of thing that would drive you to do more."

These European shows were captured and released in a live tour video called *Along the Way*. The video synchronizes recordings from fourteen different performances with audio taken from their seventh show in Germany, which was held at Kesselhalle in Bremen. The video also contains short interviews with the band members, including one where Brett goes into detail about his past struggles with drugs. The video, which was released in Germany in 1990, didn't come out in the United States until the following year.

After Germany, Bad Religion completed its European tour in London and headed back to the United States—just in time for the release of *No Control.* Jay started working at Epitaph to help out with their follow-up to *Suffer.* He wasn't a paid employee at this point and had no formal duties. "I had a pickup truck, so that meant that I could go to Alberti pressing plant and pick up the records, the physical vinyl, and drive them to the storage locker, which was below the freeway."

While Brett was occupied with the business of running a label, Jay helped out with the grunt work: fulfilling orders and moving merchandise. "In all honesty," Jay said, "I saw going to work at Epitaph not as going to work for Brett but going to work for Bad Religion. Anything that I could do to help Bad Religion would help me because I'm in the band. So, I didn't have to get paid. I would get paid down the road if I helped this process along. You do it because you believe in the product and later on you'll be rewarded."

In addition to the band and the label, Brett had something else on his mind. After he got clean, he started dating Maggie Tuch. Maggie had been seeing Hillel Slovak of the Red Hot Chili Peppers when the guitar player overdosed in June 1988. That summer, Brett reached out to Maggie and they supported each other in their efforts to stay clean, but they became more than friends. On September 10, 1989, they were married.

On November 2, Epitaph shipped twelve thousand copies of *No Control*. The success of *Suffer* translated to a large number of pre-orders for *No Control,* but as Brett well knew there were no guarantees. *No Control* sold extremely well and Brett had to work overtime to keep up with demand. Before he knew it, the record had sold over sixty thousand copies.

But Bad Religion was in a curious situation. They had just put out a new record and recently returned from a tour for their previous album, and they were in no position to go out and do it again. Greg was wrapping up his master's degree in geology from UCLA and was unable to embark on another tour until the summer. The previous year, he'd been the recipient of the Bryan Patterson Prize from the Society of Vertebrate Paleontology, an award that came with a modest cash prize and went to just one student nationwide per year. Greg was so focused on his studies, he wasn't aware of the jump in Bad Religion's album sales. He was busier than he'd ever been and had new duties as a husband to add to his responsibilities.

Nevertheless, Bad Religion maintained a tight rehearsal schedule and met at Uncle in Van Nuys once a week. It's also where they discussed band business. "It was something we felt we needed to do," Jay said. "We would get together and that's when someone would say, 'I talked to so and so. We've got a show two weeks from now.' We would meet up and talk about this stuff and then practice, and that was how we planned out what was going to happen."

Due to their limited availability, they didn't have a booking agent in the United States. They picked up local gigs that Brett, Jay, and Hetson were offered when they went out at night to see bands play. Bad Religion was also on a short list of go-to bands that Goldenvoice reached out to when punk acts from around the world came through Los Angeles. For instance, in late November and early December Bad Religion played Santa Monica Civic with the Buzzcocks. Greg recalled that he met Eddie Vedder for the first time when he was working as a roadie for the Buzzcocks and the two struck up a friendship. Vedder was a longtime fan of Bad Religion who had seen the band play on numerous occasions in San Diego, but at the time Greg had no idea that Vedder was a talented singer in his own right.

Bad Religion also traveled to Tijuana to play at Iguana's, a three-story club that had a short run as a rock and roll venue. It was located in a strip mall in the Tijuana suburbs but was just as lawless as some of the more notorious nightspots in the city center. "It was fucking crazy," Jay said. "There were no rules. I would assume that it was mostly people from San Diego, but I know a lot of people from L.A. would go down there because it was so fun. It was a lot of people who came down to get fucked up and let loose, but it was super dangerous. There wasn't really a drinking age. There was no security so people would just get onstage. There were grates in front of the stage where there may have been a fan at one point and I'd watch people fall into these holes. They'd just disappear. *What the fuck happened to that guy?*"

Although Iguana's had a capacity of at least one thousand people, as many as three hundred of them wouldn't be able to see the stage and shows were often overbooked. Despite the danger, Bad Religion loved playing to Iguana's large crowds. "All of the shows were rad," Jay said. "There wasn't a show there that wasn't rad. It sounds terrible to say this but there were broken bones and blood. 'Fuck, did you see that guy fall off the third-floor balcony?' It was just nuts."

After nearly ten years and four studio albums, things had never been better for the band, but as they would soon discover, with an increase in popularity came additional pressure.

First band photo at a church in Woodland Hills. *Doug Coss*

Frat party at USC in 1980. *Gary Leonard*

Early flyer from 1980,
designed by Brett.

Flyer for a show from 1981. The fossil skull is a clue it was designed by Greg.

(Following page) Outside the VEX in East L.A. with some friends.

Gary Leonard

Brett, Ziskrout, Greg, and Jay at the VEX. *Gary Leonard*

Live at the VEX. *Gary Leonard*

Flyer for a gig at Bard's Apollo in West L.A.

How Could Hell Be Any Worse? cover shoot in 1981.

Edward Colver

At a rehearsal studio
in North Hollywood.

Edward Colver

Brett at rehearsal.

Alison Braun

Greg and Jay in 1982.

Alison Braun

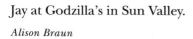

Jay at Godzilla's in Sun Valley.

Alison Braun

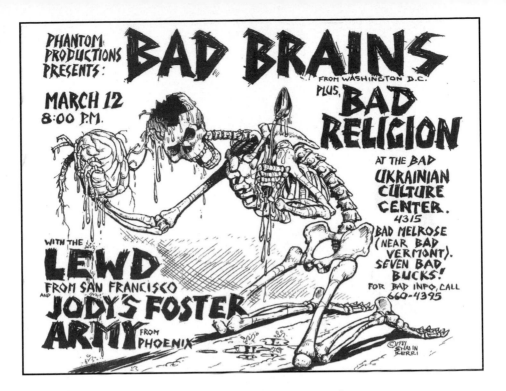

Flyer for a show with Bad Brains at the Ukrainian Cultural Center, designed by Shawn Kerri.

Flyer for a show with Circle Jerks in San Pedro, by Shawn Kerri.

Outside Westbeach during the recording of *Suffer*. *Wrye Martin*

Outside CBGB during the Suffer Tour. *Unknown*

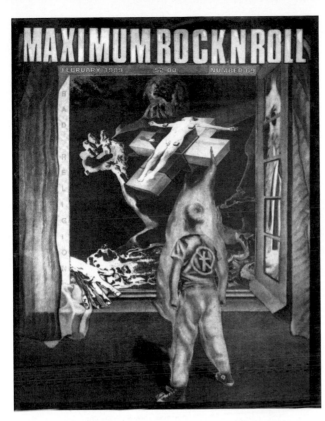

Maximum Rocknroll #69 cover.

Greg and Greg in the wild with hair. *Alison Braun*

Performing in a punk squat in Germany.

Thorsten Zahn

First European tour in 1989.

Thorsten Zahn

No Control promotion photo. *Kim Bockus*

Brett in a boat on the Amsterdam canals.

Flipside #67 cover. Photo taken shortly before Greg moved across the country to begin his PhD at Cornell.

Michele Flipside

Paul du Gre and Brett mixing *Recipe for Hate* at Westbeach in 1993. *Unknown*

Jay on the set for the video for "21st Century (Digital Boy)."

Unknown

Stranger Than Fiction photo shoot in downtown L.A. in 1994. *Dan Winters*

12

SWIMMING UPSTREAM

BAD RELIGION WAS FINALLY ENJOYING SOME SUCcess, but what did that mean exactly? There was critical success and commercial success, but in punk rock, few bands could expect either, especially in 1990.

Bad Religion had put out two critically acclaimed records in a little over a year, and by proving to their fans they could consistently deliver the goods, had won back their trust. New fans were discovering their music via skateboarding videos, surf movies, and video games—ways that wouldn't have been imaginable in 1980, when the band was starting out. And not only was the revelation of their immense popularity in Europe a pleasant surprise, it hinted at a future that was economically sustainable.

But if success is the opportunity to work harder, then Bad Religion was a successful band. When they rang in the New Year in 1990, they were already hard at work on new material for their next album.

By design, *Suffer* and *No Control* were very similar albums. Both records had fifteen songs and came in under twenty-seven minutes. Not only had Bad Religion rediscovered their roots, but they'd sharpened their sound by showcasing their strengths and making music that was instantly recognizable. They had a distinctive sound that was all their own and lyrics that rewarded the listener's curiosity by actually having something to say.

Now they had to show their fans that they could branch out and deliver songs that weren't derivative of *Suffer* and *No Control* without straying too far from their identity. Even though it had been seven years since the release of *Into the Unknown,* the aftermath of that experiment was fresh in their minds. The challenge was to write songs that were similar but not *too* similar, different but not *too* different.

"I wanted to stay relevant," Brett said. "I didn't want to make the same record every time. I was trying to show we had some dimension. This is our format, but we can take it someplace interesting."

It started with the songwriting. Brett was well aware of Bad Religion's reputation as a wordy, nerdy, smart-kid punk band, and he wanted to move away from that to some degree—an impulse that Greg, who was firmly entrenched in grad school, didn't necessarily share. "I came to have a change of heart about my lyrics," Brett said. "Using a lot of big words began to feel sort of abstruse—to use a big word to describe using big words. But I wondered if all the twenty-five-cent words weren't doing more harm than good. My favorite lyricists were always people like Elvis Costello, Bob Dylan, Joe Strummer, and Bernie Taupin. Their lyrics were painterly and poetic."

Brett wasn't about to tell Greg how to write his songs, but with his own material, he made a conscious decision to move past "thesaurus punk" and pare down the language to its essence so that fans wouldn't have to open a dictionary to understand his lyrics. The kid who idolized the enigmatic lyricism of Darby Crash had matured. He was no longer trying to prove himself to the world but was trying to stay true to the poetic impulse of songwriting in order to connect with listeners.

"*Suffer* and *No Control* have a style that's more prosaic than poetic," Brett said. "It's very on the nose. You're going to lose people if they don't understand what you're saying. I wanted my lyrics to really hit people. I decided on *Against the Grain* that I was going to make an effort to be more poetic."

Greg wrote a number of memorable songs for the record that are still part of the band's repertoire, including the title track, "Against the Grain." The song is driven by a colossal bass line and punctuated by a slithering guitar hook that complements the defiant lyrics:

> *Against the grain,*
> *That's where I'll stay.*
> *Swimming upstream,*
> *I maintain against the grain.*

Despite its rumbling bass and earworm guitar riffs, the song has a strangely mournful tone that underscores the difficulty of staying true to your beliefs when they run counter to the mainstream.

Another one of Greg's songs, "Modern Man," is a blistering rebuke of how the modern age of human existence has defiled the planet. "Operation Rescue" features Hetson's Circle Jerks bandmate, the incomparable Keith Morris, on backup vocals. Apparently, Bad Religion thought it would be fun to invite Keith for this particular song because they liked the Circle Jerks song "Operation."

In "God Song" Greg takes aim at religion, and it's the one instance where he felt he went too far:

> *Now we all see, religion is just*
> *Synthetic frippery, unnecessary*
> *In our expanding global cultural efficiency.*

It's not that Greg didn't believe in the truth behind the lyric; rather, he recognized that the song's power to effect change was diminished by reducing religion to something small and insignificant. No one wins arguments by being dismissive and didactic.

Although the album came together quickly, a lot of care and thought went into crafting the songs, and both Greg and Brett were constantly putting pressure on themselves to do better. Case in point, Brett's song "Anesthesia" was inspired by Elvis Costello's "Watching the Detectives." The inspiration came not from anything about the song itself, but in the form of a challenge. "I was trying to write a song where the lyrics were multilayered," Brett said, "with multiple layers of meaning, the way Elvis Costello would do it."

"Anesthesia" is obviously about drugs, an ode to the intoxication of mind-altering substances and what Brett called "the beguiling allure of addiction," which he knew all too well. But "Anesthesia" is also about a woman and the song can be interpreted as a murder mystery. The song functions like a short story with allegory, imagery, metaphor, and symbolism that work on multiple levels.

Anesthesia, Mona Lisa,
I've got a little gun, here comes oblivion.

"As a songwriter," Brett explained. "I was aspiring to approach the greatness of Elvis Costello. In my mind, he's the Bob Dylan of New Wave. Other people think of Joe Strummer in that way, which I agree with, but Joe Strummer was all heart, while Elvis Costello had the brains."

In an album loaded with great songs that nudged the band in new directions, one song stands out: "21st Century (Digital Boy)."

"I wanted to connect the punk scene that I came from with this new-school shit we were doing," Brett said. "I wanted to write a punk anthem."

Of course, Brett had written slower songs in the past such as "Drastic Actions" on *How Could Hell Be Any Worse?* and *No Control*'s

"Sanity," which Brett regarded as a reprise of "Drastic Actions." Plus, Greg had written "Along the Way" for *Back to the Known,* which is almost an anthem but lacks a chorus. "21st Century (Digital Boy)" is slower, longer, and has a chorus tailor-made for singing along.

Brett drew inspiration from the song "American Society" by Eddie and the Subtitles, a band from L.A.'s South Bay that had opened for Black Flag. Like their South Bay brethren the Last, Eddie and the Subtitles had a distinctive sound that was hard to pin down. When Jay first heard the demo for "21st Century (Digital Boy)," he immediately thought of "American Society." Greg, however, thought it sounded like the song "Poison" by Alice Cooper.

"21st Century (Digital Boy)" drips with irony and is loaded with arresting images. In the first verse "the way you look sometimes" is compared to "a trampled flag on a city street," which is far from the sweet and saccharine lyrics of what typically constitutes a pop song. Contrary to the song's lyrics, "my mom wasn't on Valium and my dad wasn't a lazy, middle-class intellectual," Brett clarified. "But I saw that in my world. I witnessed that suburban dystopia."

Brett recalled that not everyone in the band was thrilled with "21st Century (Digital Boy)." "We had this soundman named Kerry Faye and his nickname was Carrot. I played him a demo of the song and he said, 'You can't put that on a Bad Religion record! That's not a punk song!'"

They did in fact put "21st Century (Digital Boy)" on the record, but it was buried on the B-side. "We had no idea it was ever going to be popular," Jay said. "You never know what's going to be popular until you're out there playing it. 'People really like that, let's play that song more.' 'Let's start the show with that song.' 'Let's end the show with that song.' All of a sudden it took on a life of its own." Brett, however, felt from the start that it was a special song.

Even if "21st Century (Digital Boy)" were not so different from the rest of Bad Religion's catalog, it would still be remarkable because it's one of the only songs that features Brett's vocals. Brett sings the bridge, which is also something of a riddle:

I tried to tell you about no control,
But now I really don't know.
And then you told me how bad you had to suffer,
Is that really all you have to offer?

Embedded in these lyrics are the titles to their two previous albums. It's as if Brett realized that "21st Century (Digital Boy)" represented something of a risk. While it's catchy and melodic and has Bad Religion's distinctive "oozin' ahs," it's not as hard-hitting as the rest of the album. No one will ever mistake "21st Century (Digital Boy)" for a hardcore song. In fact, it's much closer to pop than punk, and in 1990, those were two words that didn't go together very often. By incorporating *Suffer* and *No Control* into the lyrics, Brett rewards fans for taking this journey with them.

Perhaps the most astonishing thing about "21st Century (Digital Boy)" is that it's more relevant now than it was in 1990, when the digital media that enjoys a stranglehold on our attention today was virtually nonexistent. During live performances of the song, fans raise their fists and sing along; but, more often than not, in that fist is an electronic device they use to digitally record the show so they can share it with their network of "friends." We're all 21st century digital boys now.

Bad Religion stayed close to home in the early part of 1990 and didn't go farther than the Bay Area to the north, Tijuana to the south, and Phoenix to the east. In May, they went back to Westbeach. Even though the band came to the studio with more material than usual and the songs were incredibly fleshed out, there was a lot of tension during the recording of *Against the Grain.*

"After *Suffer*," Jay explained, "the general consensus was, *This is a great album. You'll never do better.* We said, 'Yeah we will,' and we did *No Control.* Whether it's better or not is subjective, and I don't really care either way, but now the opinion was, *You've surpassed anything you can ever do.* That led to some serious damage during the recording of *Against the Grain* because we were pushing ourselves to do better and it got us into trouble. *This has to be a great record!* is the wrong way to approach any kind of art because now you're doing it sideways. It got to us and sort of fucked with us."

The history of rock and roll is full of stories of musicians melting down in the crucible of the recording studio. It's the most creative aspect of being a musician, but it can be incredibly stressful. If you make a mistake during a show, short of walking off the stage, chances are no one will notice, and if someone does, it's not going to ruin their night. But if you make a mistake during the recording of an album and no one catches it, it's forever. Being thorough in the studio is a way to make sure those forever mistakes don't happen, but focusing on the negative adds strain to the process.

Against the Grain took longer than the previous two albums to record because, according Jay, "The band was basically competing with itself and getting super picky about the way songs were being recorded. Brett was worried and stress is contagious in an artistic environment. Everybody can feel it. Eventually, you come to the conclusion that this is not a cure for cancer. This is just some dudes in a fucking recording studio making a record. But in the middle of it you can lose sight of it, and that happened."

Bad Religion was putting out records so quickly that they were recording new material *before* going out on tour for the previous record. They were a record ahead of their fans, but they seldom— if ever—played the new songs on the road. Jay had gone to see D.O.A. with some bandmates and at that particular show the Canadian punk rockers played all new material. Many of D.O.A.'s fans left disappointed, including the boys from Bad Religion. They held an impromptu meeting in the parking lot and decided on the spot that they would never do that.

"We learned that if you play stuff people don't know," Jay explained, "they're not happy. *We don't know this. We don't care. Play what we want.* The people who get excited about a new song are like three people in the audience. If Pearl Jam went out and said,

'Here's a new song that we wrote backstage!' people would lose their shit. But if we did that, we'd probably get shoes thrown at us."

When *Against the Grain* was finally in the can, they set out on a five-week odyssey that would begin in San Francisco, take them into the Midwest and the East Coast, and then continue on to Europe. In the United States, they returned to some of the venues they'd played during the *Suffer* tour. In Europe, however, they'd learned their lesson and toured extensively in Germany. Out of twenty European shows, seventeen of them were in Germany.

The European tour began and ended in Berlin. Although the Berlin Wall hadn't come down yet, the German Democratic Republic—East Germany—permitted East Germans to cross into West Germany and vice versa. Bad Religion took advantage of this situation to play at a club in East Germany. To get there they had to use the crossing point in Berlin at Checkpoint Charlie. It was only a fifteen-minute drive to the venue but it was like going into another dimension.

"It was an eye-opening experience being in East Germany," Brett said, "because it was such a stark contrast from West Germany. Brutalist concrete buildings. Abandoned streets. Desperate graffiti. Very different from West Germany, which was vibrant and creative. It really sort of drew a bright line between the two political systems. The punks that came to see us didn't like it there. They would have left if they could. They weren't fans of authoritarian government. They would have been thrilled to live in a punk squat in West Germany."

The situation left a stark impression on Jay as well. "It looked like God dumped an ashtray on the city. You drove in, everything was gray. We played and there were a lot of angry skinheads. Really vicious angry skinheads. I was like, *I get it. I get it.*"

Although Bad Religion may have been one of the first American punk bands to play in the former German Democratic Republic, the forces of consumer capitalism were even faster. Jay and Brett decided to explore East Berlin and as soon as they crossed the border they stumbled upon a 7-Eleven and a Burger King. "That was fast," Jay recalled saying to Brett.

Because Bad Religion was able to play at bigger and better venues—often with crowds larger than what they typically drew in the United States—the No Control Tour was an unqualified success that solidified their fan base in Europe and put some cash in their bank account.

When they came back to the United States, Greg learned that he'd been accepted into the graduate program at Cornell University, where he would pursue a doctorate in evolutionary biology and study with William Provine, whom Greg called "one of the most respected historians of science in the country who did groundbreaking work in the intellectual history of evolution." This new development meant that Greg's base of operations would shift from the West Coast to the East Coast in Ithaca, New York, effective immediately. The band had worked around Greg's academic schedule while he was at the University of Wisconsin and UCLA, and they would do so again.

Nevertheless, it was a big change that took some getting used to, and challenges presented themselves right away. For instance, when they took their band photo for *Against the Grain*, Greg posed in New York while the rest of the band assembled in L.A. "That established a new pattern in the band," Greg explained, "where the work was done on both coasts. We'd call each other every couple of weeks."

The move had its advantages. Because Europe's time difference with New York wasn't as severe as it was with California, Greg handled much of the communication with their European booking agents. "I just took it upon myself to really get that calendar in order," Greg said. "So I did a lot of the touring coordination through Ithaca."

On a personal level, the move to Ithaca suited Greg as it allowed him to spend more time outdoors in nature and away from the smog and traffic in Los Angeles. "I was sick and tired of living in L.A.," Greg said. "The traffic was driving me crazy. Everything's an ordeal in Los Angeles. Just going to the grocery story and taking care of basic needs. I think I grew tired of it by the time I'd finished my master's degree."

While Greg was able to make the most of his surroundings in central New York, the move to Ithaca presented challenges. "Coming [to Ithaca] meant I would have to do more moving around because I'd have to put in time back in L.A. We were an international band, so we could show up in any city and start a tour. And we did. But I was still going back to L.A. at least every three months."

With Greg in New York, Brett and Jay worked more closely than ever before, and there was a lot to do to get ready for the release of *Against the Grain*.

"I used to tell people," Jay recalled, "my thumbprint is on every Bad Religion record. There wasn't a record that went out of the warehouse that I didn't touch. We were selling them to stores and distributors. 'We'll take five or ten.' I'd count them out, put them in a box, and send them away. The thing that I can tell is it was really steady in its growth. You could tell month to month. 'We'll take 10. We'll take 50. We'll take 100. We'll take 250. We'll take 1,000.' By the time we hit *Against the Grain* our pre-orders were insane."

Meeting that demand proved to be enormously challenging. Epitaph was a DIY outfit with very few employees. Brett had to stay on top of everything. Navigating this territory required vision and sacrifice.

"If there was ever a moment when I watched Brett Gurewitz become the Brett Gurewitz that we know today," Jay said, "it was for *Against the Grain*. We were excited to take those orders, but we had to make those records and there was no financial capital to make that happen. I went with Brett to his bank and I watched him put up everything he had in the world to get a line of credit to make those records. Everything. Studio, boards, outboard gear, car. Fucking everything. He put it all out there to get this line of credit. None of us did that. *He* did that."

Against the Grain was released in late November 1990 and was a big hit with fans. The album would go on to become their first album to ship one hundred thousand copies. But another change was on the horizon that would have an immediate impact on Bad Religion.

Pete was in another band called the Fishermen, a blues rock band in the mold of the Black Crowes. Pete was the drummer but he was also writing songs and contributing lyrics, which was immensely fulfilling and a marked contrast to his role in Bad Religion.

"It was a hard band to be in," Pete said of Bad Religion. "Greg and Brett sucked up so much oxygen in the room. There wasn't much left over for anyone else. You've gotta subsume your ego when you're in that band. They're the leaders. They make the decisions. You can raise your voice once in a while, but it's their band."

The Fishermen received an offer from Atlantic Records, but it came with a stipulation: Pete could only be in one band. "I think he was given an ultimatum by his band," Greg recalled. "They told him, 'It's us or Bad Religion.'"

"I had to pick a band," Pete said. "*Should I leave Bad Religion?* I remember my girlfriend at the time, and even my mom, was like, 'Are you sure you want to leave Bad Religion?'"

Actually, Pete wasn't sure. After all he'd been through with the band he wanted to stick it out and see what came next. But the offer from Atlantic was extremely tempting. With the support of a major label, breakout success seemed plausible. What if this was his shot at the big time? Didn't he owe it to himself to find out?

Pete agonized over the decision, but a series of events pushed him over the edge. Bad Religion was scheduled to play a show on December 29, 1990, at the El Portal Theatre in North Hollywood with NOFX and Pennywise, but a riot broke out after Pennywise played its set.

El Portal was a proper theater with seats. Prior to the show, Bad Religion had requested that the first few rows of seats be removed. When the band showed up at El Portal, they learned that not only had the seats been left in place, but the concert had been over-sold. Jay recalled, "The fire marshal came in and said, 'Everybody grab a seat.' When there weren't enough seats for the people, they said, 'Okay, this is over.'"

That didn't sit well with the fans. They broke bottles, smashed windows, and ripped the seats to shreds. "I was actually out front when some fans threw a chair through the front window," Pete said. "That got the police pissed and they went in and started busting heads."

But it was more than a case of the police overreacting to rowdy fans: someone set fire to the curtains, causing serious damage to the theater. Once the fire was put out, the fire department turned its hoses on the fans outside the theater to get them to disperse.

The band couldn't leave until the theater had been evacuated and they were given the all-clear to go inside and get their gear. While he waited, Pete was interviewed by a news crew that had been dispatched to the scene. When things finally calmed down, he and Jay drove some kids home who had been stranded at the show because they'd become separated from their friends in all the pandemonium. Being from the west end of the San Fernando Valley, they knew all too well what it was like to travel a long way to see a band only to learn that the show had been canceled at the last minute. "I remember driving a brother and sister home to some place by Magic Mountain in Valencia," Pete said, "and I had a great time meeting them and getting to talk to them."

Goldenvoice rescheduled the show for the next night at the Whisky on Sunset Boulevard. They were supposed to play two shows, a matinee for the kids and a show later in the evening for the over-twenty-one crowd, but when Pete showed up, there was a sign on the marquee that read, "BAD RELIGION CANCELED." No one had called to let him know. "I felt slighted by the band once again," Pete said. "To me this was pretty much one of the final straws."

When Pete got home that night, he called Greg, who told Pete he was under the impression that Brett was going to tell Pete about the cancellation. This didn't seem right to Pete, as he was closest to Greg, who usually kept him in the loop. He decided enough was enough. It was time to go. That didn't make telling his bandmates any easier.

"I remember when I made the decision to leave Bad Religion," Pete said. "I got really drunk because I was so upset about having to choose. I wrote the guys a letter because I was too scared to tell them in person." Pete went to Hetson's house and taped the letter to the door.

Once word got out that Pete had quit the band, Greg called and urged him to consider sticking around until after the Against the Grain Tour, which was coming up that summer, but Pete had already committed to his bandmates in the Fishermen to make a record in Nashville. Brett did not take the news well. Not only was he losing a bandmate and a friend, but Pete's decision to leave felt like a rejection of Epitaph. According to Pete, Brett predicted, "In a year you guys will be dropped."

As far as Pete was concerned, that cemented his decision. "Fuck you, I'm definitely going now."

Pete's last show with Bad Religion was on February 1, 1991, with L.O.S.T., featuring the original members of T.S.O.L., and Insted at the Hollywood Palladium. The show honored tickets from both the El Portal Theatre and the Whisky. Bad Religion commented on the fiasco at the El Portal by opening the show with its take on a Beatles classic: "Give Punk a Chance."

"We killed it and sounded great," Pete recalled. "Unfortunately, it was to be my last show with the band."

Although Pete's tenure in the band was tumultuous, his role in creating the Bad Religion sound cannot be understated. Today, *Suffer, No Control,* and *Against the Grain* are regarded as a trilogy. They were written and recorded in a very short period of time with Greg, Brett, Jay, Hetson, and Pete. These three albums signal Bad Religion's shift to a two-guitar attack and are punctuated by Pete's relentless drumming. Because he was a novice, he had to create a style that suited the songs. His simple, straightforward approach helped showcase the other ways that Bad Religion was unique. He was an integral part of Bad Religion's rebirth after *Into the Unknown* and the success that followed.

Although Pete downplays his contribution, Jay is steadfast in his defense. "Pete was a better drummer than he gives himself credit for. His unique style elevated the band and set the tone for what would come."

Pete left Bad Religion and devoted all his energy to the Fishermen. Sadly, Brett's prediction had been accurate. "We went to Nashville and recorded an album," Pete said. "The record never came out and we were dropped."

Once again, Bad Religion was in the familiar position of needing a drummer—and fast.

13

ELEVEN WAYS OF LOOKING AT GOD

Y OU COULDN'T FIND TWO L.A. HARDCORE BANDS
more different than Bad Religion and the Circle Jerks.
While Bad Religion wrote songs that were socially
conscious and intellectually aware, the Circle Jerks were content to
craft the soundtrack for the punk rock party. Bad Religion wanted
to challenge their listeners to change the world. The Circle Jerks
wanted to change the keg and keep the festivities flowing. But for
all of their differences, the stories of these two bands are inexorably
linked. As Bad Religion began their search for Pete's replacement,
they turned to the protégé of a drummer who'd done time in both
bands.

Bobby Schayer was born in Encino, raised in North Hollywood,
and went to Catholic school in Burbank. The Los Angeles native
came from a family of entertainers. His great grandmother had
been a character actor who played the fortune-teller in *Mr. Smith
Goes to Washington.* Bobby's mother continued the family tradition and worked as an actor and a dancer. She was in *Blue Hawaii*
with Elvis and appeared in several Cheech and Chong movies,

including *Up in Smoke* (alongside Bobby's older brother and sister, and former Bad Religion member Tim Gallegos).

Although Bobby grew up around the business and his mother tried to get him into acting, Bobby hated it. His real passion was music, and his older siblings accelerated his punk rock education. When Bobby saw the Ramones on TV on a rerun of *Don Kirshner's Rock Concert*, he fell in love with their music. "I was watching with my sister and she had seen the Ramones play at the Starwood in '76. It was their second show in L.A. She had the record, the first album, so that's how it all started for me."

Bobby and his older brothers were learning how to play guitar, but he understood that it made no sense for all three of them to be playing the same instrument. "It was kind of silly to have three guitar players," Bobby said. "I wanted to take drum lessons so we could make some noise and play music together."

Bobby started taking lessons at Finn's Music Emporium in Sherman Oaks. Learning how to play came fairly easily for Bobby, but he had a short attention span. He was drawn to the Ramones because their songs were so short, and he would jam along to the album with his brother Steve. "We would come home from school, learn the first side," Bobby recalled. "Come home the next day, learn side two. Then come home the third day and play the whole album. That's how we did it."

He got to meet his heroes after the release of *End of the Century* at an in-store appearance at Music Plus in Hollywood. Bobby asked Dee Dee Ramone if there were any more tickets for the show at the Hollywood Palladium that night. Dee Dee told him there weren't, but if Bobby went to the side entrance, he would get him in. Bobby was skeptical, but he dutifully went down to the Palladium before the show. "The Ramones came out of their van," Bobby said, "and Dee Dee gave me his bass. 'Here. Take this inside.' That changed my life. I will never forget that."

Bobby was kicked out of the Palladium almost immediately because of his age, but if he'd stayed, he might have bumped into Greg and Brett, who were both in the audience. Bobby gravitated toward English punk even though his brother Steve was into the L.A. scene and loved X and the Germs. But the story of how a kid with no connections to Bad Religion joined the band can be traced, once again, to the Circle Jerks.

Bobby's friend Alison Braun, a photographer who went by the nickname "Mouse," had taken photos of the Circle Jerks and encouraged him to get in touch with Lucky:

ALISON: You know he's giving drum lessons.
BOBBY: He is? Can I get his number?
ALISON: You can get his number.
BOBBY: You have it?
ALISON: You have the *Group Sex* record?
BOBBY: Yes.
ALISON: Call the number of the *Group Sex* record.
BOBBY: That's Lucky's number?
ALISON: Just call it.

The title song of the Circle Jerks' first album, *Group Sex*, was based on a classified ad for swingers. Many of the words from the song were taken directly from the ad. When it came time to list the phone number, Lucky thought it would be funny to use his own number—both in the song and on the album cover. *Group Sex* was essentially Lucky's calling card.

Although he suspected his friend was playing a prank on him, Bobby called the number and, sure enough, Lucky answered. After discussing the details, Bobby found himself in a garage behind Keith Morris's house in Inglewood that was the Circle Jerks' practice space. The lesson went well and Bobby, who was only fourteen years old at the time, was able to convince Lucky to continue the lessons in the Valley, where Lucky had another drum student: Pete Finestone of Bad Religion.

Lucky eventually moved to Sherman Oaks and Bobby kept up with his lessons for approximately two and a half years, which matched up with Lucky's tenure in the Circle Jerks. Lucky would get Bobby into shows for free and Bobby witnessed the L.A. punk explosion from the inside out. Never one to stand on the sidelines, Bobby helped out any way he could, and in many ways it was like a punk rock internship. "My favorite drummers were Lucky, Spit Stix from Fear, and Robo from Black Flag. That era was just great. We were all fascinated with England. *Oh, England this and England that.* But we had our own thing here."

Eventually, Bobby started to play around L.A. He was in a band with a bass player named Tony, who had been in the Last, and whose father had written the theme music to the television show *Leave It to Beaver.* Tony told Bobby about a lounge act he was in called Too Free Stooges that included the actors Dick Rude and Zander Schloss from *Repo Man.* Bobby already knew Zander because he played bass guitar in the Circle Jerks. The band only played covers and they were looking for a drummer.

Bobby joined Too Free Stooges and started gigging around town. When he wasn't playing, he worked as a shipping clerk for A&M Records. "I was playing for the love of playing," Bobby said. "I never really had any intention of doing anything big."

Bobby came home from work one day and there was a message on his answering machine from Greg Hetson: "If you're interested in trying out for Bad Religion, give me a call." The last time Bobby had seen Bad Religion play was at Godzilla's with Christian Death a decade earlier. He was definitely interested. Bobby called Hetson back and they set up the audition.

That Saturday Bobby brought his drum kit to Uncle in Van Nuys, but things didn't go as planned. "I went down there," Bobby said, "but the day I tried out I don't think they knew I was coming. I saw Jay and Brett sitting in the lounge area. They looked at me and said, 'Who are you?'"

Bobby told them he was there to try out for Bad Religion. Apparently, they thought he was coming in the next day. He asked if he should come back but they said he might as well do it now since he was already here. Bobby set up his equipment in the rehearsal space where Colin Sears of Dag Nasty walked out after finishing his audition, and Nickey Beat from the Weirdos set up his gear. When it was Bobby's turn to play, Brett, who had blue hair at the time, announced he had to go back to work and left. Hetson asked Bobby what songs he'd learned.

"'Everything,'" Bobby replied.

Not only had Bobby taught himself how to play all of the songs, he learned them on guitar first and then the drums. "That way I knew where the verses and choruses went," Bobby explained. "It was easier for me. I knew where to put everything."

Bobby called out the songs and Hetson and Jay played along for about half an hour, and then the audition was over. On his way out, he passed the room where the Dickies were wrapping up their rehearsal. Bobby told them he'd auditioned for Bad Religion and, sensing the overall lack of enthusiasm from Brett, offered to roadie for the Dickies that summer. But when he got home, there was already a message on his machine from Hetson: "Hey, we want you to come back tomorrow. We want Brett to hear you."

Bobby went back to Uncle the following day for a second audition. After about five songs, Brett stopped him:

BRETT: Do you play chess?
BOBBY: Yes, though not very well.
BRETT: You know you're going to have to get a new drum kit.
BOBBY: Okay.
BRETT: You're in the band. I gotta get back to work.

Brett was preoccupied by Westbeach's latest move to its third and final location on Hollywood Boulevard, a half a block east of Gower. Before Westbeach took over the space, it was called the Producers Workshop, a legendary room where part of Fleetwood Mac's *Rumours* had been recorded as well as some of Pink Floyd's *The Wall*. The studio was located behind the Mastering Lab run by Doug Sax, a mastering engineer with an unbelievable discography who did Pink Floyd's *The Dark Side of the Moon*. "It was a legendary room," Brett said of the new Westbeach, "but it had fallen into disrepair by the time we arrived, and I had a lot to do to get it in shape."

Brett hadn't been planning to move, but while Pennywise was recording its debut album for Epitaph, the cops showed up and shut the session down. Although there hadn't been any been previous complaints, it was enough for Brett to start exploring his options. The neighborhood wasn't zoned for business, and they were getting too big for the little house on Vista del Mar.

"We wanted a real studio," Brett said. "The Vista del Mar location was a shoddily constructed bungalow built by a film studio in the thirties. It was just lath and plaster—you could hear through the walls. We were getting busy and I longed for a more professional situation."

This decision prompted not one but two moves: Westbeach took over the lease to the old Producers Workshop recording studio building on Hollywood Boulevard, and Epitaph moved into a warehouse on Santa Monica Boulevard.

Jay remembered it vividly. "We brought my truck to the storage locker and got all of our stuff. We were so excited. We put all of this shit into this giant warehouse and it looked like two boxes. We had all this space and no real material. But it was a start."

The first album Brett recorded at the new Westbeach was *Generator*. Jay, Hetson, and Bobby went to work on the demos Greg had provided. After a few weeks, Brett joined them for the last few rehearsals. It became immediately apparent to Brett that their new drummer had considerably more range in terms of the styles and tempos he was able to play. Plus, Bobby had memorized their entire catalog. They went through various albums, calling out songs, and found they couldn't stump him. He really did know everything.

"I would say I have a good memory if it's something that I'm interested in," Bobby said. "I always had a work ethic. That's the way I was. I don't think it was because I had talent. It just made things easier for everybody because I was prepared."

They started recording *Generator* in May 1991. Because Greg was in Ithaca, they weren't rehearsing at Uncle like they used to. In fact, they did very little pre-production work before they went into the studio, but Jay didn't see this as a problem. "I think that we'd been together long enough where there was a pretty good understanding of what the material was going to be."

The new setup at Westbeach called for a new approach. Because the old Westbeach had been so small, the musicians would record in different parts of the studio. "The studio on Vista del Mar was in a house," Jay explained. "You could track together, but the drums were in one room and you were in another room and you couldn't see each other." The new Westbeach had rooms large enough to allow for all of the musicians to be in the same room at the same time. For instance, Jay could put his amplifier in an isolation booth so that noise from his amp wouldn't bleed into the drum microphone. Then he and Bobby could play together while the sounds were tracked separately. In other words, they were recording in a professional studio.

Brett decided to take advantage of this setup by recording the band "live." The drums and vocals were recorded separately, but all the guitars were recorded at the same time—with a few exceptions.

"The day I met Greg," Bobby recalled, "we were just getting drum sounds and it took us all day to do that. Finally, it must have been around eleven thirty at night, Brett said, 'I have a song. Let's do a song!' Everyone else had left. So it was just me, Jay, and Brett, and we did 'Atomic Garden' that night. We recorded it in two takes. The next day Hetson put his part on and Greg did the singing."

"Atomic Garden" was another Elvis Costello–inspired song about the perils of nuclear proliferation in an era when the Soviet Union was dissolving and the state of its nuclear arsenal was generating concern all over the world.

The song signaled another milestone for Bad Religion: a music video. "Our first video was done by Gore Verbinski," Greg recalled.

The video aired on MTV's *120 Minutes* alongside alternative acts like Ministry, Red Hot Chili Peppers, and the Cure. Gore had been in the Little Kings, after which he sold his gear so he could go to film school and pursue a career in Hollywood. He went on to direct blockbuster films such as the Pirates of the Caribbean franchise, as well as more Bad Religion videos.

With the exception of "Suffer," which Brett cowrote, for the first time in six albums one of Brett's songs was named the title track of a Bad Religion record. It's also one of his more cryptic songs. It begins with a series of similes:

> *Like a rock*
> *Like a planet*
> *Like a fucking atom bomb*

In interviews Brett has declined to say too much about the song other than it's a metaphor for god. "Generator" compares god to everything from "turbines in darkness" to "a hummingbird in silence." There are eleven comparisons in a song that is lyrically poetic and relatively jargon free. Greg and Brett were establishing themselves as the Beatles of punk rock. If Greg was Paul McCartney, the crooner who crafted memorable melodies, then Brett was John Lennon, the poet yearning to make sense of the world. As an atheist, Greg saw things as they were. Brett, however, was more of an agnostic who hung his hopes on the ineffable.

The band went through the record one song at a time, learning the songs as they went along. When they got a take that Brett was happy with, they moved on. "I thought it would automatically be the best-sounding thing I ever did," Brett said, "because it was the most professional studio I'd ever had. But the truth is it's not the best-sounding record. I hadn't learned the room yet. At Westbeach on Vista del Mar I knew the room. I knew what it sounded like. Even though it was just a house, I could get good sounds out of it quickly and easily. I thought, *The new room is so much better, it will just automatically sound better.*"

Not only was he working in a new room, he was recording with new equipment. When Brett moved locations, he sold his old board: a Soundcraft 2400, which was a budget British board. The new Westbeach at the Producers Workshop had a Trident board, a premium brand, and it took some time for Brett to get comfortable with it.

"I thought the Soundcraft was a crap board," Brett said, "but it turns out it was a great board for rock music. Many years later I found out from Mike Campbell that they used that board to record Tom Petty's *Full Moon Fever,* which has 'Free Fallin'' and a bunch of hits on it, and it's one of my favorite records."

Generator has just eleven songs but five of them are over three minutes long. Nevertheless, the record only took three days to make. On the last day of recording, they packed up their gear and went to Al's Bar in downtown L.A. to play their first gig with their new drummer. Also on the bill was a revival band called Yard Trauma, whose bassist, Lee Joseph, helped out at Epitaph. Lee also ran the independent record label Dionysus, which specialized in garage and psychedelic rock. When Brett bought his first computer, Lee shared his mailing list with him so that Epitaph could ship records to zines, record stores, and college radio stations around the country.

But Lee wasn't the first official Epitaph employee: that distinction belonged to Jeff Abarta, who literally knocked on the door at Westbeach. He had just gotten off his shift at the drug store where he worked and was still wearing a collared shirt and tie.

JEFF: Is this Epitaph? I'm looking for a job.
BRETT: Yeah, but I'm the only employee and I'm not even
    paying myself yet.
JEFF: I'll work for free.
BRETT: You're hired![8]

8. Jeff is not only the first Epitaph employee, but the longest tenured, and works at the label to this day.

In the very beginning there wasn't enough for anyone to do full time, including Brett. "I'd make the record," Brett explained, "and then I'd ship the record out. Maybe I'd spend twenty hours over two days packaging up records and mailing them out, but nobody was calling us. It was all fairly informal. It had to be. There was very little going on."

Jeff knew how to do shipping and receiving, which proved to be an asset when Bad Religion went on tour. In the past, the mail-order operation shut down whenever the band hit the road. With Jeff in the fold, they could fulfill orders year-round.

Two days after the show at Al's Bar, Bad Religion played the Reseda Country Club with Down by Law and Jughead's Revenge. In early June they did some warm-up shows around the Great Lakes before departing for Europe for a month. Bobby had never been overseas, and didn't know what he was in for.

"When I first joined the band and we went over to Germany," Bobby recalled, "I didn't realize how popular the band was in Europe. It never really registered with me. I remember playing a show in Munich and the merch guys were freaking out because they'd sold out of every single shirt. I thought, *This is huge.*"

14

THE SWORD OF PROGRESS

IKE A LOT OF ROCK MUSICIANS, JAY HAD FALLEN into the habit of partying hard while on tour and then resuming his "normal" life at home. But in the world of independent music, and Bad Religion in particular, there was no such thing as "normal." By the time the band went on the Against the Grain Tour, things were very much abnormal.

Bad Religion was no longer a small, hardcore band from the early eighties that a handful of fans looked forward to seeing on the rare occasion the band rolled through town. When the band set out for its third consecutive trip to Europe, Bad Religion was well on its way to becoming a punk powerhouse. That's when the cracks in the foundation began to show.

"I'd been doing shit that I shouldn't have been doing," Jay said of the Against the Grain Tour. "I was doing things I'd told myself I would never do. Doing drugs that I said I would never do in ways that I said I would never do them. There's an idea that you can live this life on the road and when you get home stop. But I didn't.

When I got home, I kept that party going. But it wasn't a party. It was just drinking."

By September 1991, Jay had had enough. He was living in an apartment in the Valley at Topanga Canyon and Roscoe Boulevard with his wife, Michaela Vassos, whom he'd met when Bad Religion was recording *Suffer*, and the two were married in 1989. Jay knew he had a drinking problem, and he wasn't alone in that assessment, but he had so few responsibilities while on tour—other than the hour and a half that he spent onstage performing—that it had seemed manageable. The situation worsened once he got home.

"I was the guy who'd always be at the bar," Jay said. "My friends would close the bar and I'd stay and keep drinking until they were done with whatever they had to do. Me and another guy, who was a bartender and had the night off, went to the bar and I think we were there until five a.m. When it was time to go, I realized I'd left my dog in the car. I didn't even think about the dog the whole time I was drinking. It was nighttime so it wasn't like a dog in a hot car, but it was still a dog in a fucking car. Not cool."

Jay's excessive drinking was no longer a secret and his problem was spiraling out of control. He was extremely fortunate that when he realized he needed help he didn't have to look further than his own band to find someone who understood what he was going through. Jay went to Brett and told him what was going on. Jay later recalled that Brett was extremely sympathetic to his situation and helped him find a place to get well.

Jay wasn't the first member of Bad Religion to find himself in a difficult situation in his personal life—and he certainly wouldn't be the last—but Jay's decision to go to Brett first established a culture in which band members could reach out to one another when they were in trouble. As with most bands, the members of Bad Religion had their differences, and these differences would surface in ways big and small, but in times of crisis, they always had each other's back.

Jay went to meetings and dried out, but later admitted that he didn't fully embrace the program of recovery espoused by Alcoholics Anonymous. "I was a very bad example of a sober person," Jay said. "I didn't drink, but I was a total asshole. I didn't have anything to rely on other than willpower and a six-pack of Dr Pepper."

While his home life improved, his relationship with Brett was fraught with tension. It was an atypical employer-employee relationship. In Bad Religion they were peers, but at Epitaph Brett was the boss. This was a constant source of conflict and stress for both parties, especially when tempers flared. Things got so bad between them that, as hilarious as it sounds, they even went to couples counseling.

In one session, the therapist encouraged Jay to apologize to Brett for something he'd done that he acknowledged was wrong. Jay balked and offered an apology that was, in his view, "kind of half-ass." In other words, he didn't take the request as seriously as the therapist might have hoped. When the therapist asked Brett how he felt about Jay's apology, Brett said he was "incredulous." Jay didn't know what the word meant, but he was too proud to ask and had to wait until he got home to look it up.

"Fuck!" Jay said when he learned the meaning of the word. "He doesn't believe me!"

The incident underscored a fundamental breakdown in communication that many bands experience. As a band's popularity grows, the stakes get higher and so do the egos. There's a strong inclination to minimize issues within the band during periods of success because no one wants to rock the boat, so bad behavior goes unchecked and the pressure continues to build until tempers erupt and emotions become unmanageable. With Brett and Jay, this pressure was intensified by the demands of running a label that was becoming more and more successful, largely due to Bad Religion.

While Jay was changing his ways in L.A., another transformation was underway up the Pacific Coast in Seattle, Washington, when a little-known band by the name of Nirvana released an album that changed the rock and roll landscape. Although it didn't happen overnight, when Nirvana's "Smells Like Teen Spirit" broke through the airwaves, the world stood up and took notice. Here was a song with distorted guitars, thunderous drums, and lyrics that didn't make a whole lot of sense but were presented in a way that was arresting and in your face—and they were playing it *on the radio.* To record companies, Nirvana smelled like money, but to independent bands around the country it smelled an awful lot like punk.

For Bad Religion it was the sound of the underground finally getting some mainstream attention. As veterans of the scene, the members of Bad Religion saw past the grunge label the media was selling and heard riffs from Iggy Pop, Generation X, and Redd Kross. While Nirvana seemed to appear out of thin air for many of the band's new fans, most people in indie music already knew about them. Nirvana's drummer, Dave Grohl, came from the D.C. hardcore scene and had been a member of Scream, who had opened for Bad Religion on multiple occasions.

"I'd seen Nirvana play at Rhino Records," Brett said. "They were just a thrashy, noisy punk band. It was called grunge because the tempos were a little slower, but I thought they sounded pretty punk. Prior to Nirvana there weren't any guitars on the radio. It was all British synth-pop. Then Nirvana came along. The major labels heard them and thought, *It's time to sign guitar bands again.*"

That a band like Nirvana, who wore its punk influences on its flannel sleeves, could be a massive commercial success had a galvanizing influence on the punk community. Many thought Bad Religion was in an excellent position to take advantage of it. Although the members of Bad Religion didn't necessarily share this view, they watched what was unfolding with cautious interest.

"In that moment," Brett recalled, "the two biggest punk bands in the world were us and Fugazi. It was healthy for the scene to have two big bands and a bunch of intermediate-level bands. The

DIY scene was flourishing, and it felt good. I didn't feel like we were competing with each other."

Fugazi's relationship to its label, Dischord, was similar to Bad Religion's in that the driving force behind Fugazi's creativity and vision, Ian MacKaye, also ran the label that put out their records. Fugazi was famous for its five-dollar shows and refusal to sell merchandise like T-shirts. There were plenty of people who were eager to make money off of Fugazi's success, but Dischord refused to play along—even if it meant less money for the label. Although many record company executives courted Fugazi, there was virtually no chance the band was ever going to sign with a major label. With Bad Religion, however, the jury was still out, especially after Nirvana's breakout success.

For Brett the debate wasn't about the majors versus the indies, but between populism and elitism. There came a point where he felt that tastemakers like Dischord and *Maximum Rocknroll* had too many rules. "The view that you can't be on the radio and you can't go beyond your strictures, to me that's elitist," Brett said. "I never had a problem with my records being in the chains or my songs being on the radio. Radio is free. What could be more populist than radio? I wasn't trying to keep anything away from anybody."

Jay likened the relationship between Epitaph and Dischord to a tennis match. Each label was doing its own thing creatively, but every time Bad Religion or Fugazi released a new album they brought more fans into the fold of independent music. The question on the tip of everyone's tongue was, *How big can this get?*

"The tennis match between Fugazi and Bad Religion was trounced by Nirvana," Jay said. "It just kicked all those doors down. This was now way bigger than any of us thought it could ever be."

To put it another way, the swell that Bad Religion had been riding since 1988 was cresting into a wave that would lift them to new heights; but immediately behind them was the tsunami of Nirvana. Still, rumors swirled that Bad Religion was going to sign with a major. As record labels handed out huge deals to bands that were relatively unknown, people kept saying to members of Bad Religion: "You're next."

Jay was highly skeptical of this and could think of plenty of reasons why Bad Religion wasn't going to be next: "We're not cute. We're not Kurt Cobain. People think we're too smart. We have a name and a logo that's highly offensive and is never gonna fly in Walmart or any of the stores in the Midwest. I don't know what you see, but sure."

While everyone seemed to be speculating about Bad Religion's future, the band was looking back to its salad days. In November 1991, Bad Religion released *80–85*, a collection of the band's earliest recorded material that includes its first EP; its debut album, *How Could Hell Be Any Worse?*; its second EP, *Back to the Known*; and three songs recorded for the compilation *Public Service*,[9] which is why there are three versions of the song "Bad Religion" on *80–85*.

For the cover, they went back to punk photographer Edward Colver and licensed his photo of punk boots taken outside the Starwood. By late 1991, that iconic photograph seemed like a portal into another era that was never coming back. The photo is unusually direct in its presentation of Bad Religion as a punk band. Even the title of the compilation is slightly misleading and poses more questions than it answers. For instance, although the band formed in 1980, Bad Religion didn't release any material until the following year. So why not *81–85*? Furthermore, none of the material from *Into the Unknown* is included on the record even though it was written and recorded in 1983. Another point of confusion is the Epitaph catalog number, which suggests it was released before *Against the Grain,* but this was not the case.

Curiously, the liner notes were penned by Greg Hetson—who wasn't even a member of the band for most of 1980 through 1985.

---

9. On December 10, 1981, Smoke 7 Records released a compilation of L.A. hardcore bands called *Public Service* that included Bad Religion, Circle One, Disability, Red Cross (soon to be Redd Kross), and RF7. The Bad Religion songs "Drastic Actions," "Slaves," and "Bad Religion" were recorded specifically for the comp.

Not surprisingly, Hetson's notes contain many errors and inaccuracies. It's hard to believe this was unintentional, for although Hetson made a cameo appearance on *How Could Hell Be Any Worse?* and helped keep the band going after *Into the Unknown,* he wasn't in a position to know the band's history, much less comment on it.

The awkward title, slapdash liner notes, and on-the-nose album cover add up to a product that was clumsily conceived. Epitaph eventually put a stop to *80–85* and instead reissued *How Could Hell Be Any Worse?* with the additional EPs and extra recordings.

"I sort of regret doing it," Brett said of *80–85,* "because *How Could Hell Be Any Worse?* was the main part of that, and it never came out on CD because *80–85* subsumed it. I think that was a mistake. I should have put out *How Could Hell Be Any Worse?* on CD with bonus material. It would have been a cooler thing because *How Could Hell Be Any Worse?* is a milestone album, and by making something else out of it, I don't think it was sufficiently respectful of what that record really means."

Bad Religion's debut may not enjoy the iconic status of other early Southern California punk rock records like the Adolescents' self-titled debut or Social Distortion's *Mommy's Little Monster,* but that speaks more to Bad Religion's circuitous path and the number of outstanding records they've produced since. Most bands, if they're lucky, have only one milestone album. Bad Religion has several.

By 1992, Nirvana's breakout album *Nevermind* was dominating the airwaves. Epitaph had expanded its roster to include Coffin Break from Seattle, Dave Smalley's new band Down by Law, and the D.C. hardcore band Dag Nasty that Brian Baker had started when he left Minor Threat. Brian had to record under the name Dale Nixon because he was under contract with the band Junkyard. Why Dale Nixon? That's the name Greg Ginn used when he played bass on Black Flag's "My War."

After many delays, Epitaph released *Generator* on March 13, 1992, nearly a year after the band had finished recording it. There were a number of reasons for this, including issues with the album art, but they can be attributed to the growing pains of a band on a rapidly expanding indie label coming to terms with its own success. The delayed release allowed for a longer period of time for pre-orders. When the record was finally available to ship, Epitaph had more pre-orders for *Generator* than *Against the Grain,* which had shipped one hundred thousand units, the first Epitaph release to reach that plateau. These were huge orders for an indie label. With numbers like that, did Bad Religion even need to be on a major label?

As Epitaph continued to grow, Brett worked overtime to keep up with demand as the label signed more bands and recorded more records. He hired additional employees to ensure things wouldn't come to a screeching halt every time Bad Religion went on the road. Meanwhile, Jay continued to do a lot of the heavy lifting—literally. "I was the shipping warehouse manager guy," Jay said. "Then we got a forklift and I was the forklift operator. That was the best day of my life. The forklift was amazing!"

To celebrate the release of *Generator,* Bad Religion played Iguana's in Tijuana on April 10 and a pair of shows at the Hollywood Palladium on April 11 and April 12 with the Melvins and H.R. of Bad Brains. They spent the entire summer touring in Europe and the U.S.

The band no longer traveled in sprinter vans in Europe and cargo vans in the United States. It could now afford to hire tour buses for their excursions, which made getting around much easier and more comfortable. Bad Religion also hired people to help with their touring operation and assist behind the scenes. Their days of carrying their own equipment and lugging boxes of T-shirts and miscellaneous merchandise around were over.

This wasn't just a matter of comfort and convenience. The crowds were getting too big for them to handle all of the financial arrangements on their own. This point was driven home after a show in Germany where the band played to five thousand people in a circus tent. After the show, they couldn't find the promoter and they needed to settle up. Greg and Jay went to talk to the people who had the money. The promoters weren't punk rockers, and they didn't speak English. "You're in a room with guys in suits who are probably carrying guns," Jay recalled. *"I don't want to be here right now. This is dumb.* We realized we needed help because we were in way over our heads."

Although that was the extent of the band's touring for the year, it was a very busy autumn for Bad Religion's songwriters. Greg returned to graduate school at Cornell, while Brett had his hands full with Epitaph. On October 16, Epitaph released the Offspring's second studio album, *Ignition,* which Brett had recorded and produced at Westbeach. The following month NOFX's *White Trash, Two Heebs and a Bean* came out. In addition, Down by Law's *Blue* had shipped in June—right in the middle of Bad Religion's European tour. Even though there was plenty to keep Brett busy, he still found time to write new material for what would eventually become *Recipe for Hate,* Bad Religion's seventh studio album.

By the end of 1992, fueled by Greg and Brett's prolific songwriting and powered by a record label that was getting bigger every day, Bad Religion had produced five records in five years—four new albums plus *80–85*. With another record in the works, they were at the peak of their productivity.

The media was finally paying attention to them and, more often than not, found things to criticize. Critics either were quick to point out ways they'd deviated from their platform or criticized them for sticking too closely to it. Occasionally, music critics praised the intelligent opinions expressed in the band's lyrics. But most of these critics then took a backhanded swipe at the punk rock community by saying Bad Religion's lyrics were too cerebral or too nerdy, as if punkers weren't capable of comprehending the songs. In fact, Bad Religion's fans proved to be much more willing to engage the material than their critics.

The band members developed different strategies for dealing with the criticism—good and bad—that came their way. Jay, who handled both incoming and outgoing mail, saw more than his share of it. "I sort of came up with this philosophy," he said, "because, like every other human, I would read all the good reviews and feel good about myself and read one bad review and get all upset. I realized that I have to have the same emotion about a good review as I do about a bad review, that is, I'm grateful that you took the time to express an opinion about this art, good or bad, but I'm indifferent emotionally about whether you think it's good or not. 'I hate your band!' Thank you for having an opinion. 'I love your band!' Thank you for having an opinion. I just sort of decided to take on a flat-line approach to the media, whether it was a critic or a fan."

This strategy of stoic indifference to feedback insulated the band from the harshest criticism of all: silence. While their peers in the indie and underground music scene would get played on college radio stations, Bad Religion regularly failed to make the cut.

Interestingly, one thing that Bad Religion was seldom criticized for was its overwhelmingly negative view of Christianity. Once again, the most blatantly offensive thing about the band somehow escaped the attention of the morality police. This was surprising given the way the U.S. government and its cohorts in the media invoked Christianity during the Gulf War, which was in full swing. Bad Religion challenged this toxic combination of religiosity and warmongering in *Recipe for Hate*'s first single, "American Jesus."

The song opens with lyrics that reprise Bad Religion's earliest songwriting impulses. Written in response to President George H. W. Bush's invasion of Iraq, "American Jesus" attacks American imperialism propped up with bogus claims to Christian morality. The irony is so entrenched that it's easy to imagine someone hearing Bad Religion for the first time interpreting the lyrics as an endorsement of the values they are critiquing.

In the third verse, however, the backup vocalists present a counterpoint to the lyrics to clarify the song's position:

He's the preacher on T.V.
(Strong heart)
The false sincerity

(Clear mind)
The form letter that's written by the big computers
(And infinitely kind)
The nuclear bombs
(You lose)
The kids with no moms
(We win)
And I'm fearful that he's inside me
(He is our champion)

This brutally effective counternarrative runs throughout the entire verse to devastating effect, making "American Jesus" the album's quintessential Bad Religion song.

"American Jesus" was released as a single and features Pearl Jam's Eddie Vedder on background vocals. Greg had invited Vedder to the studio while they were recording *Recipe for Hate*. "I called him up and said, 'You want to sing backup vocals on our album? We have a couple of songs I think your voice would sound great on.'" Vedder also sings a verse on the song "Watch It Die."

Bad Religion made a video for "American Jesus," filmed once again by Gore Verbinski. The video is loaded with Christian crosses and other religious iconography. For much of the video, Greg wears a pair of goggles from a World War II gas mask. The video for "Struck a Nerve," directed by El Camino Real High School alum Darren Lavette (who made many videos for Epitaph), continues to saddle Greg with strange headgear, in this instance a neck brace. Their old friend Johnette Napolitano of Concrete Blonde belts out backup vocals during the bridge.

The title track, "Recipe for Hate," which is also the first song on the album, was written to commemorate the bogus five-hundredth anniversary of the so-called discovery of America. It's fast, ferocious, and utterly uncompromising—so much so that it would not be out of place on *Suffer*. The same can't be said about the rest of the songs on the record. The most noticeable difference is the up-and-down pace of the album. On *Recipe for Hate* the band began to make full use of their drummer's skills. Many indie bands were experimenting with time changes in the mid-nineties. Bad Religion included some atonal shifts on *Generator* and continued them on *Recipe for Hate,* but the boldest move on the album comes in "Man with a Mission" with the incorporation of the slide guitar and the twangy tropes of country-and-western music.

By the time *Recipe for Hate* was ready to go, the album had racked up a huge number of pre-orders. The record was released right before the band's summer European tour in June 1993, which was dominated by dates in Germany, including their first show at Docks in Hamburg, along with some shows in the United Kingdom. A month after they returned from their European tour, they went to South America for the first time and played a show in Buenos Aires, Argentina, with Biohazard. The following month they began a run of forty shows in the U.S., Canada, and Mexico. For this tour, Bad Religion brought along Green Day, a Northern California band that had already signed with Reprise Records and was a few months from releasing their major label debut, *Dookie.*

Record companies were paying close attention to Bad Religion's rise from a DIY hardcore band to a punk powerhouse and indie crossover contender. With the success of Nirvana's *Nevermind,* major labels were giving huge deals to punk, post-punk, and indie acts in the hopes of finding a band that could generate hits in the new alternative market. For many music industry insiders and executives, Bad Religion checked all the boxes.

Representatives from record labels reached out to Brett, and he reported their interest to the rest of the band. Once he ascertained that everyone was open to at least considering a move to a major, he set up a couple of meetings.

"Let's test the waters and see what we're worth," Jay said. "We don't have to go anywhere, but if the scenario is right, we can go somewhere."

One label stood out from the rest: Atlantic Records, which was led by Danny Goldberg. Goldberg began his career as a journalist, ran public relations for Led Zeppelin, and started his own management company with clients like Bonnie Raitt and the Allman Brothers. He signed Nirvana on the recommendation of another one of his clients, Sonic Youth. From there, Goldberg was able to parlay his success with Nirvana into an executive-level position with Atlantic Records.

"We met Danny Goldberg," Jay recalled, "and afterward Brett said, 'He doesn't blow smoke. He gets what we're doing here.' We had a pretty good rapport with the guy. We thought, *This could put us in a place where the guy who's running the show gets us, and we're not going to struggle to be understood.* It all started to make a lot of sense. The picture got really clear."

But it wasn't just up to Bad Religion's West Coast contingent. Greg needed to be on board with the decision as well. "Brett met with Danny Goldberg out in L.A.," Greg said, "and I drove down to New York City and met with him shortly thereafter."

Greg and Goldberg hit it off. Everyone in the band was ready to make a move. That didn't mean it was an easy decision to make—especially for Brett. "One of the reasons I agreed to be on a major," Brett said, "was I didn't know if Epitaph could ever make a group really cross over. Nirvana was getting huge, but I didn't know if it could be done by an indie."

Danny Goldberg recognized Bad Religion's potential to cross over into mainstream success. "I knew that the indie world had nurtured a lot of artists that I felt could reach bigger audiences," Goldberg said. "As a manager I'd had that experience with Nirvana. Atlantic wanted me to bring in new artists and modernize their rock and roll roster. Bad Religion had accomplished a lot. They had a substantial audience. They had songs with melodies and choruses that had the potential to reach this newly configured rock audience. I loved the intelligence of the lyrics and their subversive subtext, so it appealed to me personally. As a business matter, it was not a difficult call because of what they already had in the way of a following. They were exactly the kind of artist I was looking for."

Most people in the music establishment, from record company executives to music critics, overlooked Bad Religion's "subversive subtext." That Goldberg intuitively understood this about the band felt like he was a good fit for Bad Religion.

"The subtle sarcasm of Bad Religion has been missed by almost everyone," Jay explained, using a live performance of the song "You Are the Government" as an example. "When Greg sings at the end 'And I make a difference too' if you ever watch him, he holds his thumb and forefinger a quarter-inch apart. You hear the line and you think, *Yeah! I make a difference!* But then you see what's he's doing onstage and think, *Oh, shit! We're nothing!* This has always been the secret to the sauce."

Goldberg wanted to share this secret with the world. Not only did Bad Religion have an extensive fan base, he reasoned, but they wrote the kind of songs that would benefit from the exposure that Atlantic could provide.

Bad Religion gave Eric Greenspan, the band's lawyer, the green light to negotiate with Atlantic. Greenspan secured a four-record deal for a relatively small advance in favor of a higher royalty rate. Although it was a time when labels were starting to throw a lot of money at bands, this was a prudent decision. "It wasn't crazy money," Greg clarified. "We didn't take a lot up front, but we made a lot on the back end of the sales. We have a very good lawyer and he said, 'This is the way we should do it.' So that's how we did it. We've always been sensible about that."

Greenspan was also instrumental in splitting the territories. While Bad Religion felt Atlantic was the best fit for them in the United States, they believed Sony Music could do more for them in other parts of the world. So rather than give Atlantic worldwide rights to distribute Bad Religion, they negotiated a deal with Atlantic in North America and Sony Music everywhere else.

The band recognized it was in a position of strength at the bargaining table because they'd already accomplished so much on their own. They could afford not to take a lot of money up front because they weren't a bunch of broke kids who were new to the industry. Bad Religion was an international touring act that was eager to explore new regions and expand its fan base to places they'd never had an opportunity to play. With Greenspan's assistance, the band crafted a plan for long-term success rather than short-term gain.

Eventually, after a unanimous vote, the band signed with Atlantic and Sony Music. Bad Religion was officially off Epitaph, but what happened immediately afterward would create headaches for future record collectors. Atlantic was so impressed with *Recipe for Hate* they wanted to acquire it—even though the record had already been released by Epitaph. In fact, by the time the band had signed with Atlantic, close to two hundred thousand copies had been sold worldwide. Even though Bad Religion had already inked a four-record deal with Atlantic, Brett negotiated a separate deal for a fifth record that would allow the label to rerelease *Recipe for Hate* on Atlantic while the band got to work on their next album.

"After the first pressing," Brett explained, "I didn't make anymore. I gave Atlantic the parts and they handled subsequent pressings." This is why some versions of *Recipe for Hate* have the Epitaph logo and some bear the Atlantic imprint.

"You might see labels printed with Atlantic," Greg said, "but they bought that record off of Brett."

Now it was time for Bad Religion to assert their DIY sensibilities in the world of mainstream music and make a record for Atlantic that would bring new fans into the fold without alienating those who'd stood by them. This was no small task.

The notion of "selling out" had gained considerable traction in the insular world of punk rock in the late seventies. Back then it was a nervous preoccupation of fans of bands on the verge of commercial success. By the early nineties, the term had gained such cultural currency that simply signing with a major label was synonymous with selling out. But Brett and Greg weren't worried about how they might or might not be perceived in the marketplace. "We're about much more than who markets the band," Greg said.

As far as they were concerned, Bad Religion would do what it had always done: write thought-provoking songs that reflected their growth as thinkers and musicians. If anything, they were more determined than ever to make the best record they could. Signing with Atlantic and Sony was simply a matter of getting their message to more people.

After moving to Atlantic, the band immediately benefitted from increased national exposure. In November, Bad Religion appeared on *Late Night with Conan O'Brien* to perform "Struck a Nerve." Despite the band's growing popularity and continued success, it was a chance encounter on Pacific Coast Highway that made Greg realize that Bad Religion's fortunes had changed for the better. "I was driving on PCH," Greg recalled, "and heard 'Recipe for Hate' on the stereo of the car next to me. That was pretty special."

There was no turning back now. While it had been thirteen years since Rodney Bingenheimer blasted the band's demo to a devoted following of hardcore fans, Bad Religion belonged to the masses now. Only time would tell if moving to Atlantic had been a smart move. After a short holiday break, the band went on a second North American tour for *Recipe for Hate*. They wouldn't play another show in 1994 for over eight months. During that time Bad Religion, Epitaph Records, and the punk rock establishment would experience irrevocable changes.

15

A SUBTLE
FUCK YOU

IF 1991 WAS THE YEAR THAT REINTRODUCED AMERica to underground music, 1994 was when the underground broke through to the mainstream—and Bad Religion and Epitaph Records were there to give it a hard shove.

First, Green Day released *Dookie,* their third studio album and first on a major label, in February. This was followed by two Epitaph releases: the Offspring's *Smash* in early April and Rancid's *Let's Go* in June. Then came Bad Religion's major label debut and eighth studio album, *Stranger Than Fiction,* in September. It was the year that punk exploded, and Brett Gurewitz had his hand on the detonator for three of the four records.

By 1994, Bad Religion was known for their melodic hardcore sound and intelligent lyrics, but it was the latter that received the lion's share of attention in the press. The fact that the band's front man was pursuing his Ph.D. in evolutionary biology had something to do with this. Bad Religion's "punk professor" was a common theme in articles and interviews. Less well known was Brett's business savvy and entrepreneurial genius. Though it was an open secret within the band, the world was about to find out just how formidable Epitaph's founder was.

The year began with Brett's decision to expand Epitaph's operations overseas. In addition to adding more musicians to Epitaph's roster and releasing new records, Brett was looking to establish an office in Europe. He turned to one of his oldest friends and a founding member of Bad Religion: former drummer Jay Ziskrout.

After Ziskrout had left Bad Religion, he stayed in the music industry and eventually ended up working in marketing and promotion for Arista Records in New York. Brett and Ziskrout reconnected a few years after he quit the band and met face-to-face in France at an international music conference and trade show. Brett expressed his desire to open an office in Europe and Ziskrout said, "That's something I can do."

Brett enlisted his help and Ziskrout left New York to come work in the Epitaph office in L.A. They drafted a proper business plan, set down the ethos of the company, and hammered out a mission statement. Together they created a guide to what everyone in the company needed to know from an artistic and business perspective. "He actually had more record business experience than I did," Brett said of Ziskrout. "All I knew was the DIY way of doing things. I looked up to him and I needed somebody to open an office over there in Europe."

While they were working on Epitaph Europe, the Offspring were working on their new album at Track Record's new location in North Hollywood. Brett had hired his favorite punk rock producer, Thom Wilson, who had produced the Offspring's two previous records and an EP. Even though the band was writing material right up until the last recording session, early reports from Wilson were positive. Dexter Holland's vocals had the urgency of punk rock but none of the snarl, yet there was nothing candy-coated about his delivery. His voice was the loudest instrument on the record.

Ziskrout remembered Brett saying, "Jay, come here and check this out." Brett put on a demo from the Offspring's recording sessions for him to hear. Ziskrout was immediately impressed. "There were various mixes but our reaction to all of them was, *Shit, this is amazing!* We were kind of blown away by how great it sounded."

After a few weeks Ziskrout left L.A. for the Netherlands to get the business up and running. "I moved to Amsterdam to start Ep-itaph Europe—or Eurotaph as we called it. I got a flat and hired two people and we sat in the living room all day and worked on Epitaph. Then we got a small office space and then a bigger office space. One of my jobs there was to take these independent dis-tributors and create coordinated multinational marketing efforts for the business, which was something I learned how to do at the major labels."

This gave Ziskrout an opportunity to promote the Offspring's new album all over Europe. "I went to every single distributor and I told them we're going to sell five hundred thousand copies of this record in Europe," Ziskrout said. "This was very audacious of me. They thought I was insane."

Nevertheless, opening an office in Europe with everything else that was going on at the label, with his band, and in his life, showed Brett's vision and determination. While Ziskrout was beat-ing the drum for the Offspring abroad, in L.A. Brett was mixing Rancid's sophomore album *Let's Go,* twenty-three gritty, ninety-second punk ballads. Tim Armstrong's vocal delivery brings an unpolished street sensibility to the album's sound. He doesn't sing so much as spit the lyrics, which aren't nearly as in your face as the band's punk-as-fuck demeanor would suggest. Brett felt Rancid's new record had enormous commercial appeal.

The Offspring and Rancid were the yin and yang of Epitaph's brand of punk: the Offspring represented the evolution of skate punk into something tighter, brighter, and cleaner sounding while Rancid was down and dirty and definitively old-school. Both bands bore Bad Religion's imprint.

Brett believed he had something special with these albums, and he was right. The Offspring's infectious first single, "Come

Out and Play," went into heavy rotation at KROQ and exploded across the country. Epitaph's offices filled up with pallets of *Smash*, and Brett had to take out a second mortgage on his house to keep up with demand.

In the midst of all this chaos, Bad Religion was writing music and getting ready to record their new album for Atlantic. For their next release, Brett had something a bit more high-minded than what the Offspring and Rancid were putting out on Epitaph. Just as Brett had chosen to emphasize the poetry in his lyrics during the writing of *Against the Grain* and *Generator,* with *Stranger Than Fiction* he indulged his literary sensibilities.

"After music, literature is my other great passion," Brett said. "I think the songs on *Stranger Than Fiction* are some of my best. The lyrics to 'Stranger Than Fiction,' 'Hooray For Me,' and 'Infected' were heavily inspired by Kerouac and Burroughs. I loved that stuff as a young man."

The title track, "Stranger Than Fiction," has an abundance of literary references that range from the obvious to the obscure. Consider the following verse:

> *Oh yea, cradle for a cat, Wolfe looks back,*
> *How many angels can you fit upon a match?*
> *I want to know why Hemingway cracked*
> *Sometimes truth is stranger than fiction*

"Cradle for a cat" refers to Kurt Vonnegut's novel *Cat's Cradle*. "Wolfe looks back" alludes to Thomas Wolfe's best-known book, *Look Homeward, Angel,* which was a huge influence on both Brett and another writer referenced in the song, Jack Kerouac.

"These were the authors that I loved," Brett explained, "and *Look Homeward, Angel* had a big influence on me. There are plenty of other authors that I love, but in that moment of my life these were huge."

It was not the first time Brett had looked to Wolfe for inspiration. "A leaf, an unturned stone, and an undiscovered door," Brett said, "are recurring motifs in *Look Homeward, Angel*," and some of these elements also appear in the song "Suffer." It is a fitting tribute that one of Wolfe's most influential novels informs one of Bad Religion's most influential songs.

While Brett was accustomed to pushing himself to write arresting material, now he set out to write something that would thrive on the radio. Atlantic had dreams of making Bad Religion the next Nirvana—never mind that when Bad Religion started making music Kurt Cobain was just thirteen years old. Brett—always up for a challenge—was willing to give it a try.

"I tried to write something that could take the band to the next level," Brett said of his process. "Nirvana had proven that as long as the tempo doesn't freak anybody out, you can get on the radio with loud guitars. 'Infected' was my attempt at writing a grunge song. We got signed to a major and I thought, *We're a punk band, but at the same time we've gotta stay relevant, so it might be smart to write a grunge-infused Bad Religion song.* That was my approach to writing 'Infected.'"

If pop songs are essentially love songs, "Infected" explores the dark underbelly of romance. It doesn't tell a story per se; rather, it compares love to an affliction, a condition unwitting partners catch but can't shake. "Infected" is infused with resignation and despair, and much like his song "Anesthesia," it's also the story of addiction. Although the opening lines sound like a cry for help from someone on the verge of a relapse, the origin of these lyrics is much more mundane.

"I had a bit of writer's block," Brett explained, "but felt I was really on to something with 'Infected.' I decided to take my '67 Camaro and an acoustic guitar out to Joshua Tree and hole up in a little bungalow until the song was finished. My car was a radical custom street rod prone to overheating, and it was in such bad shape that as I left town, I hummed 'Now here I go / Hope I don't break down,' I was literally afraid my car would break down. These words were intended to be a placeholder, but it turned out they were a great way to start the song, and they fit the mood perfectly. The rest is history!"

The recording process for *Stranger Than Fiction* differed under Atlantic, largely because the label had more resources at its disposal. Brett had also signed a co-publishing deal with EMI publishing and had access to their studios on Sunset Boulevard. When the writing was finished, Brett met up with Jay and Bobby at EMI Studios to record some demos. The house engineer was Ryan Greene, who would go on to work on a couple of NOFX's records. They recorded demos for "Stranger Than Fiction" and "Infected," and sent them to their new producer, Andy Wallace, who had an impressive resume of outstanding records, including Slayer's *Reign in Blood,* the Cult's *Electric,* Nirvana's *Nevermind,* Sonic Youth's *Dirty,* and Rage Against the Machine's self-titled debut.

Everyone was thrilled to be working with such an accomplished producer. "He was the top rock mixer in the world," Brett said, "and now that we had a major label recording budget, it was a dream being able to hire him. I was a massive fan of his work and was eager to learn from the best." Brett asked Wallace to do a test mix of "American Jesus" as an audition.[10] "He nailed it," Brett said.

"Once we got Andy Wallace into the picture," Bobby said, "we rehearsed every day at the Alley in North Hollywood. We rehearsed for a month straight and the band got really tight."

When it was time to record, they went to Rumbo Recorders in Canoga Park. The band hunkered down in the studio for five weeks in April and May. Despite being exceptionally well rehearsed, this was the longest amount of time they had ever dedicated to recording an album. At Westbeach they'd learned the songs on the spot, but even though the band already had the songs down cold, Wallace had his own way of doing things and brought his thinking to the material. That took some getting used to. Aside from flying out to New York to sign their contract, working with Wallace was the first real indication that things had changed, and the studio

10. This track is available on the Bad Religion album *Christmas Songs,* released in 2013.

had a decidedly different feel with emotions running high and the atmosphere more charged than usual.

Bad Religion brought in a number of guests to lend a hand with the album. Wayne Kramer of the legendary MC5 played guitar and sang on "Incomplete," thrilling Bobby, who idolized the Detroit rocker. Pennywise's vocalist Jim Lindberg sang on "Marked." Tim Armstrong provided vocals on a song Brett cowrote with Johnette Napolitano called "Television," though Tim is credited on the liner notes as "Lint," his nickname when he was in Operation Ivy.

While the band was recording *Stranger Than Fiction,* representatives from the label listened to the rough cuts and expressed their concern that a song didn't jump out as a single, so they requested that the band rerecord "21st Century (Digital Boy)" for the album. Although Brett felt "Infected" was a contender for the first single, he didn't entirely disagree with "21st Century (Digital Boy)" being included on the album.

"That made sense to me," Brett said of the decision to rerecord the song. "To be honest I was so in awe of Andy Wallace, due to his recent work with Nirvana and Rage Against the Machine, that I was dying to hear what my song would sound like produced by him. So that's one of the main reasons I was for it."

In Brett's mind, "21st Century (Digital Boy)" was the perfect synthesis of punk and pop and he was excited about putting it out in front of a wider audience in this new alternative-friendly climate, but he still felt that "Infected" had a better chance of breaking out.

Despite disagreements over which song should be the first single, the band was pleased with how *Stranger Than Fiction* sounded, and they knew their fans would be, too. It wasn't a departure from their signature sound. If anything, there was *less* experimentation than on their previous two albums, and it compared favorably with *Against the Grain,* right down to the repetition of "21st Century (Digital Boy)."

"On *Stranger Than Fiction,*" Bobby said, "you can hear why everything is so precise and in the pocket because we were so well rehearsed. We went in and nailed the songs. We were a well-oiled machine."

The band was aware of their fans' concern about their move to Atlantic and knew *Stranger Than Fiction* would be heavily scrutinized for signs they had sold out. To counter that perception, they front-loaded the album with a number of Greg's up-tempo scorchers, like "Leave Mine to Me," "Tiny Voices," "The Handshake," and "Individual," many of which were destined to become fan favorites.

Everything was looking good for the Bad Religion and Epitaph camps: Rancid's *Let's Go* was released and the video for "Salvation" got significant airplay on MTV. The Offspring's *Smash* continued to soar, shattering all kinds of sales records for a band on an independent label. Both Bad Religion and Epitaph Records were enjoying a level of success they hadn't imagined possible, and—incredibly—there was room to grow.

But it was an unusually quiet summer for Bad Religion. For the first time since 1989, they weren't spending the summer in Europe. Instead, they would go overseas after the release of *Stranger Than Fiction* in September. Hetson went on tour with the Circle Jerks. Jay sold his house in the Hollywood Hills and was preparing to move his family to an island off the coast of Vancouver, Canada. His two sons, Miles and Hunter, were approaching the age when it was time to enroll in school and the Bentleys found the L.A. school system wanting.

"We went down and looked at where Miles was going to go to school," Jay said. "Zero grass. Barbed wire. I thought, *This doesn't look like fun to me. This is no way to go to school.*" The couple looked at private schools in L.A. but they were too expensive. They considered moving to Portland or Seattle before settling on British Columbia. Michaela was a Canadian citizen, so the move made sense. "It wasn't a couple of people deciding they wanted to go to Canada," Jay recalled. "It was a Canadian going home. Her family lived there. It was fairly simple. It wasn't that big of a deal."

Greg continued working on his Ph.D. and was spending time at Cornell peering at fossils through an electron microscope. He had also built up his home studio to the extent that he could not only make demos of his own music but produce records for other bands as well.

Even in Ithaca, Greg could sense the changes in the way that punk rock was perceived. "Bad Religion was in a vacuum, but the second we signed with a major label, distribution immediately improved. I could go down to the record store at the local mall and pick up a Bad Religion record. We could go to cities all over America and our record would be there. Not just at the indie record store, but at the malls. It was part of the democratization of punk that was going on at that time."

From his vantage point in far-off Ithaca, Greg could see the demographic was changing, and bands were benefitting from those changes. "I think Green Day, the Offspring, and Bad Religion expanded because the culture allowed it," Greg explained. "There was a new generation of kids who wanted aggressive music. They were buying more skateboards. They were buying more snowboards. The X Games were coming into their own. There was a whole cultural change going on that bands were able to capitalize on. It wasn't the bands leading the way. Musicians want to believe they changed the world. They didn't. They were able to thrive in that cultural milieu. That's my belief, and it comes from studying a different field and seeing how nature works. I'm an evolutionary biologist. I look at things in a different way. I see the flourishing of a species due to the environment, not the other way around."

Greg's refreshingly rational view of this sea change in the music industry explained the simultaneous success of bands as different as Bad Religion, Rancid, the Offspring, and Green Day. All of these bands were able to capitalize on the growing pool of young people entering the emerging market, but it didn't take a rocket scientist—or in this case an evolutionary biologist—to understand that many of these young fans would find Bad Religion's message to be more complex than they bargained for.

The album titles alone served as a litmus test for discourse one could expect to find on the album. If you're looking for a record that speaks to the challenges of living in an increasingly complicated world, are you going to turn to "Stranger Than Fiction" or "Dookie"? Green Day wrote songs that spoke to adolescent (and post-adolescent) concerns: fitting in, dealing with anxiety and depression, figuring out what it means to fall in and out of love. Green Day's genius was addressing concerns that were hard-wired into the teenage brain. Bad Religion didn't write songs like that and never had—not even when they were teenagers.

With Bad Religion there was always a subtext. Sometimes that subtext was sarcastic. Sometimes it was ironic. But it was always subversive and challenged the listener to think. Questioning norms and rejecting dogma were not exactly hallmarks of the formula for pop music success.

But Greg was right: punk was flourishing like never before. This rising tide changed the fates and fortunes of a number of bands. Record executives may have believed these changes constituted a new paradigm, but the players knew it wasn't destined to last. "Fun while it lasted" was the unofficial motto of countless punk and hardcore bands that rose up and flamed out. The history of punk was defined by periods of intense but unsustainable wildness and creativity. For example, the Sex Pistols, the Germs, and Operation Ivy were all fun while they lasted; but they didn't last long. The best course for Bad Religion to follow was to keep doing what they were doing, and nobody knew this better than Bad Religion.

Naturally, somebody had to throw a wrench in the works, which was exactly what happened when Brett Gurewitz and Jay Bentley got into an argument that changed the course of Bad Religion.

Like most breakups, it started with a fight over a trivial matter that in retrospect didn't make a whole lot of sense. In this case, it concerned a guest list. Epitaph was gearing up for the Epitaph Summer Nationals at the Hollywood Palladium. The idea was borrowed from Dischord: to put on a show of Epitaph bands and only charge a few bucks for the ticket. The Epitaph Summer Nationals ran for three nights. Headliners included the Offspring and Down by Law on July 27, Pennywise and Rancid on July 28, and NOFX and Bad Religion on the final night of the show. It would be a simple affair: just the bands and their fans. Because the dressing room at the Palladium was so small, the backstage area was restricted to the bands, their crews, and Epitaph staff. That meant no guest lists. Unfortunately, Jay didn't get the message.

He called the Epitaph offices and asked for his wife to be put on the guest list. When the request was denied, he became understandably indignant. After all, he was a member of Bad Religion, the band that built Epitaph, and until very recently, an Epitaph employee. Because the tickets for the Summer Nationals were so cheap, they'd sold out immediately. Without a guest list, if you didn't have a ticket, you weren't going to the show. Jay couldn't— or wouldn't—wrap his head around this. He said some not very nice things and hung up the phone.

A few minutes later, Brett returned Jay's call. They went back and forth about the guest list. Jay was incredulous that he couldn't bring his wife to the show. Brett was upset that Jay had cursed out one of Epitaph's employees. The argument escalated, both parties accused each other of being unreasonable, insults were exchanged, but Brett delivered the coup de grâce: "I quit."

Jay thought Brett was joking when he said, "'I don't need this shit. I quit.' I kind of laughed and he said, 'No, I'm serious. I'm fucking out.'"

Just like that, Brett was no longer a member of the band he'd cofounded.

Later that day Bobby got a call from their manager, Danny Heaps, who informed him that Brett had quit the band. He told Bobby that Brett and Jay had gotten into an argument with the result being that Brett had quit Bad Religion. Danny wanted Bobby to call Brett and talk him into staying in the band. Instead, Bobby called Jay to find out what had happened.

Over dinner that night, Jay gave Bobby the rundown. Now that he'd had a chance to reflect on his argument with Brett, Jay felt one of two things would go down. Either he would be kicked out and Brett would return to the band, or Greg would quit too and that would be the end of Bad Religion. "That was where my brain went," Jay said. "I automatically thought Brett would say, *I'll come back, but Jay has to go.* I thought for sure that was going to happen. Why would they keep me in the band instead of Brett? He writes songs and owns the label. Who am I?"

Bobby didn't agree. As the newest member of the band, he was able to assess the situation without all the emotional baggage. "I saw it coming," Bobby recalled. "We went to a major and they were expecting us to do a lot more. We knew we were going to tour more and there was no way Brett was going to be able to do it. When the Offspring took off, it was huge. Just massive. There was no way he was going to be able to tour with Bad Religion and run a label. You can't do both. It's overwhelming."

While Bobby and Jay were commiserating, Brett called Greg and explained what had happened. "'Me and Jay got in an argument,'" Greg recalled Brett telling him, "'and I hate what he said to me. I'm not going to tolerate it and I can't be in this band.'"

Greg took the news about Brett's fight with Jay with a grain of salt because he knew what was going on at Epitaph and understood the incredible pressure that Brett was under. Once Greg took the emotion out of the equation, it came down to a very simple question: "Do you want to be a record mogul or do you want to be in Bad Religion? I never got that mad at him because he wasn't saying, I can't work with you, but he said in as many words that he'd rather captain the ship at Epitaph than cocaptain Bad Religion."

Once it became obvious that Brett wasn't interested in returning to Bad Religion, the rest of the band began to wonder what Greg's response would be. Would he quit too? Was this the end of Bad Religion?

The news was particularly upsetting to Greg because he wasn't just losing a band member and a friend, but a creative collaborator. There's no good time to lose a key member of your band, but for Greg it was doubly devastating. Unbeknownst to the rest of the band, when Greg received the news that Brett was leaving Bad Religion, he was dealing with marital problems that would ultimately lead to the breakup of his marriage. It was already a trying time for Greg without the added drama of Brett's untimely exit from the band.

"I really felt the weight of his departure," Greg said. "*Shit, man, are we really going to dissolve the band the minute after we take the step up to the next level? Literally the minute after?* I said, *No way. I'm going to redouble my efforts.* But it wasn't easy. As sad as it sounds, I had to make myself believe that we could go on without Brett. In the midst of tragedy, you soldier on without self-reflection, but it felt like everything was washing away."

Though Greg was stunned by Brett's decision, he never considered bailing out of the band. If anything, he was more determined than ever to push forward. No one else in the band wanted to jump ship. They'd made a commitment to Atlantic and, more importantly, to each other, to record three more albums, and that's what they were going to do.

This begs the question: with so much at stake, why did Brett *really* leave?

Everyone had a theory. While the argument with Jay over a guest list may have been the trigger that set Brett off, obviously there were deeper issues at play. First and foremost was the decision to sign with Atlantic. Moving to a major label was supposed to relieve Brett of his duties as the band's label, but now more was expected of him as a member of Bad Religion.

Atlantic wanted the band to tour more often and make more appearances. For almost as long as the band had been in existence, its ability to play shows had been determined by Greg's availability. After Bad Religion signed to Atlantic, Greg said he would put his graduate school studies on hold so that the band could travel longer and farther. But with all of Brett's responsibilities at Epitaph, this wasn't something he was able to do. Greg's limited availability was what allowed Brett to be both a member of the band *and* run its label. Greg's reversal put that in jeopardy and may have generated some friction between the two songwriters.

Jay found himself caught in the middle of this dispute. "I remember very vividly thinking, *I can go out on the road and play bass in this band or I can sit at that desk and answer telephones and drive a forklift.* I thought, *I wanna go on the road and be a bass player.* That for me was the beginning of the unraveling of the team."

Looking back, Brett's departure also explained the unusual amount of tension during the recording of *Stranger Than Fiction,* especially between Greg and Brett. "All of a sudden," Jay said, "you couldn't say something to someone without them yelling at you. It was fucking weird."

Bad Religion had considerable experience making records under all kinds of conditions, and they often pushed each other to give their absolute best performance, but the atmosphere in the studio had changed.

"The state of the band during the making of *Stranger Than Fiction* with Andy Wallace was of dysfunction and passive acrimony," Brett said. "We were four guys and if one guy left the room—say Hetson—then, Greg, Jay, and I would talk shit about that guy. Then if he came back and Jay left the room, me, Greg, and Hetson would talk shit about Jay. And then if Jay came back and Greg left the room, then me, Jay, and Hetson would say the meanest things about Greg. I can't verify, obviously, that when I left the room they were saying things about me, but I would be shocked and disappointed if that weren't the case. The only thing we had in common was how much we hated each other."

The members of Bad Religion, Brett and Greg especially, were victims of their own high standards and outstanding work ethic. Between 1987 and 1994, Bad Religion recorded eight studio albums and toured constantly, which took a toll on the band members' relationships with one another. Greg maintained his academic career while Brett grew his businesses. Greg, Brett, and Jay had all gotten married and started families during that period of intense productivity. From the standpoint of how hard they were pushing themselves, something had to give.

"I think I was living on four hours' sleep a day," Brett said. "I came down with chronic fatigue syndrome. I'd run myself into the ground. I was clean and sober for most of it and was using work as a drug, which had its benefits, but it had some steep trade-offs and one of those was harmony within the band. The whole situation was fraught, and I extricated myself from it in a fit of anger—not my finest moment."

Ironically, the reason Brett agreed to go along with the other members of Bad Religion and sign with a major label was because he didn't know if an indie—much less Epitaph—could push a record to bona fide mainstream success. But with the unprecedented success of *Smash,* that's exactly what happened.

"The truth is," Brett said, "I think we'd made the best record of our career, and I was proud of it, but Epitaph had become insanely successful, more than I ever thought possible. I didn't have to be in a band. I was thirty-two years old. I hated for it to happen that way, but it was the perfect time for me to move on."

The success of the Offspring must have been extremely disruptive for Brett. Epitaph reached a point with *Smash* that each record sold pushed the band and the label into unknown territory. When all was said and done the album would go double platinum, selling over eleven million records worldwide. The Offspring did what no other band signed to an independent record label had done. It was a historic achievement of epic proportions and it simply wouldn't have happened if Brett had continued to split his time between Bad Religion and Epitaph.

Jay eventually came to believe that Brett left Bad Religion for the same reason people quit their jobs every day: lack of appreciation. Brett wrote half the material—not just the music, but the lyrics as well—but because Greg sang all of the songs fans assumed that Greg wrote them all. "I think Brett felt he wasn't getting the credit he deserved," Jay said, "and maybe there was a little bit of Brett saying, *Fuck it. I'm doing my own thing.*"

Because of Epitaph, Brett's finances weren't tied to the band. For him Bad Religion was a creative outlet, but it clearly wasn't as satisfying as it had once been. The deal with Atlantic made things worse because now he had less control over how the music was made into a product. A big part of Bad Religion's success was its distinctive sound, a sound that Brett painstakingly crafted in the recording studio. Now those creative decisions were being made by other people.

There were also intangible elements that weighed on Brett's decision. In the mid-nineties, signing with a major label was the ultimate sellout for a punk band. While the success of Nirvana had ameliorated this to some degree by empowering advertisers and producers to put noisy guitar rock, including punk songs, in commercials and on television shows, there was still a strong stigma in the punk community against selling out. Even Green Day, who didn't have anything close to the history of Bad Religion, was criticized for selling out by its fans when it moved to Reprise Records, part of the Warner Music Group. It irked Brett to pay the price of signing with a major, only to have one of Epitaph's bands achieve success without it. As Brett put it, "Bad Religion left right before the miracle happened."

"I think he must have been tortured," Greg said of Brett's decision to leave. "Here's your band that you love so much. Here's your artistic expression of who you are, and you're getting ready to take the next step, but at the same time the label that you nurtured is now exploding. He probably didn't know what to do, but the decision was made, and I respected his decision."

Brett's feelings about the band going to Atlantic were more conflicted than he let on to his bandmates. "I was in favor of it. My self-esteem was low enough to think that a major label could do more for the band than I ever could. Like many recording artists, I always wondered if the majors had some kind of secret sauce that they weren't sharing with the rest of us. Turns out they don't. At the same time, I was also hurt. Somewhere deep inside I wanted the band to say, *We'll never go to a major! Epitaph for life!* In my secret heart of hearts, I wanted my band to say that, but I couldn't ask them for that because that's like asking someone to love you. It wouldn't have been real."

Once Brett made the decision to leave Bad Religion, he gave everything he had to Epitaph. It was a tremendous amount of work and no small amount of financial risk. The massive, global success of the Offspring meant that he had to transform Epitaph's operations overnight. Then, when the industry took notice of what Epitaph had achieved, it came gunning for him. Record labels sent representatives to sign the Offspring and Rancid away from Epitaph. Rumors circulated that the pop star Madonna tried to seduce Armstrong with nude photographs to lure Rancid to her label. One night in New York Greg watched Madonna buttonhole Armstrong for twenty minutes backstage.

Despite the internal conflict and headaches of being in a band, producing records, and running a label, all of Brett's endeavors were extremely successful. The record he'd just cowritten, *Stranger Than Fiction,* was poised to do great things with Atlantic, and Epitaph was far and away the biggest independent record label on the planet. This made Brett very wealthy, but it was a bittersweet moment. Nor did his new fortune make the old demons disappear. Brett relapsed and started drinking during the making of *Stranger Than Fiction,* and he would eventually go back to using drugs again.

It's difficult to know exactly what impact this may have had on his decision-making at the time, but he was experiencing intense pressure in all areas of his life: from the band, with the label, and at home. More and more was expected of him and it ultimately got to be too much.

Jay insisted it was unfair to blame the breakup of the band on any one member's erratic behavior because the move to Atlantic brought out the worst in everyone. "It was exactly why bands break up. Everyone was way out of control, myself included. We were all pretty fucking crazy."

Greg, Brett, Jay, Hetson, and Bobby took the stage together for the last time at the Epitaph Summer Nationals at the Hollywood Palladium. Rumors had circulated about Brett leaving the band, and people were curious to see if he would play one last show with Bad Religion. "He'd officially quit the band," Greg said, "but he did come onstage for that show."

The Summer Nationals were Brett's last hurrah and Bad Religion's final show under Epitaph, and there were plenty of hard feelings between Brett and the rest of the band. "It had already been established that everyone was on the outs," Jay said, "and it was going to be the last thing that we were going to do, but we still played it."

It may have been an awkward scene, but it was a clean break. One of the remarkable things about Bad Religion was they weren't a tight group of friends. They each had their own interests and agendas, and at times they were very frank about putting these priorities ahead of the band. For years Greg's academic schedule dictated when the band could play. Similarly, Brett's availability was limited by his duties as a producer and label head. Even Hetson would take time away from the band to tour with the Circle Jerks. These competing interests would have spelled the demise of many bands, but not Bad Religion.

"It's a very good thing," Jay said, "and it's always been a very Bad Religion thing, that we have never been a group in the sense that we live together, we eat together, we breathe together, we do everything together. We don't. We do everything separately and always have—except the band. That's something we have for ourselves, and when it's over, whether it's a rehearsal or a tour, we all go live our separate lives. And I think that is very important to everybody."

So when Brett stepped away, the rest of the band didn't fall apart. They forged ahead, convinced there was a bright future for Bad Religion. After all, they'd gone through lineup changes before. In fact, for Greg and Hetson, playing without Brett was nothing new. It was something they'd done for years and years between *Into the Unknown* and *Suffer*. The first time they replaced Brett, Hetson slid into place like a key in a lock. As Jay had said of Pete Finestone, "He was already there." But this time would be different. There was no one standing on the sidelines. To replace Brett, they would have to bring someone in from outside the band.

16

COLLAPSE

THE NIGHT OF BRETT'S LAST SHOW WITH BAD
Religion, his replacement watched from the audience.
Brian Baker was already part of the Epitaph family
when he was invited to join Bad Religion. Brett had put out a
record by Brian's band, Dag Nasty, in 1992. In fact, Jay recalled
that Brian started lobbying for a spot in Bad Religion while he was
recording with Epitaph. "He told me, 'If Hetson ever leaves, call
me.' He said to Hetson, 'If Brett ever leaves, call me.' It was really
funny because when Brett left, both me and Hetson were like,
'Brian wants the job.'"

Of course, Brian wasn't as well known for his guitar work with
Dag Nasty as he was for being one of the founding members of
what was arguably the most important hardcore band to ever plug
in an amplifier: Minor Threat.

Brian started playing guitar when he was eight years old. He
learned to play at the same time as his best friend, Michael Hampton, another influential guitar player in the D.C. hardcore scene,
who would go on to play in State of Alert with Henry Rollins

and the Faith with Ian MacKaye's brother Alec. When Brian was twelve, he joined his first band, Silent Thunder, which basically just played KISS and Aerosmith covers in the drummer's basement. "I think we might have played one show," Brian said, "but I know we had T-shirts!"

The Bakers moved to Michigan, where Brian formed a band called Hameron with some other kids at his school. This time it was Cheap Trick and Ted Nugent covers. When Carlos Santana came to town, the drummer's dad secured backstage passes for his son, who brought Brian along. Before the show, they were given a tour of the entire backstage area where Brian made his presence felt by picking up one of Santana's guitars and jamming on it. Instead of being escorted out of the building, the crew brought Brian an amp and encouraged him to keep playing. That would be the highlight of any kid's night, but this was just the warm-up. Right before the second encore, one of the guitar techs slung a Les Paul guitar around Brian's neck and pushed him out onstage. Brian ended up playing a couple songs with Carlos Santana in front of twenty-five thousand people.

However, Brian's newfound fame in Michigan was destined to be short-lived because not long afterward he moved back to Washington, D.C., where all his friends were now into punk rock. For most kids, listening to punk made you an outcast, but at Georgetown Day School punk was cool. The first time Brian saw real punks outside of his circle of friends was when he saw the Cramps play at the Ontario Theatre on August 21, 1980. "I felt a visceral tingle," he said. "I felt like I was on fire."

After the Teen Idles broke up, vocalist Ian MacKaye and drummer Jeff Nelson started a new band. They invited Lyle Preslar to play guitar, and recruited Brian to play bass. This was approximately the same time that Bad Religion was forming on the other side of the country. Like his future bandmate Jay Bentley, Brian was a guitar player who was asked to switch instruments for the sake of the band. Brian was only fifteen years old, by far the youngest member of the band.

"I'd never played bass," Brian said. "I was a guitar player. I suppose I was asked to join the band because there was no one else available who had an instrument and wasn't already in a band. Our scene was so small. I went to high school with the guitar player who was two grades above me. I played bass because I was the last one there. I started playing chords on it. They told me, 'No, you play one note at a time.'"

Most scenes are defined by one or two bands, but the D.C. punk community was exceptionally vital with a large number of bands for such a small city. Dischord, the label MacKaye co-owns with Jeff Nelson, was the epicenter for the scene, but it sometimes seemed as if everyone Brian knew was making music.

"I was part of this group of twenty or thirty people in Washington, D.C., and everyone had a band," Brian said. "That whole experience was really profound. I was in Minor Threat and my friends were in the Faith. These guys were in Void and these guys were in Marginal Man. Everyone was in their own band. Someone would play a show and we'd all go watch. Our band would play and they'd come watch us. It was all the same. Minor Threat would play and it would be the same thing if Government Issue were playing. The same people would go to both shows. The only difference was who was onstage."

Much like the L.A. scene, each band had its own distinct sound, but it was Minor Threat that broke out of the pack and rose to prominence in D.C. and beyond. As the youngest member, Brian downplayed his contribution to the band. "I could play and Lyle could play," Brian said. "I mean we knew how to play our instruments, but we had the best drummer in town and Ian wrote great songs."

With a mix of sledgehammer riffs and howling intensity, Minor Threat set the bar for hardcore punk. Musically, Minor Threat made other bands sound tame in comparison, but the clarity and coherence of MacKaye's message was never compromised.

Although it didn't feel like it at the time, being in Minor Threat was a watershed moment that set the stage for the rest of Brian's career. "It was a classic case of right place, right time," Brian said. "It was a lightning-in-a-bottle situation. My high school band that jammed at the guitar player's mom's house after school got to be one of the most influential punk rock bands ever. And always will be."

After Minor Threat broke up, Brian collaborated with Glenn Danzig in the infant stages of what would become Samhain, though Brian left the group before they played their first show. Brian also did a stint in the Meatmen while "sort of" going to college before leaving school for good and forming Dag Nasty in 1985. After Dag Nasty broke up in 1988, Brian went on to join Junkyard, an L.A. hard rock band. They did two records for Geffen and toured extensively in the United States before being dropped in 1992. Junkyard fizzled out soon after that and Brian moved on to his next project.

Next, he started a band called Careless, an alternative rock band with what Brian described as "a weird crossover of styles." Major labels were throwing around stupid amounts of money in the hopes of signing an alternative act that could deliver a hit. "We were Weezer before Weezer," Brian said. "Not metal. Not grunge. Whatever the fuck we were. The problem was whatever the fuck we were didn't get a record deal." The band was very close to being signed—they had a publishing deal with Virgin—but it didn't happen.

Brian decided to take a hiatus from playing music at this point. "I realized I'd been in a band consistently for fourteen years," Brian said. "It was time to step back for a bit and recharge my batteries." He started working full time at Cole Rehearsal Studios in Hollywood. Cole was a pro-am studio, meaning they rented to professionals and amateurs alike. A band like Danzig might have a practice space locked out for a month while a bunch of kids just off the bus from Tulsa rented the room right next to it by the hour.

"It was entertaining," Brian said. "I was basically the front-of-house guy. When you came into Cole, I was the guy at the front desk. 'You're going to be in B. Your mics are set up, and if you need anything let me know.' I was basically a concierge. I think it helped that people would recognize me. 'Oh my god you're Brian from Minor Threat!' So that was interesting to them."

Brian was a talented guitar player with an affable personality who was willing to do whatever was necessary to assist. It didn't matter if you were on your way up or crashing back down to earth, Brian had been there and was willing to lend a hand. "I was a kind of goodwill ambassador," Brian said. "Lending my experience and trying to be funny and lightening up the process. That's what I did."

At Cole, Brian struck up a friendship with Tommy Stinson of the Replacements, who'd formed a new band called Bash & Pop and was looking to recruit some musicians for a follow-up album. Stinson asked Brian to join his band, and for a while they wrote music and played shows together in L.A. Around this time Brian met Scott Litt, who was working with Juliana Hatfield. Litt enlisted Brian's help during preproduction of Hatfield's new record. It turned out that Litt had produced a number of R.E.M.'s albums, and he was so impressed with Brian he introduced him to the R.E.M. camp. The rockers from Athens, Georgia, were looking for a fill-in guitar player for their next tour.

Brian met with Michael Stipe and, like a lot of tryouts Brian had been on, the subject turned to Minor Threat. It helped that Brian was a really good guitar player, but Stipe and MacKaye were also friends, and Brian discovered he and Stipe knew a lot of the same people. Brian formally tried out and was offered the gig.

"I was still working at Cole and life was looking good when I got a conference call from Greg Hetson and Greg Graffin asking if I wanted to try out for Bad Religion. They had a new record coming out and they were touring immediately. They needed someone right now and they didn't want some random person. Because of Brett's importance in the band, they felt they needed someone with a pedigree."

In a matter of days, Brian went from being a guy who worked at a rent-by-the-hour practice space to being offered gigs in R.E.M.

and Bad Religion. Brian loved Bad Religion; they were his favorite West Coast punk rock band. "When I bought my first Bad Religion record, I got *How Could Hell Be Any Worse?* and Black Flag's *Jealous Again* the same day. I really liked 'We're Only Gonna Die.' I thought that Black Flag were more powerful, but I preferred the singing in Bad Religion."

Despite his affection for the band, he felt the honorable thing to do was tell Greg that he'd already accepted an offer to tour with R.E.M. Greg countered by matching the salary that R.E.M. was going to pay him and offering him a chance to become a full member of the band. That made the prospect of turning down R.E.M. much easier.

"It meant being part of a team and not an outside guy," Brian explained. "It meant being an equal partner in what we decided to do and where we decided to go. In some camps you can be hired for a tour and let go. You're not pretty anymore or someone's wife is looking at you the wrong way. There are all kinds of things that can happen. But being a member of the band you're a partner. You have security you don't have as a side player."

In addition, he already knew several members of the band. He was acquainted with Brett and Jay from Epitaph when Dag Nasty's *Four on the Floor* came out, and he knew Hetson from around town. "Hetson was a local Lothario barfly like me," Brian said. "He was someone I'd see at bars. We knew each other from Circle Jerks and Minor Threat. He was a punk icon. I was a punk icon. We'd go to bars and be punk icons."

Brian's audition took place at Cole while Greg was in town, and he played with the full band. It was something of a foregone conclusion that he would get the gig because they didn't bring anyone else in for a tryout. It was Brian's job to lose.

"It was great," Brian said. "They found out I'm a real person. I'm not just this myth."

After the audition, he was officially offered the gig. Brian would now get his first taste of Bad Religion's bicoastal arrangement. In L.A., he rehearsed with Jay, Hetson, and Bobby—or whoever was available. Then he flew out to Ithaca to work with Greg on some songs. The next time he would play with the entire band would be at his first Bad Religion gig for a one-off show in Germany. The airline lost one of the two guitars that he'd brought, which made his first trip to the European continent more nerve-wracking than it needed to be.

"I flew to Europe to play the Bizarre Festival with Bad Religion," Brian said. "My first show was a forty-five-minute set at a big European festival with sixty thousand people. I walked out on the stage to play with Greg and the whole band for the first time, and I'd never played in front of that many people ever. It was insane. It was absolutely insane."

A number of Epitaph bands were playing the festival, and Brett watched Brian's debut from the soundboard. It was like the Epitaph Summer Nationals only this time Brian and Brett had traded places.

Brian's performance at the Bizarre Festival changed the narrative from despair over Brett's departure to excitement about Brian's arrival. Minor Threat had never played in Europe, so Brian joining Bad Religion was a very big deal over there. Bad Religion received considerable media attention and a lot of it centered on Minor Threat.

"Publicly," Jay explained, "when someone leaves the band and people want to know what happened, my answer is, 'You'll have to ask him.' But when someone like Brett leaves and you've lost one of your songwriters, you can't just go, 'You'll have to talk to him' because that's not going to fly. So having someone like Brian Baker from Minor Threat helped get us out of that awkward conversation. 'What happened? Here's Brian!' It buffered the situation without completely ignoring that we'd lost a major player in our band by replacing him with another major player."

The festival also opened Brian's eyes about how Bad Religion was perceived in Europe. "I knew Bad Religion was a successful band. I knew they were a punk band, but I did not know they were a *big* band. I knew they played the Hollywood Palladium in L.A.

and they could play Roseland in New York. I thought of them as nowhere near as big as the Offspring or Green Day, but at that Replacements, Soul Asylum level. Then I went to Germany and was like *Jesus Christ*. I had no concept."

The Bizarre Festival, though intense, was just a warm-up. The moment Brian got off the stage, he had less than a month to prepare for what they were calling the Ain't Life a Mystery Tour, which would take them to eleven European countries in five weeks.

Brian asked for help and he turned to an unlikely person: Brett Gurewitz. Brian didn't have copies of Bad Religion's back catalog, which he needed so he could learn the songs. Brian had avoided getting involved in the dispute between Brett and the band, and the two remained on good terms. That didn't stop Brett from issuing Brian a warning: "Those guys are crazy. You won't last three months."

Stranger Than Fiction was released in early September, a few weeks before the European tour. KROQ put "Infected" into heavy rotation despite Atlantic pushing "21st Century (Digital Boy)" as the first single from the album. It was a less than ideal situation to have the most powerful rock and roll radio station playing one song while the record label promoted another. Neither song gained the momentum necessary to break out nationally, and it had a negative impact on sales.

Before Brett's departure Bad Religion shot two videos for the album, both by Gore Verbinski. "Stranger Than Fiction" features a random cast of characters who have assembled for a book burning under a bridge in downtown L.A. The exceptionally strange video for "21st Century (Digital Boy)" required covering the band members with blue paint and submerging them in a pool of green slime, which would act as a liquid green screen. "Unfortunately," Brett recalled, "the idea didn't work and it looked like we were drowning in weird blue liquid." Life isn't always a mystery, but the video certainly is.

In late September, the band embarked on its first European tour without Brett. The tour started in France and proceeded to Spain. In San Sebastian, at a show at Discoteca Erne, calamity struck. When the band entered through the ground floor of the building, they assumed that the structure was being renovated because portions of the second story, where the club was located, were supported with jacks. Bad Religion had been touring Europe for six consecutive years, and they'd performed in plenty of dodgy venues. From rundown squats to buildings that weren't up to code, the band had grown accustomed to playing in places that would have been shut down in the United States.

The band opened up with "Recipe for Hate" and the fans immediately started jumping around and dancing to the music. Right at the song's climax, the left side of the floor suddenly collapsed. "We started playing the show," Greg recalled, "and a big hole opened up in front of me on the dance floor and bodies started falling into the hole." The people who had been standing in front of the stage disappeared into the space where the floor had been.

Bad Religion stopped playing and the people on the right side of the dance floor shouted in protest, unaware of what had happened. But the screams of those who had fallen or were in danger of falling drowned them out. A huge cloud of dust rose from the lower level and people continued to tumble into the pit.

The band was quickly ushered off the stage and out of the venue while fans and club personnel attended to those who had been injured. The hole that had opened up in front of the stage was enormous: approximately seventy feet long by forty feet wide and between fifteen and twenty feet deep. Hundreds of fans fell into the chasm created by the collapse. Between the lights and the dust and the screams from below it resembled a scene out of a disaster movie. It took twenty minutes for the first ambulance to arrive and two hours to get everyone who'd been hurt out of harm's way. Although hundreds had been injured, thankfully there were no fatalities.

The band had questions and demanded answers. What happened? Had the show been oversold? Did the venue have the proper permits? The disco's promoters insisted the venue had held events in the recent past with 3,500 and 4,000 guests. By the band's count, fewer than three thousand people had come through the door to see Bad Religion. In retrospect, the presence of temporary jacks to help support the joists was a huge red flag that the structure was unsound and the venue unsafe.

Bad Religion's soundman, Ronnie Kimball, took photos of the scene to document the damage, but on his way out of the venue, his camera was confiscated and the images were lost. Neither the club's owners nor the local police wanted word to get out about what had happened, and they were eager to see Bad Religion leave San Sebastian.

Much to the band's surprise, the incident received minimal media coverage in the weeks that followed. Less than two weeks later, an incident occurred at a Pink Floyd concert in London where a section of the bleachers collapsed. Nearly one hundred fans fell but no one was hurt. This story generated major headlines across the United States and Europe. The silence out of Spain struck Bad Religion as odd.

"To this day," Greg said, "when we go to Spain, people tell us, 'I was there. I was at that show.' We get asked about it all the time."

It's a minor miracle that the show will go down in history as one of Bad Religion's shortest performances and not its deadliest. Although the tragedy was widely known in Europe, few fans in the United States were aware of it until the band discussed the incident in their newsletter, *The Bad Times*, which enjoyed an intermittent eleven-issue run from 1994 until 2001.

Although the band, the crew, and the majority of the fans escaped unscathed, Bad Religion had experienced enough upheavals over the last few months, and they were eager to leave behind the feeling of the ground giving way beneath their feet.

17

FASTEST DRIVER DRIVES THE CAR

BY THE END OF THE AIN'T LIFE A MYSTERY TOUR, IT was obvious to everyone in the band that bringing Brian Baker into the fold had been a brilliant move. He was an even better player than advertised and could do things with a guitar that no one who'd ever played in the band could do. He also had professional rock experience that his bandmates, being new to the majors, didn't have.

"When I joined Bad Religion," Brian said, "I had the most major-label experience, I had the most tour bus experience. I had done big records with Junkyard. I had already done the major label, big studio, famous producer thing. *Stranger Than Fiction* was their first time working at that level. I'd already done that. It was familiar to me. I didn't have any trepidation."

In other words, the stage wasn't too big for Brian. But he offered more than indie cred and big-league rock experience: he brought a welcome personal dynamic to Bad Religion. He was smart, sharp, and had a caustic wit that was endlessly entertaining—unless you were on the receiving end of it. Bobby, who lived for rock and roll trivia, was thrilled. "Wow, I'm in a band with a guy from Minor Threat!"

While talent and a solid work ethic are essential qualities for a touring musician, character is just as important. Professional musicians only spend a few hours together onstage per week, but the rest of the time, the so-called down time, is just as important to the longevity of a band. A sense of humor, an easygoing nature, and a short memory are essential to long-term sustainability and success. Character is everything.

"After playing a few shows with Brian," Jay said, "we realized that we'd made the right choice. We couldn't replace Brett, so we went and got a fucking great guitar player with a great backstory who turned out to be a really great guy. He became a guy that I really liked and cared about. We had a lot in common even though we were complete opposites. In all honesty, I think the weirdest thing about Brett leaving was that when Brian joined the band I got a brand-new best friend."

Although Jay was sober, Brian most certainly was not. He enjoyed the rock star lifestyle and wasn't shy about it. As Brian put it, "I wanted to do tons of blow, fly first class, and play huge festivals. I made the best of it and had a great time. I wasn't a fucking mess. I wasn't a tragic alcoholic yet." Jay enjoyed spending time with his new bandmate even when Brian was drinking. "He had a great time all the time," Jay said, "so I didn't mind being around Brian while he was drinking and partying because it was fun. I didn't have to drink to participate."

Brian arrived at a time when Bad Religion's popularity was growing. Much of this was predicated by their labels' efforts to capitalize on the global commercialization of punk, but not without some backlash from fans. In Germany some enterprising punks sold crossbuster T-shirts with the caption "THIS ISN'T PUNK ROCK. IT'S SONY." Despite the uproar, the increase in ticket sales and the size of the venues the band played in were significant.

For example, Bad Religion played a show at the Lisebergshallen in Gothenburg where the opening acts were SNFU and

Green Day. "They hadn't broken in Europe yet," Bobby said of Green Day. "They were nothing in Europe. We were playing in Sweden and I remember walking in and thinking, *This place holds six or seven thousand people. We're not going to sell this shit out.* Later that day there were eight thousand people in there."

Immediately after the European tour, the band geared up for the first leg of the North American Stranger Than Fiction Tour. The six-week tour included two dates in Jay's new hometown of Vancouver. In 1995 Bad Religion went to Japan for the first time for a series of shows in Osaka, Nagoya, Tokyo, and Sendai. A show in Sapporo was added because a devastating earthquake hit Kobe two months before the band was scheduled to play there. They also played two dates in Hawaii before heading home.

The band had logged the better part of six months on the road. They were spending a lot of time together on tour buses, in dressing rooms, and at hotels, and looking for ways to keep themselves entertained. One of the more surprising diversions Bad Religion became preoccupied with was NASCAR. While stock car racing might seem like a strange hobby for a bunch of punkers, there are a lot of similarities between a racing team and a rock band. Both have lots of expensive gear that they have to move around the country quickly and efficiently. Both require specialized technical skills in high-pressure situations. Both focus on a single event and when it's over you pack your gear and move on to the next one. You're in competition with your peers, but they're also your community because no one understands the ups and downs of this strange world like they do.

The ideology of racing teams became a source of inspiration for the band and one of its organizing principles. "'Fastest driver drives the car' is a Darrell Waltrip quote from watching the Southern States 500," Brian explained. "What that means is the guy who can get the job done the most efficiently and waste the least amount of time is the person for the job. That's been our ethic and it's stayed with us."

This mantra applied to everything the band did on and off the stage, and cultivated a spirit of can-do bonhomie and adjusting on the fly that served the band well. It also encouraged band and crew alike to check their egos. The best way to hold on to a job was to do it well without causing a lot of friction. If not, it would go to someone else.

The band's interest in cars and their crews also led to an unsettling discovery about one of their bus drivers, a good old boy whom everyone liked. He had a tendency to ride the brakes and wasn't a particularly good driver. Brian also noticed he was constantly sipping on something, and Brian was fairly certain it wasn't water. "I'm an alcoholic," Brian said. "I notice these things." Brian was convinced their bus driver was drinking on the job and driving while impaired. He brought this to the attention of the rest of the members of the band. They had a discussion with the driver and gave him an ultimatum. Brian recalled the conversation like this:

BAD RELIGION: Here's the thing. We love you but you're going to have to make a choice. You can stay with us and not drink, or you can go home.
DRIVER: Nice knowing you, boys!

Finding a new driver wasn't a problem because Bad Religion was in demand like never before. That summer, the band went back overseas for a short European tour before joining Pearl Jam on their much-maligned Vitalogy Tour.

Pearl Jam had taken a stance against Ticketmaster and had boycotted the service and the venues that supported it. The band had to organize every facet of the tour, which required an enormous amount of effort. This took a toll on the band's passionate front man, Eddie Vedder. When Vedder got sick, a number of the shows had to be canceled, upsetting fans. Despite these hassles, Bad Religion got to play in front of massive crowds for people who may not have been familiar with their music.

"The Vitalogy Tour was a big deal," Greg said. "There were a hundred thousand people at Soldier Field and a hundred thousand people at Golden Gate Park. Some of the biggest shows we'd ever played."

While Bad Religion was eating up the miles, Greg continued to write songs. As the sole songwriter in the band, he felt the pressure to deliver an album's worth of material to Atlantic and he was fully committed to the task. Greg took a break from working on his Ph.D. to prepare for the new album. Bobby and Brian both flew out to Greg's home studio, now called Polypterus Studios, in Ithaca to get ready for Bad Religion's ninth studio album, *The Gray Race.* Hetson was unavailable because he was touring with the Circle Jerks in support of their own major label debut—and final Circle Jerks release—*Oddities, Abnormalities and Curiosities,* about which the less said, the better.

"Greg said, 'I got some songs. Come out to Ithaca,'" Bobby recalled. "Brian and I went up there and rehearsed for about two weeks. Greg pretty much had the layout of what he wanted to do. We added our input to it, and it came out great. We had a great time doing it. It was all positive."

The experience was new for Brian. Although he'd flown out to Ithaca before the Ain't Life a Mystery Tour for what he called "vocal camp," he hadn't sat down with Greg to collaborate on new material. "I had never really written like that," Brian said. "I wrote lyrics when there was no one else to write them, like in Dag Nasty because we didn't know who was going to sing. But I never really thought of myself as a lyricist. I think I can do a pretty good imitation of a meaningful lyric because I'm not stupid, but when I wake up in the morning with an idea, it's a guitar riff. I'm never thinking about what the singer's gonna do."

This was the exact opposite approach that Greg took when crafting a song. "The song comes from a feeling," Greg said. "You have to somehow find the words to capture that feeling. The music is accompaniment. It's the sound you have in your head to accompany melody, and the melody is secondary to the feeling. So finding the words is everything."

In spite of their different approaches to songwriting, they made it work. Brian brought musical ideas he had stockpiled over the course of the tour. Greg picked some of the riffs he liked, and they made songs out of them. A change here or a suggestion there would transform a hook into something greater. Brian estimated he contributed to a quarter of the songs on *The Gray Race* in some meaningful way.

"I love the song called 'Nobody Listens' that we collaborated on," Brian said, "and also the song 'The Gray Race.' But some of my favorite songs on that record I had nothing to do with. I just play them. 'Drunk Sincerity' is one that I really love that Greg already had."

The bulk of the songwriting was done by Greg, and he approached it as rigorously as he did his academic work. "When it comes down to it, songwriting is self-control," Greg explained. "Most of what you spend your day doing, you have to throw away at the end of the day. It's not good enough. You think it sounds cool, but it's just not good enough. It's hard work. It's not fun. It can be torture, but when you get a song right it's the most life-affirming thing. It's pure elation."

For Greg, the writing of *The Gray Race* was an intense experience, and in interviews he referred to it as the band's most emotional album. Although it's not a concept album, the title track serves as an organizing principle for the rest of the record. The gray race is the human species because we are the only species on the planet that can see things in terms other than black-and-white, e.g., fight or flight, kill or be killed, et cetera. Humans can perceive a middle ground that encompasses a wide range of emotions like love, empathy, kindness, and other altruistic impulses, i.e., the feelings that give life meaning. Despite this ability, our species continually creates systems that encourage (if not enforce) a black-and-white duality to existence that is responsible for war, sickness, starvation, and a host of other maladies that could be prevented if we worked together as a species. The album's message is simple: either we have to create new ways of coexisting in the world or we are doomed to destroy one another.

Songs like "Them and Us," "Empty Causes," and "Nobody Listens" expand on this thesis. "Punk Rock Song," the most upbeat-sounding song on the record, is ultimately the most pessimistic:

> This is just a punk rock song
> Written for the people who can see something's wrong
> Like ants in a colony we do our share
> But there's so many other fuckin' insects out there

"Punk Rock Song" is a protest song that's aware it's preaching to the choir. It's also one of the few instances when a Bad Religion song expresses frustration at those who *can't* see that something's wrong. In other words, punks in name only. The song suggests it's not enough to buy tickets and T-shirts; you have to do more. If you're not working to improve our shared environment, then you're part of the problem. To drive the point home, the final verse is a catalog of statistics that illustrates the way the gray race fails itself and how we fail each other:

> 10 million dollars on a losing campaign
> 20 million starving and writhing in pain
> Big strong people unwilling to give
> Small in vision and perspective
> One in five kids below the poverty line
> One population runnin' out of time

Once the band was satisfied with the material, they worked with their management team to find a producer for the album. They decided to go with Ric Ocasek, the front man for the Cars. Ocasek had worked with punk legends Bad Brains and had recently done the breakout album for Weezer. Most importantly, he was an active producer and talented songwriter, which was very important to Greg.

"I think Bad Religion albums always need collaboration," Greg said. "Everything is collaboration. When Brett left, I knew I was going to need someone to fill his shoes and be a songwriting advocate, but also a critic. Someone who could steer the creative ship. And Ric was great at that."

Given the position that Greg was in, it would have been understandable if he insisted that he was captain of Bad Religion now. He very easily could have hired a producer who would follow his lead in the studio. To his credit, Greg sought out someone who was both experienced and esteemed and could be counted on to provide constructive criticism. Greg understood he couldn't do this on his own.

Bad Religion began recording *The Gray Race* in October at Electric Lady Studios in Greenwich Village. The studios were built by Jimi Hendrix in 1970, and countless legendary artists had recorded there over the years, from Led Zeppelin to the Clash to U2. Greg was invigorated by the newness of it all.

"I was thrilled to be working with great people," Greg said. "We had a good manager. We had a great label. We could just go down to Rockefeller Plaza and pop in at the label. It was a thrilling time for me. I had two young kids, and they'd come down and visit me in the city. It was a blast."

The band moved into long-term rental apartments at Fiftieth and Third. As the group's musical historian, Bobby was quick to point out this wasn't far from where Dee Dee Ramone had worked, first as a construction worker and then as a street hustler.

The band's newest member loved everything about the experience. "I was living in an apartment in New York City," Brian recalled, "and recording in one of the most famous studios in the world with an incredibly great producer and cool dude, who was also in a pretty amazing band. Things were firing on all cylinders and I was living the rock and roll fantasy. You're in Manhattan, you're going out for drinks with other musicians down in the Village after a long day in the studio. It was the stuff you read in books about rock and roll bands except it's your band."

It helped that Ocasek was a fellow guitar player who appreciated Brian's talent. They liked a lot of the same music and Brian was a great admirer of the Weezer record that Ocasek had produced. "He was very laid back," Brian said. "He was confident and knew exactly what he wanted things to sound like, but he wasn't an asshole. He'd done it many times before and had written a lot of big songs. We got along well enough that he asked me to be in his solo band afterwards."

The experience of writing and recording *The Gray Race* validated the band's decision to keep going after Brett left. Whatever doubts they had about losing a founding member and creative contributor were fading in the rearview mirror. They'd had a series of successful tours, written an album's worth of new material, and were having a quintessential New York experience—all while the band's popularity continued to climb. This suggested that the abruptness of Brett's decision to leave Bad Religion mattered more to them than it did to their fans.

"Brett's departure didn't cripple us," Greg said. "We can talk about everything that Brett and I had in our relationship that was special, our partnership as songwriters, and this bond that we had as intellectual companions, but if you want to talk about business, the fans don't pay attention to that. To this day you can ask our fans 'Who wrote that song?' and they'll say, 'The singer.' They don't know. They don't know who wrote what. They just love the music. They don't care about the songwriting."

Perhaps the only member of the band who didn't have a great experience during the recording of *The Gray Race* was Hetson. During the period when Greg, Bobby, and Brian were collaborating in Ithaca, Hetson had sent them a demo with two songs on it. Bobby strongly encouraged Hetson to fly out to Ithaca for a few weeks. "You should come up," Bobby said. "We need you here." But Hetson replied that he was still tied up with the Circle Jerks.

Greg had already written ten of the songs for the new album and was working on more. He also didn't think too highly of Hetson's songs, one of which wasn't even complete. "They weren't appropriate," Greg said. "They weren't Bad Religion songs. They weren't even Circle Jerks songs."

That wasn't going to fly, especially with Brett gone. Greg put a great deal of blood, sweat, and tears into the songs. Never one to take his responsibilities lightly, Greg was intensely focused on writing the best songs he could so that loyal Bad Religion fans wouldn't notice Brett's absence when they listened to the new album. There was virtually no chance he was going to lower his standards to appease Hetson.

The situation came to a head at Electric Lady. Hetson was adamant about putting one of his songs on the album. The band felt that if Hetson wanted to contribute to the album, he should have accepted Greg's invitation to come to Ithaca—like Bobby and Brian did.

But Hetson wouldn't budge. Greg diplomatically suggested that it was the producer's call, but also added there probably wasn't room for Hetson's songs at this late stage in the game. Hetson abruptly left the studio. They were scheduled to begin working with Ocasek the following day, and they had their final rehearsal without Hetson.

In the morning they held a band meeting, and Greg revealed that he'd talked to Hetson, who informed him he was going to quit the band after they finished recording the album. The band agreed that if Hetson was going to quit, he should leave now. They gave Hetson an ultimatum: if you're at the studio tonight, we know you're in the band; if not, you're out. Hetson showed up, and that was the end of that.

The band wrapped up recording in November and the members went back to their respective homes. Whereas once all of the members of Bad Religion had lived close to one another in the Valley, now they were spread out all over North America. Greg went upstate to Ithaca, Jay flew to Vancouver, and the three "newest" members of the band—Hetson, Bobby, and Brian—returned to L.A.

18

A TANGLED WEB OF LOGIC AND PASSION

AS GREG AND BRETT'S PATHS DIVERGED, WITH Bad Religion going one way and Epitaph going another, they both fixed their attention on the future. But the former collaborators also spent a considerable amount of time looking back on the legacy they had created together. As Bad Religion's songwriters, Greg and Brett had a reputation for being hyper-intelligent lyricists. They didn't cultivate labels like the professor and the record mogul, but they didn't shy away from them either. The way the two songwriters went about celebrating the band's legacy after their breakup revealed they were no less susceptible to intense emotions.

Toward the end of 1995, Epitaph released *All Ages,* a compilation of Bad Religion songs spanning from *How Could Hell Be Any Worse?* to *Generator,* celebrating ten years of Bad Religion records. (Songs from *Recipe for Hate* and *Stranger Than Fiction,* even those that Brett had written, were left off because they no longer belonged to Epitaph.) *All Ages* also includes two live tracks, "Do What You Want" and "Fuck Armageddon . . . This Is Hell," that were recorded with Brian Baker during the Ain't Life a Mystery Tour the previous year. From a business perspective, *All Ages* was a way for Brett to put a "best of" album in the stores at a time when Atlantic and Sony were spending a lot of time and money marketing and promoting Bad Religion. Releasing *All Ages* was a smart move from a savvy entrepreneur, but it was also a way for Brett to exercise creative control over a decade's worth of material.

Meanwhile, in the Bad Religion camp, *The Gray Race* was released in February 1996. After a few shows in California, Bad Religion immediately went to Germany to kick off a series of European club shows. In an effort to recapture the magic of their first European tour in 1989, they played at smaller, more intimate venues across Europe for performances that were more like album release parties. Their German fans rewarded the band for starting the tour in Europe by making the album's first single, "Punk Rock Song," number six on the German charts. *The Gray Race* was also a strong seller in Scandinavia. In fact, *The Gray Race* was Bad Religion's best-selling album outside of the U.S.

These dates were only the beginning of their longest and farthest-reaching tour to date. After two weeks in Europe, Bad Religion spent the next seven weeks traveling throughout the United States and Canada. Greg was a regular, if not religious, reader of the band's fan mail, and was aware of the many fans who complained that Bad Religion had never played in their town. The band spent that spring playing venues all over North America, hitting many cities for the first time.

After a month off, Bad Religion hopped around Europe, North America, Asia, and South America for the rest of the year. They came home for a well-deserved rest over the holidays before flying to Australia for another sold-out slate of shows. By the end of the tour, the band had played over 110 shows on five continents in under a year. They'd come a long way from playing frat parties and warehouse shows with their friends. They were a bona fide international act with fans all over the world.

The result of this extensive touring was an audio document that eventually took the form of the live album *Tested.* Like a scientist conducting an experiment, Greg wondered what it would be like to capture the sound of a Bad Religion show at various venues and then compare and contrast the recordings. Would the recordings reveal something useful that could be implemented in the future?

Greg was eager to find out. He packed his ADAT (Alesis Digital Audio Tape) multitrack recorder and, with the aid of the band's soundman, Ronnie, was able to capture the Bad Religion experience in clubs and concert halls all over the world.

After listening to a few of these recordings, the idea of a live album began to take hold. Greg wasn't interested in using overdubs and other studio effects to enhance the sound or trick the listener into thinking they were hearing a seamless live performance; he insisted on authenticity. By featuring songs from different venues, *Tested* became a "best of" The Gray Race Tour record. There's no crowd noise. What you hear is Bad Religion at the top of their game playing twenty-four songs at various venues from Baltimore to Berlin, Melbourne to Montreal.

The album also includes three previously unreleased studio tracks recorded at Greg's home studio in Ithaca: "Dream of Unity," "It's Reciprocal," and "Tested." The last takes its name from the notion that things that endure have stood the test of time, which certainly could be said of Bad Religion. The title also suggests that Greg felt The Gray Race Tour tested the band's mettle in terms of endurance and quality control. Greg wanted quantitative evidence that Bad Religion was just as good without Brett as it was with him.

The album wasn't released on Atlantic. The label wasn't as enthusiastic about the project as Greg was and declined to release or distribute it. (Later, representatives from the label said they weren't informed of the band's desire to release a live album and claimed they would have approved it.) Bad Religion put the album out with Sony and Atlantic agreed to sell it in the U.S. as an import. *Tested* was released in January 1997 as a double gatefold album and CD with a twenty-page booklet from the tour.

Most of the songs included on *Tested* were written by Greg even though the album drew from material all the way back to *How Could Hell Be Any Worse?* Now that the shock over Brett's decision to leave the band had faded, a feeling of mutual bitterness between the two founding members set in, and that may have played a part in Greg's decision to leave many of Brett's songs off of the album. While Brett had said uncharitable things about the band, Greg was careful not to take his feelings public.

"I never went on record as saying, 'That dick! He left the band right when we needed him the most!'" Greg said. "I guess I'm arrogant. I thought, *You want to fucking quit? I'm going to show you that we don't need you.* That's arrogance perhaps. But you know what? It probably saved me from the pit of despair. Instead of taking a self-destructive path, I thought, *We've got to kick it into high gear and make the best album we've ever made!*"

Whether it was arrogance or a coping mechanism, Greg transformed his pain into a source of motivation. Although Greg understood why Brett felt like he needed to step away from the band, Brett's criticism still stung. Despite the band's relentless touring and promotion, *The Gray Race* did not sell as well as *Stranger Than Fiction* in the United States. However, the record did extremely well worldwide.

By this time Danny Goldberg had moved on and no longer had a hands-on role with recording artists contracted to Atlantic, but his opinion of the band hadn't changed. "I think they're one of the great American bands," Goldberg said. "They didn't have the pop crossover success of Green Day or the Offspring but their songwriting has real depth to it, even more so than some of the other bands that were successful."

While *Stranger Than Fiction* was Bad Religion's best-selling record by far, it fell short of Atlantic's expectations for the album, which surprised Jay not at all. "My goal was to double our sales at Epitaph," Jay said, "and their goal was to sell seventeen million records. Those two things weren't even close to being the same. When we didn't sell seventeen million records, they were bummed. The climate for us didn't change. The expectations changed."

Seventeen million is a bit of an exaggeration, but the stratospheric success of Green Day's *Dookie,* the Offspring's *Smash,* and Rancid's *Let's Go* also contributed to the unrealistic expectations for the record. This created an odd dynamic: Bad Religion had never been more popular, and this newfound popularity had generated a wealth of opportunities for the band, but from the label's perspective they were falling short.

"I think a lesser band would have thrown in the towel at that point," Greg said. "We were banging our head against the wall. We'd been together for fifteen years and had inspired all these other multi-platinum artists. We took them on tour with us and Brett marketed their albums through Epitaph, but we weren't sharing in the windfall. What were we doing wrong?"

It was a question that a lot of punk rockers were asking themselves, but few bands could claim the kind of influence that Bad Religion had exerted on the new wave of nineties punk. While it was true that Nirvana played a big role in ushering in the punk explosion of 1994, their impact is often mischaracterized. Nirvana changed the music industry by removing the barriers that prevented popular indie rock bands from breaking out. But Nirvana didn't inspire the punk rock bands that soon became household names. Bands like NOFX, Rancid, and the Offspring were already out there, making records, playing shows, and hitting the road, and the band that inspired them was Bad Religion.

When *Suffer* came out in 1988, it helped resurrect punk from the dead and breathed new life into music meant to be played loud and fast. The album inspired a lot of bands from around the county, particularly on the West Coast, and changed people's minds about what punk rock could be in the late eighties and early nineties. *Suffer* was both a stake in the ground and a road map for the way forward.

However, the band whose intelligent lyrics and uncompromising stance on a wide range of issues was not getting its due, even though Bad Religion practically invented the format that other bands were using to catapult them to success. Greg was right to feel indignant, but he recognized that if he were to discuss Bad Religion's influence on the bands that were essentially eating their lunch, it would come off poorly.

"It would have looked like sour grapes," Greg said. "But you know what? I always consider the long view and I have no regrets. I'm just glad I didn't talk about it. We just clammed up, put our nose to the grindstone, and toured a lot."

Still, when the time came to begin preparations for the next album, they did so knowing that the last two albums had missed the target Atlantic had set for them. Whether that target was realistic or not, there was now the distinct possibility that Atlantic could drop them if they didn't deliver an album the label felt would sell well. Bad Religion's deal with Atlantic had been structured so that their advance for the second record was larger than the first, and so on. But while the advances were going up, the sales were going down, which added to the pressure.

Because major labels were more concerned with blockbuster hits then doing right by their artists, they allocated marketing, promotion, and publicity resources to the bands at the top of the food chain. As soon as a band's sales started to slip, the label stopped promoting them. There was also reason to believe Atlantic kept Bad Religion on their roster so they could use the band's name to recruit other indie acts.

Before turning to the next Bad Religion record, Greg pursued a more personal project: a solo album that dealt primarily with the end of his marriage. His thoughts had moved away from politics and taken a more introspective turn. In an essay written for *Details,* Greg speculated on how his punk rock upbringing had prepared him to challenge dogma and question authority but had sabotaged his ability to maintain intimate relationships. Despite several attempts at marriage counseling, including while Greg was in New York recording *The Gray Race*, the Graffins divorced.

Greg poured out his heart in a series of songs written over the course of several years that explored everything from the divorce of his parents ("Opinion") to holding out hope for reconciliation ("Maybe She Will") to brutal self-recrimination ("In the Mirror"). Greg played the piano or acoustic guitar with the drums dubbed in after the fact. The album also includes "Cease," one of Greg's songs from *The Gray Race*, only this version is much slower.

Sad and soulful, the album isn't a cathartic attempt to use a painful chapter of his life to spread his wings and show the world what he can do as a songwriter. Rather, the record, which he titled *American Lesion*, feels like the mournful howl of a man compelled to confront the reality of his divorce the only way he knows how. Everyone looks in the mirror every day, but few have the courage to sing about what they see there.

The album title is a statement about how capitalism turns everything into a commodity whose value is determined by the marketplace. Products that aren't profitable, regardless of their artistic merit, are cast aside and considered a blight on the economy. The album's art illustrates this idea with an American flag whose stars are replaced by dollar signs and whose stripes form a field of broken hearts.

Greg wrapped up the recording of *American Lesion* in time for Bad Religion to hit the road and return to Europe for a short three-week tour in June 1997. They played a number of festivals, including Go Bang! in Munich, where they opened for David Bowie and were joined onstage by Biohazard for a rousing rendition of "We're Only Gonna Die." But they also played smaller venues in Austria and France.

Never one to wait, Greg had already started working on material for a new Bad Religion record. In fact, the recording of Bad Religion's next album commenced as soon as the band returned from Europe.

It was a confusing time for Bad Religion. On one hand, punk rock was providing the band with a steady source of income that allowed its members to do things like pay their mortgages, have health insurance, and take care of their families. On the other hand, punk rock had reached a plateau and was now more or less mainstream. More people were buying punk CDs, punk T-shirts, and tickets for punk rock shows than at any other time in the genre's troubled history. As a result of this cultural shift, punk's emphasis had moved away from its primal impulse to reject the status quo in favor of creating more commodities for the subculture to consume. That's not what Bad Religion was all about. The members of Bad Religion were no longer teenagers (or even what teenagers considered young), but their message hadn't changed. They were still calling for personal accountability in their own intelligent but uncompromising way.

Bad Religion did not survey the new punk landscape and try to come up with ways to broaden their appeal, but the punk community often reacted as if it did. The rise of the Internet allowed the band to reach out to its fans and inform them of what was going on, but it also permitted fans to provide feedback, which the band encouraged, read, and frequently answered. While many of the messages they received offered support for the band or contained questions about a song lyric or an upcoming show, many lashed out at them for changing or selling out.

It was beginning to feel like a damned if we do, damned if we don't situation. Their label wanted them to be more like the bands cranking out hits; their fans wanted them to be more like the band that produced *How Could Hell Be Any Worse?* or *Suffer* or whatever album had brought them into the fold. Neither of these aspirations was realistic.

The band felt the best thing they could do for their new record was to go back to their DIY roots. After working with Brett in studio environments they were familiar with, their last two albums were recorded by people they didn't know in places they'd never set foot in before. Greg wanted to get back to a simpler, more hands-on approach. What better place to do that than at home?

There was also a practical reason for wanting to record in Ithaca. After logging so many miles during their world tour, Greg was eager to spend more time in New York. In addition to his self-produced solo album, Greg had been producing more bands' albums, including Unwritten Law's *Oz Factor* for Epic Records, at his friend Alex Perialas's studio Pyramid Sound. A well-respected producer of thrash metal, Alex had worked with a number of popular bands, including Anthrax, Overkill, Testament, and many others. With more experience under his belt and additional resources at his disposal, Greg pushed to make the new Bad Religion record in Ithaca.

Over the next several months, Jay, Hetson, Bobby, and Brian came out to central New York to write songs and record tracks. Sometimes they recorded at Pyramid Sound, other times they worked at Polypterus Studios at Greg's home. Compared to the previous record, the making of *No Substance* had a decidedly different feel and reflected a more laid-back approach. As with *The Gray Race,* Greg collaborated with Brian on several songs. "I came in with musical ideas," Brian said. "Greg had songs in his file, as was his way, that were completely his."

Unlike with the previous record, they didn't work off demo tapes. Instead, they arranged the songs as they went. It was more spontaneous than previous Bad Religion albums with plenty of opportunities for collaboration. Jay is credited on a song, and Hetson contributed to two. After the completion of *The Gray Race* and *American Lesion,* fears as to whether Greg could shoulder the songwriting load on his own had subsided. Surrounded by talented musicians, engineers, and producers who brought their skills to the table, Greg felt inspired by their collaborative spirit.

"To me it was always a creative outlet that everyone was allowed to participate in," Greg said of the making of *No Substance*. "I was willing to offer the creative freedom to anyone. I sort of looked at it as a loose consortium of people who came together to share our creativity. That's a lot different than those who run things with an iron fist. It's kind of like a family in that sense. It's important to acknowledge that making a record is a privilege and not something that you have to maintain control of at all costs. I think that's the secret, or part of it, to our longevity."

In other words, the fastest driver drove the car.

In September, they took a break from recording *No Substance* to play a series of shows at smaller venues throughout New York. All of the shows were five dollars a ticket, and they issued a special-edition T-shirt to commemorate the "tour."

Afterward, they returned to Ithaca to put the finishing touches on *No Substance*. When they were done recording, the album was sent to Chris Lord-Alge in L.A. to be mixed. Lord-Alge was a renowned audio specialist who, along with his brother Tom, had worked on some huge records that produced massive hits. Bad Religion was pleased with his efforts, and the consensus was that together Greg, Ronnie, Perialas, and Lord-Alge had succeeded in re-creating the early Bad Religion sound while continuing to make full use of the band's talents by experimenting with various styles and tempos.

In interviews Greg explained that *No Substance* addressed his concerns with a culture that was becoming increasingly superficial. People were overly focused on trivial concerns to the detriment of their social conscience and political awareness. *No Substance*, he hoped, would serve as a wake-up call.

Each song on the album tells a story about a facet of American history and expands on Greg's interest in combining the aggression of punk with folk storytelling and pop sensibilities. "The Greatest Killer in History" paints a grim picture of the American military-industrial complex and specifically names Edward Teller, who, along with Robert Oppenheimer, developed the atom bomb.

"The State of the End of the Millennium Address" expands on the opening of "The Voice of God Is Government," a song from their debut album, in which a fake evangelist preaches, "Neighbors, no one loves you like he loves you . . . " But instead of launching into a hardcore song as "The Voice of God Is Government" does, "The State of the End of the Millennium Address" continues in the mode of a spoken-word piece that would make Jello Biafra proud, delivered over a soundtrack of churning guitars.

In "The Hippy Killers," Greg waxes nostalgic about L.A.'s punk scene. The song isn't about Manson-like suburban assassins, but the kids who killed off the Flower Power generation with "good days during horrible times." Greg was very much interested in connecting punk to the tradition of protest music. The title track, "No Substance," exemplifies the style of message-driven punk ballads by bands like Sham 69 and Stiff Little Fingers that were so inspirational to Bad Religion in their early days.

As the band members went their separate ways for the holidays, Greg soldiered on. *American Lesion* came out in November 1997 with little fanfare. No singles were released, and promotional copies of the record were issued without any kind of explanation. That month Greg played three solo shows for *American Lesion* at the Knitting Factory in Brooklyn, the Haunt in Ithaca, and the Viper Room in Los Angeles. Greg performed a mix of songs from the album as well as soulful acoustic versions of a few Bad Religion tunes like "Struck a Nerve," "Punk Rock Song," and "God Song."

The record drew support from friends like Jack Rabid of *The Big Takeover* in New York and former drummer Pete Finestone in L.A., but the album didn't crack *Billboard*'s top 200 list and didn't get much traction at radio stations. The public was caught off guard by these sad, slow songs.

Although Atlantic had offered Greg an advance on the album, he turned it down in favor of greater creative control. He'd written all the songs and played all the instruments, and then released the record as if he were still on an indie label that lacked the resources of a major. By going back to his DIY roots for this gritty, heartfelt, and intensely personal album, Greg's message was clear: take it or leave it.

19

UNTETHERED FROM REALITY

DESPITE BAD RELIGION'S REPUTATION AS THE smartest band in punk rock, its members (and former members) possessed a proclivity for self-destructive behavior that expressed itself in ways that seemed the opposite of intelligent. While Greg was wrestling with personal issues in Ithaca, Brett was doing battle with demons of his own in L.A. His drug use was becoming increasingly problematic and, unlike the past, when he was limited by his income and work schedule, Brett was now an extremely wealthy man.

In 1994, the year that punk rock went mainstream, Epitaph did $60 million in business. Brett, who came from a middle class family and had never owned a new car before, was completely unprepared for how quickly things changed. "Punk was blowing up," Brett said, "and I had platinum records hanging on the wall." Suddenly, investors were offering him $50 million for half of his company. Jimmy Iovine, the cofounder of Interscope Records, invited Brett to a meeting whose attendees included Suge Knight of Death Row Records and Bryan Turner of Priority Records. Iovine believed that if Epitaph, Interscope, Death Row, and Priority teamed up to form a mega-independent label, they'd be as big as any major label. Brett considered it, but declined to join, and lived to tell the tale.

Nevertheless, rumors swirled that Brett was going to sell Epitaph, which he had no interest in doing. Brett listened to offers but was committed to staying independent. He also enjoyed the perks of being a self-made mogul. He'd bought a house in the Hollywood Hills just above the Sunset Strip and a stone's throw from the House of Blues, the Roxy, and the Troubadour, making it easy to attend shows and host after-hours parties for the bands on his label.

But after seven and a half years of sobriety, Brett had slipped. When he started drinking during the recording of *Stranger Than Fiction,* he kept it a secret. He had a more serious relapse with heroin but he didn't go off the rails and become a full-blown junkie—at least not right away. "There was a period," Brett said, "in the first few months of me getting loaded again when I was just chipping. I was only using on the weekends. I was attempting to be the oft-romanticized gentleman junkie."

But what started as a weekend romp soon turned into a daily habit; the disease of addiction had come roaring back. He recalled being high during the mixing of the Pietasters' LP, and the demos for Rancid's *Life Won't Wait,* their follow-up to . . . *And Out Come the Wolves,* which Brett regards as "the *Born to Run* of punk rock."

Although Brett was still putting out records and growing his business, the pace had slowed somewhat from the manic days when the Offspring and Rancid were climbing the charts. His lifestyle may have been manageable by music industry standards, but it wasn't conducive to family life, and on July 10, 1997, he and Maggie were divorced. Once again, Brett had developed a serious drug problem, only this time he had his two kids, Max and Frida, to consider. He was powerless to do anything about his overwhelming need to get high.

"I wasn't showing up anywhere," Brett recalled. "There was a period of time when I was checked into the hotel across the street from my house on Sunset Boulevard. People were trying to do interventions, and I didn't want them to find me, so I hid in hotels."

Brett's run came to an end while he was at his house in the Hollywood Hills. He spent most of his time in a bathrobe with two large pockets: one for his heroin, the other for his crack cocaine. He would alternate between the two while *Scarface* played on repeat. One morning there was a loud knock on the door and when he looked out the second-story balcony he saw his front yard was filled with police officers outfitted in tactical gear. Brett naively assumed that there had been a bank robbery or home invasion in the neighborhood, and calmly opened the front door.

POLICE: Are you Brett Gurewitz?
BRETT: What's going on? Is everything all right, officer?
POLICE: I repeat, are you Brett Gurewitz?
BRETT: Yeah, that's me.
POLICE: Do you have any drugs in the house we should know about?
BRETT: Don't you need a warrant for that?
POLICE: Yes, I have a warrant for your arrest.
BRETT: Well, yeah, the drugs are right here in my pocket.

The police were convinced that Brett must be a drug dealer because they couldn't believe that someone who made punk records could afford to live in the Hollywood Hills. Brett couldn't believe it either, but he got a cold dose of reality when he was sent to L.A. County Jail.

On December 21, 1997, Brett was ordered by the court to go to a drug and alcohol rehabilitation center in northeast L.A. with a reputation for hard-nosed tactics where his friend and former Bad Religion drummer John Albert had gotten clean. To say that Brett was reluctant to go would be an understatement. "I was strung out, and I was getting high all the time," Brett said. "I'd spent the last year trying everything I could to stop, but nothing worked, and in the end I gave up in despair. I was going until the wheels came off."

That meant right up until the moment Brett set foot in rehab. After he was arraigned, Brett went home and came up with a plan. He made an offer to his connection, a long-time street junkie named Chuck, whom he thought of as a friend. "'I'm going into rehab and get my life together,'" Brett said to Chuck. "'If you want to do that, too, I'll pay for you. Let's get in there together.'" Chuck had been in and out of L.A. County Jail dozens of times, and that's how he got clean. Chuck accepted and they went to rehab together.

Fletcher Dragge of Pennywise drove them to rehab in Brett's Suburban, while Brett and Chuck smoked crack cocaine in the back and the Bobby Fuller Four's "I Fought the Law" played on the sound system. "We blasted that song over and over," Brett said, "and smoked crack the whole way. At one point we had a cop car behind us. The Suburban was completely full of smoke and Fletcher was sweating bullets!"

When they arrived at the facility, Brett threw his crack pipe on the sidewalk, shattering it, and stomped on the glass as a symbol of his determination to break with his old way of life. After a couple of weeks of rehab, Chuck realized it wasn't for him. At many drug and alcohol rehabilitation centers, it was relatively easy to get drugs, but not at this one. "Nobody gets high there," Brett said. "It just doesn't happen. It's very high security—the Pelican Bay of rehabs."

While Brett was struggling to adjust to the harsh conditions and inflexible discipline, a local newspaper ran a cover story on Brett that described his latest run-in with the law. The newspaper showed a caricature of Brett emerging from a grave, and the tombstone was an Epitaph logo. A staff member showed it to Brett and asked, "Is this you?"

Although the rehabilitation center had strict security and was run like a jail, with high walls and no phone calls, unlike Brett, Chuck hadn't been ordered by the courts to be there. He could leave at any time. When Chuck told Brett he was done, they cooked up a plan so that Brett could have one last hurrah. "This shows what a terrible but creative drug addict I was," Brett confessed.

Brett asked Chuck to wrap some crack and heroin in some foil, put it in an orange, and throw it over the wall at midnight the following day. Chuck agreed. The next night, Brett lay awake in his bed after lights-out, waiting for the minutes to pass. At midnight, he got out of bed and snuck outside to the wall, and there was the orange. Brett crept back to his room, went into the bathroom, and started getting loaded. He alternated between the crack and heroin. When it was all gone, he went back to his bed, but sleep was out of the question. He wanted more, but the only way to get more was to leave.

He walked up to the office and confronted the staff. "I knew if I told them I was high," Brett said, "they would kick me out and I could go home and continue getting high." But by admitting he was high he'd put himself in a bind. The facility couldn't release him for insurance reasons because if they kicked him out and he got hurt after admitting he was impaired, they would be liable.

While they looked for someone to take Brett home, word of Brett's exploits spread throughout the facility. "I became a bit of a legend because I managed to get high in the house," Brett said. "No one had ever done that before, and no one knew how I did it."

A staff member drove Brett home and he wasted no time scoring. Brett was getting high in his house alone when his attorney called:

ATTORNEY: What are you doing?
BRETT: I'm getting high.
ATTORNEY: You can't do that. You've struck a deal.

BRETT: I know I fucked up.

ATTORNEY: You better hope they take you back.

BRETT: I don't want to go back.

ATTORNEY: If they don't take you back, you have to go
straight to jail.

BRETT: Oh.

In his altered state of mind, Brett had forgotten about his pre-
dicament. "I wasn't thinking about the court order," Brett admitted, "which meant that if I tested dirty or messed up, I'd automatically have to serve six months in jail without a trial because I'd
already pled guilty."

They accepted him back, and Brett returned to rehab. The following morning Brett was informed that he was being taken to the
courthouse as a result of testing positive for cocaine and heroin.
The judge sent Brett to jail for a few days but warned him if he
tested positive again, he'd have to do the full six months. "I really
knew I had no more chances left," Brett said.

He was taken to a drug court pod in Lynwood Jail, where he
shared a cell with an inmate named Pee Wee who was not only a
drug offender but a veteran of home invasions. After a few days
with Pee Wee, he was brought back to rehab. Brett was finally
ready to surrender. He embraced his recovery and stayed clean.

Six months passed without any further incidents and Brett was
moved into a halfway house in the San Gabriel Valley for three
months, after which he was finally able to return home. He was
still in drug court, however, and was tested five times a week, but
his outlook had improved considerably. "After six months of being
clean, I snapped to and became myself again. I was doing very well
and going to a lot of meetings. I had truly been out of my mind
from so many mind-altering chemicals. I just wasn't myself at all,
but now I wanted to stay clean."

Brett didn't know if his drug addiction could be attributed to
a disease or a lack of will power. In the past this would have inter-
fered with his recovery, but now he realized the distinction didn't

matter. He recognized that he was impatient, impulsive, and easily distracted. He was at the pinnacle of success when he fell off the wagon. Unless he learned to appreciate the fruits of his achievements while working on his flaws, he would always be susceptible to relapse. Brett made a lifelong commitment to staying clean, which he did and continues to do to this day.

Brett returned to Epitaph with a new outlook on life. During his time away from the music industry, the bitterness he felt toward his old band receded. While drugs didn't play a role in his leaving Bad Religion, getting clean helped him let go of the resentment that had a stranglehold on his relationships, and that paved the way for reconciliation with his former bandmates.

There was cause for celebration in the Bad Religion camp, too. While *No Substance* was being mixed, the band learned in March 1998 that *Stranger Than Fiction* had certified gold, meaning that it had officially sold five hundred thousand copies. Bad Religion finally had a gold record, a milestone that the band, Brett, and the label could all be proud of. Together, they'd achieved something undeniably special, and no one could take that away from them.

It was one thing to be told you'd won an award, but quite another to receive evidence of it, and few awards were as impressive as an actual gold record. Each member of the band received five gold records, with which they could do whatever they pleased. Most hung one up in their home and stashed the rest, but not Bobby.

Bobby gave all of his gold records away, including one to his mentor Lucky and another to Wayne Kramer of the MC5. "I love Wayne," Bobby said. "When *Stranger Than Fiction* went gold, I gave one to Wayne. I was very proud of that. One of my proudest moments. He was a hero of mine. That was my way of saying thank you to him." Bobby also had to make good on a promise he made to Bad Religion's balding merch guy, Paul Glackin, that if *Stranger Than Fiction* went gold, he'd buy Paul hair. Although this promise was made as a kind of joke, Bobby did not renege, and he bought Paul a hair transplant from Bosley. "Stupid me and my big mouth," Bobby said, "but it was all in good fun."

The band was in a celebratory mood. Bad Religion got ready for the No Substance Tour with a series of one-off gigs in New York, Canada, and Spain, but the event in Edmonton was the most unconventional as it featured a charity hockey game between the Bad Religion Hockey Club and the Musician's Hockey League of Canada, which included members of SNFU, and had been organized by a Bad Religion fan.

This wasn't Bad Religion's first foray into competitive hockey. Greg Graffin grew up playing the sport in Wisconsin, and Jay and Hetson, a long-time L.A. Kings season ticket holder, had formed a hockey team in L.A. called the Hollywood Tornados—a group of musicians that included Taime Downe of Faster Pussycat, Tony DeFranco, and Riki Rachtman. The Tornados competed in a Pickwick Ice hockey league in Burbank. That they were regularly beaten by teams fielded by the L.A. County Sheriff's Department and a women's group in Simi Valley was beside the point.

With Greg leading the team in scoring and Jay guarding the net, the Bad Religion Hockey Club shocked its Canadian rivals by going into overtime before being defeated in the shoot-out. The audience was thrilled that a Southern California punk band was able to mount such an entertaining challenge. The event was written about in the local paper the next day, the band raised a lot of money for the local food bank, and a good time was had by all.

In April, Bad Religion embarked on their biggest tour yet: 120 cities with gigs ranging from the smallest clubs in the country to the largest arenas in the world. The No Substance Tour began in the U.S., where they played a series of smaller venues—in some cases much smaller. For example, they performed at Linda's Doll Hut, a tiny Orange County landmark in Anaheim, California, that was one thousand square feet and had a capacity of forty-nine people. Greg also squeezed in a couple of *American Lesion* shows, including a performance at California State University, Northridge, where he'd started his college studies, which were still very much on his mind.

Earlier that year, the band had launched the Bad Religion Research Fund. The idea was to give $3,000 to $5,000 to a graduate student working in the sciences with a promising project in need of funding. Applicants submitted a description of their project and the band picked the best one. When Greg was a student at UCLA, he'd used a variety of grants and awards to fund his fieldwork. The Bad Religion Research Fund was created to help foster interest in scientific study. While the band toured from city to city, the musicians read applications and awarded the first Bad Religion Research Fund to Lena Sharon Nicolai, a student at the University of Michigan, Department of Biology. (The Bad Religion Research Fund had a successful run until 2000, after which it was discontinued.)

No Substance was released on May 15, 1998, in the middle of Bad Religion's club tour. The first single, "Raise Your Voice," features Campino, the lead vocalist from Die Toten Hosen, Germany's biggest and best-known punk rock band. Formed in 1982, the band established a reputation for their irreverent style while tackling important social issues without taking themselves too seriously. The song was popular in Germany, especially when Campino joined Bad Religion onstage during their two-week European tour immediately following the release of *No Substance*. It was a fitting way to celebrate the tenth consecutive year that Bad Religion had played in Europe.

As veterans of the European festival circuit, Bad Religion lamented that they didn't have the same kind of opportunity at home. If only there was something like it in the U.S., a series of festivals of like-minded artists in all the major cities. How great would that be?

That's more or less what Kevin Lyman had in mind when he started the Vans Warped Tour in 1995. "The Warped Tour brought Southern California to the rest of the world," Jay explained. "We play music and drink beer and skateboard in pools. This is what we do."

In the summer of 1998, Bad Religion was finally able to participate in the great parking lot punk festival alongside Cherry Poppin' Daddies, Deftones, NOFX, Rancid, Reverend Horton Heat, and the Specials. The tour got underway in Phoenix, Arizona, lasted from June 30 to August 9, and had thirty-four dates.

By this time Bad Religion had made some changes to the way they traveled around the country. The band had learned through trial and error that the most effective way to travel was to drive their tour bus to the next venue immediately after the gig. By traveling through the night, the band saved money on hotel rooms while they slept on the bus and ensured the crew was ready to set up on time the following day.

Greg tried to fight this for a while by having two buses, one for the band and another for the crew, but he discovered that bus travel, like air travel, was terrible for his voice. The solution that worked best for all parties was for Greg to sleep in a hotel each night after the show and make his way to the next venue by plane, train, or automobile the following day. "My only job is to get to the next city," Greg said of his travel schedule. "My work day is from six p.m. to eleven p.m. but my commute to the office is often 250 miles or more."

One of the quirks of the Warped Tour was that all of the bands had the same travel schedule, so there was a lot of bus swapping and ride sharing. The fun of the Warped Tour never let up, even when the bands were on the road. This made it even more imperative than usual for Greg to protect his voice by getting plenty of rest when he wasn't onstage, something that was easier said than done amidst all the revelry the Warped Tour encouraged. It also didn't help that the members of Bad Religion were typically ten years older than their punk rock peers. "Being a singer is like being a pitcher in Major League Baseball," Greg said. "All they get is a hundred pitches. Even throwing a little bit is detrimental. So they rest that arm and rejuvenate so they can do it again."

But the band had to do something with all that downtime. Rather than sit on the tour bus between gigs, they set up the Bad Religion festival tent, which, incredibly, was open to the public. The band would hang out, grill food on the barbecue, and interact with fans. When traffic was slow, Greg would catch up on some light reading, like Richard Rhodes's *The Making of the Atomic Bomb*. The tent was also headquarters for No Substance Radio, a pirate radio station with a three-mile radius. It played punk rock bands from the seventies and eighties that influenced Bad Religion and occasionally opened the airwaves for local musicians to play their demos.

To assist with these extra duties, their manager, Michele Ceazan (now Michele Ceazan-Fleischli), who had started out as Danny Heaps's assistant and then took over after he left for RCA, brought Rick Marino into the Bad Religion camp. Rick was the can-do guy who helped out with the barbecue, the radio station, or whatever needed to get done. The Warped Tour was the perfect environment for someone with that attitude and it endeared him to the band. "They just wanted to make it fun," Michele said of that first Warped Tour. "They created their own world and all the bands worshipped them."

Although playing the festival circuit in Europe helped prepare Bad Religion for the rigors of the Warped Tour, it was its own animal with a unique set of challenges. "The Warped Tour was literally summer camp with our friends," Jay said. "There were plenty of egos involved, but you put that aside to make it happen. Whatever your grind was, you figured out how to make it work."

Over the years, the members of Bad Religion learned they could trust people who'd been on multiple Warped Tours. It was a proving ground of sorts. It said something about an individual's work ethic and willingness to check his or her ego at the door. A lot of the things that went on behind the scenes to make a rock tour a success were out in the open during the Warped Tour. Bands had to make sacrifices they would not be asked to make if they were touring on their own, and their crews had to pick up the slack.

"There were no working lights on the Warped Tour," Jay said. "They never carried lights. The show was supposed to end before it got dark. Do you know how many times we played in the fucking dark? We'd have two work lights on the side of the stage and guys holding flashlights. Whatever. Make it work. Make it go. That's the magic of the Warped Tour. Everybody worked together to make it happen, but it took a lot of work to make it great."

Just as the Warped Tour exposed bands to new fans around the country, it gave the bands the opportunity to witness the effects of punk's new popularity. While it was gratifying to connect with new fans, it was disheartening to see people at the festival whose sole purpose was to cash in. "Why the fuck are you here? What are you bringing to the party?" Jay recalled asking. "Oh, nothing, you're just here to sell shit."

Still, magical moments took place from time to time. In Montreal, Bad Religion was preparing to play "Generator," but the band wasn't ready to go so Greg started without them. He sang the entirety of the first verse a cappella. "It turned into a sing-along that sounded very cool," Jay recalled. When the rest of the band came in after "It's the generator . . . " the place went bonkers. The band that liked to keep things interesting was still capable of surprising their fans—and themselves.

After the final Warped Tour show in Austin, Texas, Bad Religion headed back overseas for the first Warped Tour Europe. While Europe was a new experience for many of the Warped Tour veterans, it was familiar territory for Bad Religion.

Nevertheless, back-to-back Warped Tours took a toll on some of the band members. Despite Bad Religion's popularity and *Stranger Than Fiction* going gold, Jay was in a bad place. "By the end of the '98 Warped Tour in Europe," Jay said, "I was hating my life. I was bummed and sad and miserable. We'd been on tour forever and my personal life wasn't that great and my marriage wasn't that great. I was really sad and I didn't have anything to fight off the sadness."

Jay fell off the wagon, but as relapses go—at least by punk rock standards—his return to drinking was comparatively mild. "My biggest problem is my head," Jay explained. "Sometimes I just want to shut my brain down. I don't want to hear it. I was sitting on the bus and I was pissed that I couldn't stop my brain, and I thought, *I know what will stop it.* I opened up a bottle of wine and had a glass of wine. That was it. I had one glass of wine and that's all. *This is cool,* I thought. *I'm a grown-ass man. I can do this. I don't have to drink like a moron. I can have a glass of wine and be cool.* I would have one glass of wine every night after the show. That lasted about six weeks before I thought, *A shot of vodka would be way better.*"

The band returned home for a much-needed rest, but they weren't done traveling—not by a long shot. Their next album would take them away from the continental United States and far out of their comfort zone.

20

PARADISE LOST

GREG STOOD AT THE TOP OF A HILL OVERLOOKING the city and watched the lights wink off, block by block, from the jungle to the coast. The city of Santos, perched on the edge of São Paulo, Brazil, plunged into darkness. Heavy rains had knocked the power out at Jump, the club where Bad Religion was scheduled to perform that night with White Frogs, an energetic Brazilian punk band.

It had started raining after sound check and didn't let up. After an hour, the local punks started to look anxious. Tarps and canopies covered the stage and sound equipment, but the four thousand fans who had come to see Bad Religion were left to stand in the downpour. After two hours, the lights went out backstage, and then the stage went dark. Even the music playing through the club's sound system cut out. Despite the rain, the fans stayed, but now their anxiety had given way to anger. In Brazil, refunds weren't issued for cancellations due to weather, and the soaking wet fans were getting pissed.

The smart thing to do, Bad Religion reasoned, was to play an acoustic set, but the band hadn't prepared for this contingency and without operational microphones it wasn't going to work. When the manager got the news that the storm had pummeled the coastline and power was out in the entire state of São Paulo, a region of some twenty million people, the musicians were advised to leave the area before the fans took their anger out on them. This was easier said than done.

A single, twisting two-lane road connected the club with the rest of the city, and with the power out, the road was flooded with people coming down the mountain, trying to get home. The band eventually made it to their hotel and went to bed, but at around 1 A.M. they received a call from the venue: "The power is back on! You must return!"

It was a strange situation, but they had no way to gauge how unusual. "Nobody was going to Brazil and South America back then," Michele explained. "No one was doing that, but Bad Religion was up for it, and we had four thousand kids waiting in the jungle."

They got back in the car and made the treacherous trip up the mountain. While the club may have had power, the rest of the city did not. The streetlights were out and the roads gridlocked. People streamed up and down the mountain road on foot as word spread that the show would go on.

Bad Religion arrived at around 2 A.M., just as White Frogs finished their set. The band took the stage and appropriately opened with "Generator," for it wasn't an act of God that permitted them to play that night, but a petrol-powered machine.

In 1999, Bad Religion followed the pattern they'd established in 1997 of maintaining a relatively light touring schedule the year between album releases. In Zurich, Brian Baker once again got to show off his Carlos Santana licks during a short set that included a cover of "Black Magic Woman," but the majority of the spring and summer was dedicated to getting ready for the final album of their four-record contract with Atlantic.

Although sales for *No Substance* were not substantial, Atlantic exercised its option to release the next Bad Religion record and complete the contract. "Raise Your Voice!" was popular in Germany, but it didn't take off in the U.S. The second single from *No Substance*, "The Biggest Killer in American History," didn't get much airplay in the U.S. either. The band's next album would commemorate their twentieth anniversary, and it would have been disappointing to be dropped by their label. "Greg really respected the label and wanted to do a good job for them," Michele said. "I don't think Atlantic appreciated it."

Atlantic blamed *No Substance*'s poor sales on its low-budget production. Major labels were infamous for courting indie artists and then overproducing their work. They fixed problems, both real and imagined, by throwing money at them. Atlantic sought to remedy Bad Religion's independent impulses by hiring an expensive big-name producer for their next record.

Jay didn't agree with Atlantic's assessment of *No Substance*. "The record didn't suffer because we didn't spend money on it. The record didn't do well because we didn't take it seriously. When we went into the studio, no songs had been written. We didn't know what we wanted to do. It was very piecemeal."

Be that as it may, Greg had entertained the idea of working with Todd Rundgren as early as 1997, when Greg was recording *American Lesion*. His manager had sent demo tapes to Rundgren's team and word came back that Rundgren liked them. It was no secret to the rest of the band that Greg idolized Todd Rundgren. "If you were to ask me," Jay said, "'Who is your musical idol?' I know that Greg's would be Todd Rundgren."

Even Keith Morris knew how much Todd Rundgren's music meant to Greg. When they were first getting to know each other in the early eighties, Keith gave Greg tapes of Nazz, Todd Rundgren's psychedelic rock band in the sixties. "He knew that I really liked Todd," Greg said. "'Dude, you're gonna love these.' And I did."

Since he was nine years old, Greg had been a fan of the Philadelphia native. Rundgren had written a number of hits in the seventies, including "Hello It's Me" and "I Saw the Light" before "Bang the Drum All Day" broke out in 1983 and became a staple at sports arenas and stadiums, including at Greg's beloved Lambeau Field, home of the Green Bay Packers. Rundgren also had a long list of impressive producing credits that included Grand Funk Railroad's *We're an American Band,* the New York Dolls' self-titled album, Meat Loaf's blockbuster *Bat Out of Hell,* and the Patti Smith Group's well-regarded *Wave.* Rundgren's mixing engineer, Bob Clearmountain, also had a punk rock pedigree: he had produced and played guitar on the Dead Boys' first album.

Greg was looking for someone who could get the most out of his songs and push him to create original-sounding music to combat the perception at Atlantic that Bad Religion's melodic hardcore approach to punk rock had gotten stale. Rundgren, who was regarded as a wizard in the studio, fit the bill.

Greg couldn't have been more excited to be working with one of his musical heroes. However, at this stage in his career, Rundgren worked exclusively from his home in Kauai in the Hawaiian Islands. He also had a reputation of being difficult to worth with. If Greg wanted Rundgren to produce the next Bad Religion album, the band would have to decamp for the Western Pacific for an extended period of time. Greg jumped at the opportunity. "We were getting paid a lot of money to go live in Kauai for two months and do what we love, which is play music," Greg said. "What's the downside?"

Greg had begun to mend fences with Brett, who was now completely clean and sober again. The consensus among the band was that it didn't feel right to celebrate Bad Religion's twentieth anniversary without Brett, and they discussed asking him if he'd be interested in contributing a song to the album. That job fell to Greg.

"I think it started with a lunch," Brett said. "Greg reached out to me. He was one of my oldest friends from high school and we were in a band together for years. The truth is even though we got on each other's nerves terribly, we loved each other and it was a nice lunch."

They talked about Bad Religion's plans for the new record, working with Rundgren, and all the new developments in audio technology since they'd recorded *Stranger Than Fiction* together. Finally, Greg broached the subject of collaborating with Bad Religion again and asked Brett to write a song for their new album. "I'd gone three or four years without writing a song," Brett explained. "For eight years straight, I was writing all the time, but when I quit the band, I just stopped writing. When he invited me to write a song I thought, *I wonder if I still can.*"

Brett went to work. Before Greg left for Hawaii, he met with Brett again, and Brett played the song he'd written. As soon as Greg heard it he said, "Let's do it." Brett gave him the demo and Greg took it with him to Hawaii. Inviting Brett to be a part of Bad Religion's twentieth-anniversary album was a simple gesture, but one that went a long way toward establishing a dialogue between Brett and his old band.

Bad Religion arrived in Kauai with more material than they could use. Not only did they have a new tune from Brett, they had a surplus of songs to ensure they made the most of their time in the studio with Rundgren. Although Greg had expanded his home studio and made significant upgrades to his digital equipment and outboard gear to create a project environment for recording demos, it was nothing like the setup that Rundgren had in Kauai.

To record Bad Religion, Rundgren had rented a barn so Bobby's drumming wouldn't disturb the neighbors. He'd installed all of his recording equipment in the barn, along with a great deal of computer equipment. Rundgren was known for his innovative sound recording techniques for the music he made and the records he produced. "New technology was coming out in digital recording," Greg said, "and Todd was always an early adopter."

But Bad Religion didn't hire Rundgren to experiment; they hired Rundgren to bring out the best in Bad Religion. So, when the band arrived at the facility, they were alarmed to find a building on the site of an old sugar plantation that was more barn than studio. To make matters worse, the building wasn't equipped with air conditioning and lacked many of the amenities of a professional studio. To keep the air flowing, they had to leave the door open, which let in mosquitos that feasted on the intruders from the mainland, with Bobby bearing the brunt of the onslaught. Brian characterized the setup as "primitive."

Even more concerning, there wasn't an amplifier in sight. Rundgren insisted on using Pods, digital guitar amplifier modelers, which were fairly new at the time. It dawned on the band that everything was going to be done on the computer without any outboard gear. This didn't sit well with the guitar players. In Greg's words, "They were miserable."

Rundgren knew what he wanted and wasn't shy about being vocal when he wasn't getting it. Some producers take their cues from the band, but not Rundgren. He made it clear from the get-go that this ship only had one captain, and he was it. No one was spared from his criticism—not even Greg.

"He's notorious for being honest," Greg said of Rundgren. "I have always respected him for that. Todd's extremely talented, a legend. He's an honest artist, but perhaps like myself, he's not very good at people skills."

They went to work on Greg's songs and Rundgren pushed for changes not just in the song structure, but in the lyrics as well. Rundgren felt that the lyrics came from a place of anger at the world and suggested a somewhat more hopeful outlook. After all, they weren't teenagers anymore.

Greg was caught between two conflicting desires: to stand up for the work he'd created, or follow the advice of an artist he'd looked up to all his life. Whether he was collaborating on a song with his bandmates or working on his doctoral thesis, Greg was accustomed to receiving constructive criticism, but this was a whole new approach from someone for whom being fun to work with wasn't a priority.

Greg's bandmates recognized their front man was in a tough position. "When Greg has a song on his demo," Brian explained, "it's pretty much done. He'll give me some latitude in solos and things, but in general he wants me to play his ideas, only better because he knows his limitations as an electric guitar player. But he's not into experimentation."

Unlike on the previous two albums, Brian did not contribute any songs to *The New America*. "They didn't hire me to bring things to the table," Brian said. "I was offering to bring a side. I have these great green beans. I can do some stuffing. I did that for two records and I kind of noticed on the second record they weren't eating my sides. I would get the dish back and it was full."

Despite the challenges inside the studio, the band was determined to make the most of the experience. Greg flew his family out to Kauai and his mother even came for a visit. "Hawaii was gorgeous," Greg said. "I'm a naturalist. I was in my element. I'd go hiking. I'd go bird-watching. I'd go beachcombing and forget the time. *Oh, yeah, I gotta be in the studio at two o'clock!*"

Jay and Brian were equally forgetful, though with them it was a case of selective amnesia. They treated the trip like a working vacation—with the emphasis on vacation. During recording sessions there was always plenty of downtime and Jay and Brian were infamous for disappearing from the studio to go hang out at the beach.

As always, Bobby was on point and in the pocket—despite being attacked by mosquitos. He had a showman's work ethic: he was always prepared and seldom complained when things didn't go as planned, which was always. Nor did he have issues with substance abuse. Like Greg, he didn't partake in drugs or alcohol—not even in a tropical paradise.

"For me it was all work," Bobby explained. "Here's the gig, let's get up and do it. It took me ten years to get there. When I got there, I didn't want to fuck it up. That's the last thing you want to do."

In the middle of September, they took a break from recording to fly out to Honolulu and play the Big Mele festival with the

Offspring, Fun Lovin' Criminals, the Vandals, and AFI. Then it was back to work.

For Brett's song, the musicians learned their parts and Greg sang the vocals. They wanted Brett to record the guitar solo, so they sent him a tape and he sent it back with his part. Despite all the technology being used to record *The New America,* the tapes were shipped back and forth across the Pacific via airplane. The song was "Believe It," and everyone was happy to have a track from Brett on the record.

The songs on *The New America* are more personal than political. "1000 Memories" riffs on moving on from a relationship and "Whisper in Time" is an ode to nostalgia for things that have been lost to the past. "A Streetkid Named Desire" channels Greg's earliest memories as a punk, when all it took to earn the enmity of his peers was a ripped-up T-shirt and a short haircut.

Playing in places like Brazil, where the kids who showed up at their shows wore dyed clothing held together by patches and pins, brought back memories of Greg's own punk rock awakening. Part of Greg's early identity as a punk was transforming his white T-shirts and thrift store boots into badges of honor. As a fourteen-year-old kid in a single-parent home, he had to find creative ways to demonstrate his rejection of the status quo and allegiance to the heady music, art, and fashion scene that was punk rock. But in the new America, a kid could purchase a punk outfit—online with his or her parents' credit card—and then fire off an email to Bad Religion criticizing them for selling out.

Although many of the songs on the new album are fueled by the songwriters' longing for simpler times, it sometime feels as if Rundgren was trying to push the band into the twenty-first century. The most unusual song on the record, and perhaps in the band's entire catalog, is "I Love My Computer." Filled with double entendres, the song takes a playful stab at online romance. The familiar sound of distorted guitars is accompanied by the disconcerting noise of computerized bleeps and bloops.

When the album was complete, the masters were sent to Clear-mountain in California. Greg and Brian were on hand to assist with the transfer from digital to analog, and that's when they learned of the engineer's connection to the Dead Boys. Clearmountain, who shared the band's appreciation for old outboard gear, was particularly fond of the song "1000 Memories," which opens with something of a tribute to the Dead Boys' "Sonic Reducer."

Thankfully, there weren't any Y2K glitches, and the album was ready to go, but there were a few hiccups with their label. Atlantic rejected the art that the band proposed for the cover. The image featured children holding one hand over their hearts, as if recit-ing the Pledge of Allegiance, while clutching a handgun with the other. They ended up using this artwork for the European release and went with an image of a swarm of attack helicopters descend-ing on a row of urban brownstones.

Overall, Greg was pleased with *The New America*'s loud, crisp sound. He likened Rundgren's input to working with a strong ed-itor, but this telling quote in *Rolling Stone* published shortly after the album's release suggests Greg's estimation of Rundgren had changed after working with him. "He used to be my hero," Greg said, "and now he's just my friend."

The New America shipped in May 2000 with a novel promotion for the record: free entry to a show that spring with proof of pur-chase. This idea suffered a setback when the band abruptly can-celed its mini-tour due to a development that shocked many long-time fans: Bad Religion was hitting the road as the opening act for the pop punk band du jour Blink-182.

Brian's first Bad Religion show at the Bizarre Festival in 1994.

Thorsten Martin-Edingshaus

Graffin, Ocasek, Jay Bentley, Brian Baker, Greg Hetson and Bobby Schayer (from left)

Recording *The Gray Race* with Ric Ocasek at Electric Lady in New York City. *Kevin Mazur*

Bobby Schayer in New York.

Walter St. Clair

(Opposite page) Jay and Brian on tour with Pearl Jam in Sacramento, California, in 1996.

Walter St. Clair

Ronnie Kimball creating live audio magic during the 1996 Gray Race Tour. You can still find him at the board today.

Walter St. Clair

Bad Religion and Pearl Jam at Chicago's Soldier Field in 1996.

Michele Ceazan-Fleischli

Jay in the pajamas he wore
for every show in 1998.

Olaf Heine

Hetson in Europe.

Olaf Heine

Greg in 1998.

Olaf Heine

On a rooftop in
São Paulo in Brazil
for the European
promotion photo
for *The New America*.

Olaf Heine

Hanging out at a Favela in São Paulo, Brazil, in 2000. *Olaf Heine*

Jay, Brian, Greg, Hetson, Brooks, and Brett during the *Process of Belief*
photo shoot. *Unknown*

In a junkyard in the San Fernando Valley for the *Process of Belief* promotion photo. *Unknown*

Live show circa 2002. *D.J. Farley*

Riding some Milwaukee Iron in Milwaukee during the
Warped Tour. *Unknown*

Greg in the studio during the recording of *Dissent of Man*. *Unknown*

Brian, Brooks, Greg, Jay, and Mike. *Lisa Johnson*

Tour manager Rick Marino and Greg in Medellin, Spain, in 2016. *Walter St. Clair*

Making demos for *Age of Unreason* in Brett's home studio in Pasadena.

Walter St. Clair

Jay and Greg with Oulun Kärpät Captain Lasse Kukkonen in Oulu, Finland, in 2018.

Rick Marino

(Top left) Mike displays his sartorial flair at the Download Festival in Donington Park.

Clair McAllister

Jay and Brian. *Jim Wright*

(Bottom left) Jamie at the Download Festival in 2018. *Clair McAllister*

Old pals in Hollywood.

Rick Marino

Bad Religion in Mexico
City in 2019. *Greg Stocks*

Jay, Jamie, and Greg at the Hollywood Palladium. *Steve Albanese*

Taking a break during the recording of *Age of Unreason*. *Alice Baxley*

21

A SHITTY BAND
LIKE YOURS

WHEN *HOW COULD HELL BE ANY WORSE?* came out in 1980, Mark Hoppus, Tom DeLonge, and Travis Barker of San Diego's Blink-182 were eight, five, and five years old, respectively. Nevertheless, they asked Bad Religion to join them on the Mark, Tom and Travis Show Tour in the late spring and early summer of 2000. Blink-182 specialized in a fast, melodic, and radio-friendly style of pop punk, and their 1999 album, *Enema of the State*, had been a huge hit. Their brand of irreverent, and at times highly sexualized, lyrics was extremely popular with young fans, many of whom hadn't been born when the boys from the San Fernando Valley were practicing in the Hell Hole.

While their fans may not have been familiar with Bad Religion, Blink-182 certainly was. They had opened for Bad Religion on a few occasions and praised them as an important influence when *they* were high school kids playing in their parents' garages. In fact, at the band's earliest rehearsals it jammed Bad Religion covers.

Like every punk band that signs with a major label, Blink-182 was criticized by its fans for selling out, and magazines like *Punk Planet* ran articles criticizing the band's blatant misogyny. Inviting Bad Religion, who had also faced criticism for signing with a major label, was a way to bolster Blink-182's punk credibility. As for Bad Religion, they saw it as an opportunity to play in American stadiums and arenas with crowds comparable to those at the European festivals they played every year.

However, in order to participate in the Mark, Tom and Travis Show Tour, Bad Religion would have to postpone the dates for their spring mini-tour of the West Coast until later in the year when they embarked on a considerably longer North American tour.

The Mark, Tom and Travis Show Tour began on May 11 in the San Diego suburb of Chula Vista and ended on July 2 in Milwaukee, Wisconsin. The band was blown away by the money Blink-182's corporate sponsors put into the production. Still, there were die-hard fans from both camps who were against Bad Religion opening for the intellectually inferior Blink-182.

Bad Religion's drummer wasn't one of them. Bobby understood the historical context of what the band was trying to accomplish. "You're trying to reach out to people you never thought would like you," Bobby said. "Like the Ramones opening for Black Sabbath, Jimi Hendrix opening for the Monkees, or even Prince opening for the Rolling Stones. It's kind of the same thing. People booed them, but these are shows you never forget. At the end of the day, the Blink guys treated us well. I'm happy with that."

Wherever they traveled, Bobby was interested in the rock and roll history of the region they were visiting. Sometimes this meant taking a side trip into or out of the city, like when he visited the Rock and Roll Hall of Fame with Hetson. Other times it meant taking the tour bus on a detour, such as the time they went to the Rose Hill Cemetery to see where Duane Allman and Berry Oakley were laid to rest after dying in motorcycle accidents a year apart.

On the Blink-182 tour, the band was driving through Georgia for a show in Atlanta, but they didn't have to be there until late in the afternoon. Bobby asked the bus driver if they were going through Macon. When the driver enquired why he wanted to know, Bobby mentioned his desire to see the grave of Berry Oakley of the Allman Brothers Band. The driver enthusiastically agreed to take them.

The driver, who was a southerner, had called ahead so that when they arrived at the cemetery the driver's sister, her husband, and a cousin were waiting at the gates with a pickup truck. They drove Bobby, Jay, and the driver right to the graves where Duane and Berry were buried side by side. The driver was moved by Bobby's interest. "'That's respect,'" Bobby recalled the driver telling him afterward. "'I never met anyone who liked the Allman Brothers, especially a shitty band like yours.'"

After the Blink-182 tour, Bad Religion had a month off before they began to promote *The New America* in earnest. One advantage of having spent so much of the summer playing with Blink-182 was they were well rehearsed and had the new songs down cold for the European tour. *The New America* had peaked at number 88 on the *Billboard* 200. The album also concluded the band's relationship with Atlantic. "It was a clean break," Greg explained. "They said, 'We're done with the contract.' We never presented another album to them, and they never asked for one."

At the conclusion of the South American leg of The New America Tour, morale was low. No one was particularly happy about how the band's relationship with Atlantic had petered out. Although there were no hard feelings between the label and the band, the experience of recording *The New America* under such unusual circumstances had left a sour taste in the mouths of some of the members. Could the end of the contract trigger the end of the band? "I was really mad that we might actually end on this fart," Jay said.

There was a growing feeling within the band that perhaps Rundgren had been too quick in his embrace of some of the technology used on *The New America,* and that Bad Religion would have been better served by a more analog approach. Others felt burnt out from the challenges of being on a label that didn't support them.

As defeated as they felt, they weren't willing to throw in the towel. There was a feeling of unfinished business, but everyone was so exhausted from spending most of the previous year on the road that no one knew what the next step should be. The tour had gone on for so long that Greg had started writing songs on the road, but he wondered if it made sense to work on them without a record label. Bad Religion was at the proverbial crossroads. For the first time in their long career, they didn't have a label, and no one was quite sure what to do next.

The New America had a well-known and somewhat surprising detractor: Fat Mike of NOFX. The singer was very vocal about his feelings about the album and declared that it was not up to snuff. Brett believed Bad Religion's decision to sign with a major label stirred up a lot of conflicting emotions, not just within the band, but also with the other bands at Epitaph. "My leaving the band became very polarizing for a lot of my artists," Brett said. "It's like a divorce: some friends are on team wife and some friends are on team husband, except in the most modern and open-minded divorces where everyone remains friends and has Thanksgiving together. We weren't that enlightened, and in the moment some people were saying the band had betrayed me, they weren't loyal to Epitaph, and going to a major was a sellout. I didn't agree with any of that."

Before they'd left for Hawaii to record *The New America,* Jay had gotten a strange call from Brett:

BRETT: Do you remember the Ramones' thirteenth record?
JAY: No, I don't.
BRETT: Me neither and I'm a huge Ramones fan.
JAY: What does that mean?
BRETT: You guys need to make a great record.
JAY: You can't just say that!

Jay thought about this conversation a lot and wondered what it meant. Although Brett had retracted his critical statements about the band, was he implying that Bad Religion was no longer making great records? Did his comments reflect a desire to do more on the new record than contribute a song? If nothing else, it sent a message to Jay that Bad Religion's legacy was still important to Brett. Jay decided to take it as genuine encouragement from his old friend and bandmate and leave it at that.

When they were preparing *The New America* for production, Jay had called Brett to ask him how he wanted to be credited on the album for "Believe It." They had a pleasant conversation, and it felt to Jay that they'd moved on from the anger and animosity of the past, and that things were back on the right track. "It seemed like we were all okay," Jay said. Things were going so well, in fact, that Brett came out to see his old band play on a few occasions during the North American leg of The New America Tour.

After the final show in Porto Alegre, Brazil, the band discussed their future before they went off in different directions, which were more far-flung than ever before. Brian was now back in Washington, D.C., and Hetson had moved to Texas. Only Bobby Schayer still lived in L.A.

Jay suggested to his bandmates that he go to L.A. and have a talk with Brett about Bad Religion returning to Epitaph. "What if I go meet with Brett? It seemed like Brett and I were the ones who had the biggest problem. If I go back and meet with Brett and sense any sort of weirdness with him, we won't do it, but what if it's great?"

It was a tantalizing proposition. Jay believed that Epitaph was where Bad Religion belonged. It was where they started and it was where they did their best work. Even if things were occasionally tense between Epitaph and Bad Religion, it would be better than their relationship with Atlantic had been. With Epitaph, both parties knew what they were getting. It only seemed fitting that they go back—if Brett would have them.

They all agreed this was a good idea. Jay flew to L.A. and spent a couple of days with Brett at Epitaph. It was immediately apparent that the past was the past and that Brett was willing to turn the page. Jay was surprised to learn that not only was Brett open to bringing Bad Religion back to Epitaph, he wanted to be a contributing member of the band.

"It was absolutely a no-brainer," Brett said. "Of course, Bad Religion should come back to Epitaph and I should write the records with Greg like we did in the old days. What I'd realized through the process of writing 'Believe It' was I missed writing. I really enjoyed it. Not only that, but as a record executive I recognized that the band reuniting—not just with a former member, but with their former label—would be a story. It would create a moment and be a great opportunity to make a record and have everybody interested in it."

While Brett was indeed sincere in his interest in Bad Religion's musical legacy, he was also serious about his commitment to Epitaph, which had grown in Bad Religion's absence. Brett loved writing songs and he wanted to make a record with Bad Religion again, but he had no interest in touring. Could they work out an arrangement where the band would come back to Epitaph and Brett would contribute creatively but not tour?

This seemed like a win-win situation for Bad Religion because it meant the person putting out their records would have skin in the game. Not only did Brett want Bad Religion to do well from a business standpoint, he wanted to make great records. And who knew how to make great-sounding Bad Religion records better than Brett?

"So we had a situation," Jay said, "where here's a guy with a label who doesn't want to tour but who wants to write songs. It dovetailed nicely with our touring operation." Brett's reluctance to tour wasn't going to be a problem because the band already had two world-class punk rock guitarists in Greg Hetson and Brian Baker.

"The first thing they did after Brett came back," Brian quipped, "was they decided that I should stay. That was really the watershed moment."

But could they make this work? Brian Wilson of the Beach Boys was the most famous example of a creative contributor who didn't tour with his band, but in all of rock and roll there wasn't much of a precedent for having a band member who wrote songs *and* was in charge of the label but didn't actually play with the band.

Jay didn't think this was so strange. To his way of thinking, it was far more remarkable that Bad Religion had stayed together after Brett left in 1994. Considering what was going on at the time in the world of punk music, it would have been easy, if not expected, for one or all of the band members to jump ship. No one did, and by sticking it out together something remarkable happened: they matured.

"The funny thing is when Brett came back," Jay said, "the scenario hadn't changed at all from 1994 when Brian came into the band. Nothing had changed. What changed was our ability to deal with scenarios that at thirty we couldn't. We were emotionally immature and didn't know how to say, *You're a great songwriter. You don't have to come on tour. You have a label to run. We can figure this out. We'll hire Brian and make it work*. We couldn't get our heads around that. Everything was all or nothing until it finally blew up."

After twenty years, they'd finally figured it out.

But in Porto Alegre, Brazil, Bobby blindsided them. He informed his bandmates that he would not be going on the final leg of The New America Tour in Europe. He had been dealing with a painful shoulder injury that would require surgery if he was to continue as Bad Religion's drummer. His doctors were advising him to stop playing altogether because, even with the surgery, there were no guarantees he'd be able to play at the same level again. Rather than go through an expensive surgery and a lengthy recovery and still not know if he'd be able to cut it, Bobby decided to call it quits.

"What did me in at the end was two things," Bobby said. "My arm was killing me, and I was burning out. I just stopped being a fan of the music. When it started to be about lawyers and accountants, you kind of lose sight of what made you a fan in the first place."

Bobby was wearing down—physically and mentally. Being a professional rock drummer is like playing catcher in baseball. You've got more gear and more responsibilities, and it's the most physically demanding position on the field. Your body breaks down faster than everyone else's around you. It's a grind. Brian put it best: "Drummers wear out."

While opening for Blink-182, Bobby had an epiphany: "I accomplished everything I wanted out of being in a rock and roll band. I got to tour Europe. I got to play England. I got to play CBGB and the Whisky. I got to put out records, and I took care of my family." But for Bobby, a lifelong Angeleno, getting to play the Los Angeles Forum was a dream come true. "Even though we opened for Blink-182," Bobby said, "after playing the Forum, I could die happy."

It was important to Bobby to leave the band on his own terms. So, instead of having surgery on his rotator cuff and going through a potentially long rehab that would have left the band in limbo, he decided to bow out gracefully.

"My last words were, 'Thank you,' not 'Fuck you,'" Bobby said. "That to me was the perfect way to end it."

Once again, Bad Religion needed a drummer. Before they set out on their European tour in the summer of 2001, the band arranged auditions and brought in musicians who could do more than play punk rock songs. "Brett saw it as an opportunity to get someone with a higher level of technical skill," Brian explained. "Bobby's a great drummer, but he's a Clem Burke drummer. He's a Tommy Ramone. I think Brett was more interested in a different kind of musicianship."

Brooks Wackerman was the fifth drummer to audition that day. It was clear after just a few songs they'd found Bobby's replacement.

The Southern California native was raised in Seal Beach and went to Los Alamitos High School in Orange County. Like his predecessor, Brooks grew up in a musical family. His father was a lifelong music teacher and his brother, Chad, was an acclaimed percussionist who had played and recorded extensively with Frank Zappa. As a result of his upbringing, playing drums had been a part of Brooks's life for as long as he could remember.

"There wasn't ever a defining moment," Brooks said. "My family threw sticks in my hands as soon as I started walking. It became a daily activity in the house. I'd wake up, eat my Wheaties, and figure out my way around a drum set."

Brooks started taking private lessons from a jazz and classical music teacher when he was just six years old. "I think there's definitely something to be said for being a child and navigating around the instrument and not having an education," Brooks said. "The classic example is Jimi Hendrix. If he went to the Berklee College of Music, he probably wouldn't be Jimi Hendrix. I wonder what I would sound like if I didn't have my dad who's been a music educator for over sixty years. But I love how well-rounded my background was in terms of studying all these different styles because I had a grab bag to pull from and add something different to how punk rock is performed."

With a foundation in Latin, jazz, and reggae, Brooks started playing in jazz bands in high school. But it was Brooks's brother who had the biggest influence by exposing his younger sibling to the Sex Pistols and the Ramones, which opened the door to all kinds of punk, metal, and progressive music.

Brooks started his professional career in the band Bad4Good, which was managed by axe maestro Steve Vai. While he was still in high school, Brooks was recruited to play drums in the Huntington Beach punk rock band the Vandals, where he received a different kind of education.

"The Vandals' bass player, Joe Escalante," Brooks recalled, "threw the CD *Stranger Than Fiction* on my lap. He said, 'You should listen to that.' *Stranger Than Fiction* was my introduction to Bad Religion."

Brooks left the Vandals and played with Suicidal Tendencies for two years, but he'd been a free agent for about a year when he got the opportunity to try out for Bad Religion. During all his time in the Vandals and Suicidal Tendencies he'd never shared the same stage as Bad Religion. "We played a lot of the same festivals," Brooks said, "but it was always on different days." In fact, the first and only time he saw Bad Religion perform before he joined the band was with Blink-182 at the Universal Amphitheatre, where he was struck by the difference in size between Jay Bentley and Greg Hetson.

Though Brooks was relatively young—he was only twenty-two years old—a number of musicians had recommended him to Bad Religion. "From what I heard," Brooks said, "Travis Barker, Josh Freese, and Fletcher from Pennywise all threw my name in the hat." Brett's assistant called and asked if Brooks would be interested in coming down to Cole Rehearsal Studios. Because Brooks didn't drive, his dad drove him to the audition.

The members of Bad Religion could see right away that Brooks had more than an impressive resume: he was a supremely gifted musician. "He was a child prodigy," Greg said. "His family is a really talented group of people. Brooks helped elevate our sound and made us more modern." Everyone was impressed with his style of play. "Brooks was an anomaly," Jay said. "He was one of those super talented people who was going to make a mark on the world no matter what he did." Brett said it most succinctly: "He was a dynamo."

Brooks was so good, in fact, they worried he'd slip away. Once they ascertained that he was interested in being a full-time member of the band, they hired him on the spot. For Brooks, it was all a whirlwind. When he auditioned, he didn't even realize that Brett was back in Bad Religion.

"When I first got the call, I didn't put two and two together. I wasn't under the impression that he was coming back to the band.

I talked to him later on that week and he told me, 'You know I'm coming back. I'm producing and writing.' It was exhilarating to join the band at that time."

With a new drummer in the fold and the remainder of the summer off, Bad Religion went to work on the new album. For the first time since *Recipe for Hate* was recorded nearly a decade before, the band assembled at the old studio at Westbeach Recorders to make a new record.

22

THE HURTING GROUND

FOR BAD RELIGION, RETURNING TO EPITAPH RECORDS was like a homecoming. "Epitaph was a smaller, family operation," Greg said, "and we had a lot of friends there. It had a California vibe. They weren't corporate people. They were like people from the scene. It was like going back to our old friends."

There was a feeling within the band that, because of the label's influence and/or the direction from outside producers, some of the songs from the Atlantic era hadn't been developed as fully as they could have been, that they'd been let down and led astray by their label. "To be honest," Brian said, "by *The New America* I was lazy. I was lazy and drunk, and I took the easy way out. I guess that's why I have a bad taste in my mouth with *The New America*—specifically because there are so many great ideas, but they're all in different songs. I'd love it if some of those ideas were all in one song because that's what you call a hit."

That said, Brian didn't dislike any of the songs from that period and took a warts-and-all approach to their catalog. "I don't think there's anything the band has done I abhor, that I don't get behind," Brian said. "I can't do that. I don't have that in me. They're all our kids no matter how fucked up they are. It's like, *All right, go do what you're gonna do* . . . There are things that I don't like. Maybe it's the structure, or I think the chorus isn't strong. I've got my opinion about things, but I don't hate things. They can't all be winners."

For the new record, which would be called *The Process of Belief,* they wrote shorter, faster songs. The first three songs on the album, "Supersonic," "Prove It," and "Can't Stop It," are all well under two minutes. Together, they come in at a total of four minutes and twelve seconds. These songs also demonstrate what Bad Religion's new drummer was capable of doing behind the kit. "Having Brooks was a great asset because he could play anything," Brett said. "I always had to write stuff that I thought Bobby could play or Pete could play. Then we had this great virtuoso in the band, and I thought, *I should write something where he can just go nuts.*" A good example of that is "Can't Stop It," a furiously fast song.

Jay welcomed the return of their signature sound, but it was the attitude and intensity that gave the recording sessions a slightly different feel. "I can tell you some of my favorite moments in the band," Jay said, "were the recording of *Suffer* and *The Process of Belief.* The reason I look at those times is because that's when no one gave a shit about us at all, and we were making records for no reason other than making them for us. When we made *Suffer,* no one gave a fuck about Bad Religion. When we made *The Process of Belief,* people had written us off. We'd had our moment on the tidal wave of punk rock and by the time *The New America* was done, we were just sort of a parody of ourselves. I hated it. Making *The Process of Belief* we had that feeling again. No one came to the studio to say hi or popped in to see what was going on. No one gave a shit about what we were doing."

But not all of the songs Brett and Greg brought to the studio were red-hot scorchers. Brett's song "Sorrow" and Greg's

"Epiphany" both have atypical beginnings. "Epiphany" starts out slow and mournful before the pace picks up while "Sorrow" begins with a three-note harmonic on the guitar that sounds like a spring coming unsprung, and a drum and bass combination right out of a reggae number. The echo on the rhetorical question that opens the song—"Father can you hear me?"—makes "Sorrow" stand out from the rest of the album.

But "Sorrow" didn't always start that way. "It had a much heavier intro," Brett explained. "It was still half-time but had a heavy, chunky guitar. My cousin was at my house and I said, 'Hey, you want to hear my new song?' I took her downstairs to my little demo studio and I played her the intro and a little bit of the beginning. She said, 'I love it. It reminds me of Pat Benatar!' That bummed me out so bad that I had to change it. I had to make it completely different so that it couldn't possibly be compared to Pat Benatar."

Brooks recalled how upset Brett was by the comparison to Pat Benatar. "He came to me and said, 'Listen, I want to change this. I don't want us to sound like Pat Benatar. What if we did something in the reggae style?' That's when I started experimenting with some Stewart Copeland–esque rhythms. Stewart Copeland does a lot of cross stick. It's when you put the stick on the rim. It gives you that high-end piercing sound. That clicking sound in the intro is the stick on the rim. Stewart studied a lot of Lebanese and African rhythms. He is notorious for that type of drumming."

To craft the new intro, Brett swapped the kick drum and the snare drum so that it would have more of a reggae beat, and he asked Brooks to play some dotted eighth note fills, which Brooks was more than capable of doing.

"It all came together very magically," Brett said.

When Brett wrote the song, he was inspired by his son, Max, who was just a little boy. "I was playing around on the guitar with Max and the chords to 'Sorrow' came out. That was the genesis of the chord progression and the melody, which I felt right away. I thought it had a melancholic feeling, so I thought, *Okay, I'm going to write a sad song. What would be a good subject?"*

Brett turned to a strange place for inspiration: the Bible. The story of Job from the Old Testament is sometimes referred to as the saddest story ever told. To summarize, Job was a loyal and faithful believer. The Devil felt he could tempt Job, but God believed Job would be resolute no matter what the circumstances. The Devil wagered that he could convince Job to sin and God, in his unshakable confidence, took that bet.

Brett felt like this was a messed-up situation. "Who could worship such a despicable god?" he said. "A god that would take his one loyal creation and sell him out to evil? Why wouldn't God protect Job? Why wouldn't he say, 'Fuck off, Devil! Keep your hands off Job! He's a good dude!' But God didn't do that. The despair in the story of Job is that the creator of the universe turned his back on man. That's sorrow."

The first two verses of "Sorrow" tell the story of Job without being too explicit about it:

Father can you hear me?
How have I let you down?
I curse the day that I was born
And all the sorrow in this world

Let me take you to the hurting ground
Where all good men are trampled down
Just to settle a bet that could not be won
Between a prideful father and his son

"It's very primal," Brett explained. "A kid talking to his father, Job talking to God. I thought it was really powerful because it's very, very sad. A kid letting his father down. It's Job talking to God, but anybody can relate to what it feels like to let their father down. On some level, all of us are trying to impress our parents when we're little. They're our gods."

The story of Job is the story of humankind. We yearn for pro-
tection either from our parents or from a supernatural entity, only
to be let down when we find ourselves vulnerable and alone.

"It's not meant to be a depressing song," Brett said. "I'm actually an optimist, and I think there's a solution to the suffering
associated with the human condition; I just don't happen to think
it can be found in a savior. 'Sorrow' is me attempting to write a
spiritual song for punk rockers. I was trying to write something
with the emotional impact of John Lennon's 'Imagine,' but for
my generation."

Even Brett's bandmates were blown away by what Brett had accomplished. "I'm in the band," Jay admitted, "and it took me until
'Sorrow' to recognize what a great songwriter Brett Gurewitz is. It
took a long time for me to have a moment and realize *This guy's
a genius.*"

Originally slated for an October release, *The Process of Belief* was
pushed back to 2002 because the record wasn't ready. Another
factor contributed to the band's decision: on September 11, 2001,
a terrorist attack on the Twin Towers in Manhattan, the Pentagon
in Washington, D.C., and onboard Flight 93 killed nearly three
thousand people and injured many more, making it the deadliest
attack of its kind on American soil.

After 9/11, it became clear which song would be the first single. When Brett presented "Sorrow" to Greg, the singer immediately recognized its subtle power, but he didn't realize how important it would become to the band. "It's a great song," Greg
said, "but because it came out on the heels of 9/11, we couldn't
have predicted the impact it would have. 'Sorrow' ended up being
a defining song for Bad Religion."

Brett was actually working on "Sorrow" when he first learned
of the attack. "I remember it like it was yesterday," he said. "I was
mixing 'Sorrow' at Larrabee East with the TV news on when the
towers fell. It was happening live while I was putting the finishing
touches on the mix."

Initially, Brett didn't think "Sorrow" was a single. He believed the beat was too fast for radio. He thought "The Defense" or "Broken" were the top contenders from the album. But it was Andy Kaulkin, the president of Epitaph's sister label, Anti-, who suggested that "Sorrow" be the first single. "He said to me, 'I think this is a single because it really captures the zeitgeist of where our country is post-9/11. This is what it feels like today.' I think he was right."

The song's promise of a world without sorrow, while acknowl-edging all the suffering going on, struck just the right balance between hope and regret at a time when so many people were reeling from the aftershocks of 9/11. The song turns from dark-ness to light in the chorus:

There will be sorrow
Yeah, there will be sorrow
And there will be sorrow no more

Of course, in typical Bad Religion fashion, the end of sorrow in our time comes with a lengthy list of ironic prerequisites.

When all soldiers lay their weapons down
Or when all kings and all queens relinquish their crowns
Or when the only true messiah rescues us from ourselves

The likelihood of any of these things happening, much less all of them, makes the end of sorrow a dubious proposition at best.

While "Sorrow" doesn't have the tenor of a sing-along—it's not a happy song, nor is it joyful or carefree—it's structured like a call-and-response that beckons the listener to answer. Emotions drive the audience's participation, and the song is a high point of every live performance. At the sound of its unorthodox opening, a roar washes over the crowd that quickly gives way to a hushed silence. Because of its simple, straightforward chorus and slower tempo, if you don't know the lyrics at the beginning of the song, you do by the end. Singing "Sorrow" along with hundreds and thousands of people became a cathartic experience for fans coming to terms with post-9/11 reality.

Although 9/11 hadn't happened when the song was written, some fans mistakenly believe the song included direct references to the tragedy. During the chorus, a sample of an explosion plays between "There will be" and "sorrow." Brett has always maintained that this was a production touch to add emphasis to the chorus, but it has a surprising influence: the Simon & Garfunkel song "The Boxer." In that song, the sound of a crash breaks up the chorus.

"I always thought it was so cool," Brett explained. "The way they did it was they put a drum in an elevator shaft. I didn't have an elevator shaft so I used a sample of an explosion."

The Process of Belief was released in January 2002 to positive reviews. It reached 49 on *Billboard*'s top 200 album chart, and also did very well abroad, especially in Ireland. Brett's instincts were right: Bad Religion's reconciliation with Epitaph and his reunion with his bandmates were big stories. Fans welcomed Brett back, but more importantly they relished the return of short, fast songs. While critics noted that many of the songs would not have been out of place on albums from the band's so-called glory days, *The Process of Belief* represented a new milestone: it was the first album that was cowritten and co-produced by Greg and Brett. It also outperformed the records Bad Religion had released after Brett left the band.

"I personally feel that Bad Religion is better with me and Greg as a writing team," Brett said. "I think Greg is one of the great punk rock songwriters and singers of all time, and I think he wrote some very good songs and made some very good records for Atlantic, but Bad Religion is better when we're together."

The Process of Belief contains all the things that make Bad Religion great, and while the songwriting and production benefit from Greg and Brett's collaboration, their timing was impeccable. September 11 was a defining point in our country's history with a clear delineation between before and after. Brett's return to the band was a boost to Bad Religion fans, many of whom viewed the rise of bands like Blink-182 as the end of punk. "It was more than a reunion of friends," Brett suggested. "It was like the return of the prodigal son." That two of the most intelligent songwriters in the industry were collaborating again and had created Bad Religion's first nationwide radio hit was a cause for celebration at a time when there was a scarcity of good news.

The Process of Belief also marked a shift in the way the songwriting credits were recorded. In the past, they made it clear in the liner notes which artist wrote what song. When Greg and Brett got back together, they decided to take a different approach. "We share songwriting credit," Brett explained. "We started doing the Lennon and McCartney thing, and we don't say who wrote what. It just takes the politics out of it."

Brett was extremely pleased with how the record came out. Of all the records he'd worked on at Westbeach, including Rancid's *Let's Go* and NOFX's *White Trash, Two Heebs and a Bean* and *Punk in Drublic,* he thought *The Process of Belief* sounded the best, and Westbeach had a lot to do with it. "The drums weren't done there and the mix wasn't done there," Brett said, "but all the overdubs were done at Westbeach. *The Process of Belief* is probably the best-sounding record that I've produced, and a lot of it was done in that room."

The return to Epitaph signaled two important shifts for the band: Jay began to spearhead the band's touring operation and took an active role in planning and organizing their intense schedule, and Greg resumed his academic career. He'd stalled on writing his dissertation when Bad Religion signed to Atlantic so that they could tour more, but now that they were back with Epitaph, Greg decided it was time to complete his Ph.D.

For his dissertation, Greg had settled on the topic of evolution through the lens of religion. He was interested in exploring the religious beliefs of prominent evolutionary biologists. However, because this data didn't exist, Greg had to go out and collect it.

That meant conducting dozens of interviews—both in person and on the phone—and gathering the information he needed. Luckily for Greg, traveling was something he was accustomed to doing. This dissertation would eventually be called *Evolution, Monism, Atheism, and the Naturalist World-view.*

Bad Religion kicked off The Process of Belief Tour in late January 2002 with a series of small shows in the United States. Although much was made of Brett joining the band but not touring, he did play these shows. He also went overseas with the band for six shows in Europe. Then it was back to the United States in March for a proper North American tour, at which point Brett returned to L.A.

Despite the fact that it was a short tour, a great deal had changed. "We were supposed to tour after the record was mixed," Brooks said, "but we took the rest of the year off. When we started touring again, it felt different with the extreme security checks. Traveling overseas as an American was weird. It was just a different mood. Not much was said, but this catastrophe happened, and it had a somber feel in some of the countries that we traveled to."

During the spring festival circuit, the band received a surprise. Sony Records released a "new" Bad Religion record with songs released between 1994 and 2000. This anthology was given the uninspiring title *Punk Rock Songs* and featured an image of Uncle Sam brandishing a weapon on the album cover. Bad Religion was neither consulted about the record nor advised of its release, but there was little the band could do. The album includes a German version of "Punk Rock Song" and live versions of "Change of Ideas" from *No Control,* "Leave Mine to Me" and "Slumber" from *Stranger Than Fiction,* and "Cease" from *The Gray Race.*

After a short rest, Bad Religion geared up for another Warped Tour from late June until mid-August. In September, the road warriors played the Inland Invasion, a massive two-day festival in San Bernardino that featured a reunited Sex Pistols, though the English punk rockers were outshined by their fellow countrymen the Buzzcocks.

One of the advantages of being back on Epitaph was that Bad Religion had more control over their schedule. They'd always insisted on complete creative control within the parameters of their collaborations, but now they could determine when to write, when to record, and when to tour—and, more importantly, for how long. It was time for a well-deserved break, but the newly elected President George W. Bush had other ideas.

23

SHOCK AND AWFUL

O
N MARCH 20, 2003, THE UNITED STATES
launched an attack on the presidential palace in
Baghdad, Iraq. Although the troops represented
a coalition from the United States, United Kingdom, Australia,
and Poland, the invasion of Iraq was led by George W. Bush's
White House and the American military. The justification for this
unprovoked attack changed throughout the buildup to war, but it
was ultimately attributed to the need to eradicate Iraq's weapons of
mass destruction (WMDs). Most of the free world saw this for what
it was: a shameless show of brute force by an imperialist power that
needed to flex its muscles after the September 11 attacks.

While there was considerable support in the United States
for the war, which technically lasted less than a month but whose
aftermath would drag on for years, most forward-thinking Ameri-
cans were appalled. Iraq, after all, had had nothing to do with the
planning or execution of Osama bin Laden's plot on the World
Trade Towers, Pentagon, and Flight 93 on 9/11. Now bombs were

raining down on Baghdad, indiscriminately murdering men, women, and children in their sleep.

Bad Religion was among those outraged by America's unprovoked incursion into Iraq. "We went into Iraq under false pretenses," Brett said. "When 9/11 happened, we had Bush in office, who seemed more like an unwitting puppet of Dick Cheney and Karl Rove than a real president. These guys saw an opportunity to go into Iraq, turn it into a democracy, and make it a U.S. outpost in the Middle East with oil. This story about them having WMDs turned out to be trumped-up bullshit to wind us up to war while everyone was mad about 9/11."

What made the invasion so horrific was how unnecessary it was. The politicians built their case for war on the cable news networks and—once they felt they had sufficient support from the public—they let the bombs fly. For those opposed to the war, the years following 9/11 were marked by a feeling of helplessness as flag-waving "patriots" beat the drum and called for supporting the troops. In the wake of 9/11, protest was painted as unpatriotic.

The members of Bad Religion felt just as powerless as their progressive peers, but they had something that most protestors did not: a voice. The band went on a six-week tour of North America in support of *The Process of Belief* from early April until mid-May, and then in September they did a West Coast tour with most of the shows held in Southern California. Whether it was due to anti-American sentiment abroad or a sense that they had work to do at home, Bad Religion did not go to Europe.

In November, the band assembled at Sound City in Van Nuys to begin recording their thirteenth studio album, *The Empire Strikes First*. "We don't really make topical records," Brett said. "Our lyrics have generally been personal or sociological in nature, but *The Empire Strikes First* was a polemical record and most definitely inspired by the U.S. preemptively, and needlessly, striking Iraq."

The title of both the album and the song comes from how unprecedented it was for the United States to make an unprovoked attack on an unwitting enemy. The band's anger at the administration was outpaced only by its incredulity that a simpleton like Bush could get elected in the first place. This was a man who, during the presidential election, couldn't remember the title of a single book he admired, and was so out of touch with the American people that at one campaign stop handed out dollar bills to the common folk who came to see him. With another election coming up in 2004, Greg, Brett, and the rest of the band were determined to do their part to make sure Bush wasn't reelected.

As usual, Brett and Greg dished out heavy doses of irony in their scathing critique of America's imperialist adventures, but with songs like "Let Them Eat War," "To Another Abyss," and "Boot Stamping on a Human Face Forever," which comes from a quote by the writer George Orwell, there was no disguising how Bad Religion felt about the war. To combat the xenophobia the administration was cultivating, the band felt it was necessary to be as explicit as possible.

"Everyone gets more conservative and warlike when they're scared," Brett said. "Research proves that fear makes people more conservative. And when people feel safe, they become more liberal." A pervasive feeling of protest sparked the band's collaborative spirit and multiple members contributed to songs on the album. Brian, for instance, wrote the main riffs for "The Empire Strikes First" and "Let Them Eat War," which also featured Sage Francis, a recording artist from Anti-. "He was a slam poetry artist," Brett said. "He was in the early backpack hip-hop scene, the early slam poetry scene. He was a fan of Bad Religion so I thought it would be cool to have a little bit of cross-pollination."

Not all of the songs on *The Empire Strikes First* were political. For all its apocalyptic imagery, "Los Angeles Is Burning" isn't about the war. "L.A. might be the only city in the world that has a fire season," Brett explained. "Some cities have a rainy season, but L.A. has a fire season. I'm a third-generation Angeleno so I thought it would be interesting to use L.A.'s fire season as a metaphor for the waves of people who come to L.A., seeking fame and fortune only to have their lives ravaged by the vanity and superficiality they find there."

The album came together quickly, with one notable exception. Brett wasn't happy with the guitar solo in "Los Angeles Is Burning." He and Brian both took a few shots at it, but to Brett's mind it wasn't quite there, so he called in reinforcements. "One of my great heroes," Brett said, "is Mike Campbell from Tom Petty and the Heartbreakers. He's truly one of the greatest rock and roll guitar players of all time."

Brett got to know Mike through friends in the industry, namely recording engineers and record producers who all spoke highly of him. Mike's son was a big fan of Rancid and other Epitaph bands, and Brett recalled seeing him in the balcony at the Palladium. Brett called Mike and asked him if he would play on the record, and he agreed. "I honestly think the solo makes the song," Brett said. Brett was such an admirer of Campbell's guitar work that he put out an album by Campbell's surf band, the Blue Stingrays. In fact, Brett created a new label to release it—Epitone.

Bad Religion has never been afraid to experiment with their sound and see how far they can take their brand of melodic hardcore. In the past, those experiments typically yielded a slower, softer, more radio-friendly song, from the pop sensibilities of "Infected" and "21st Century (Digital Boy)," to the country twang of "Man with a Mission," to the folk-infused songs of the Atlantic years. But *The Empire Strikes First* represents the first time the band experimented with a heavier, faster sound. Part of the reason was they were angry at the Bush administration for leading the country into a senseless war, but the other factor was that Brett and Brooks made their presence felt in new and arresting ways.

"On that particular record," Brooks said, "I started feeling comfortable in the band. I'm proud of *Process of Belief*, and to this day 'Sorrow' is one of my favorite songs, but once we got into *Empire*, that's when I started feeling comfortable as a musician and a member of the band."

Brooks collaborated with Brett on "The Quickening" and "Beyond Electric Dreams," the rare Bad Religion song that is over four minutes long. (Both songs were cowritten by Chris Wollard of Hot Water Music.) "Beyond Electric Dreams" is about the Sierra Nevada Mountains, a place that Brett has felt connected to since he hiked 190 miles of the John Muir Trail when he was a teenager. "The mountains are my church," Brett said. "They're my place to escape cultural conventions and recharge spiritually."

The song has the same theme as "Generator," but where "Generator" uses metaphors to describe a condition of godliness, "Beyond Electric Dreams" employs more prosaic language to address what Brett calls "the mystery of the cosmos." "I'm always finding spirituality in nature," he said. "Even though I'm not really particularly interested in metaphysics, I think the existence of consciousness in the cosmos is the great mystery, and I've always been completely captivated by it."

Musically, "Beyond Electric Dreams" was inspired by Frank Black, and it even includes the use of a megaphone. The song also has a free-flowing middle section that complements its premise of the rejuvenating power of nature but is otherwise uncharacteristic for the band. "When we played that song live," Brooks said, "it was always interesting and fun because I could take it as long as I wanted to or shorten it if we wanted to get to the next song. It definitely had a spontaneous factor where every night it was different."

Another song that showcases Brooks's considerable talent is "Sinister Rouge," a scathing indictment of the Catholic Church. It's a blisteringly fast tune that pins your ears back and makes the jackhammer drums of the *Suffer* era seem slow in comparison. The song represents a fresh approach to a subject the band had been addressing for decades. "That song in particular stood out the first time I heard Greg's demo," Brooks said. "It had this Bad Religion goes Goth element to it, which I thought was unique and different."

Recording lasted from November 2003 until February 2004. The album was released in June but by then Bad Religion had already hit the road. They spent the entire month of May in Europe to make up for not playing any shows there the previous year. They made their feelings about the war in Iraq clear by urging audiences to encourage their American friends not to vote for Bush because they didn't want to be part of an empire that strikes first.

Bad Religion returned from Europe in time for the Warped Tour, which lasted six weeks. While Brooks may have been Bad Religion's newest and youngest member, he was no stranger to the festival. He played his first Warped Tour with Suicidal Tendencies in 1999 in Australia—the only year the festival went Down Under.

To make up for the spartan accommodations, Brooks recalled, the buses for Bad Religion, NOFX, Pennywise, and Lagwagon would park in the shape of a square, creating an impromptu courtyard for the bands. They only played for thirty or forty minutes a day, which left a lot of downtime, and that took some getting used to.

"I don't like to be at the venue the whole day," Brooks said. "I want to go to a museum or walk around. I feel very stale being at the venue for ten hours. As a musician, I would have a better show if I wasn't hanging out at the venue for the whole day. I needed some type of battery recharge. Once I got in Bad Religion and saw how Greg traveled, I thought that was definitely more civilized. On that particular tour, I was on the bus half the time and with Greg the other half because he liked staying in the city and getting a rental car and driving to the show the following day. I would be his wingman, and I got to know him."

After the Warped Tour, the band set out on a five-week tour of North America in October to support *The Empire Strikes First*. Both the Warped Tour and The Empire Strikes First Tour did double duty as grassroots get-out-the-vote efforts. Bad Religion was one of the two hundred punk bands aligned with Punkvoter.com, Fat Mike's campaign to register young voters and get Bush out of office, and they also contributed to both volumes of the compilation *Rock Against Bush*. Unfortunately, after a contentious election marred by voting irregularities in Ohio, Bush was reelected.

The election cast a shadow over the remainder of the tour, which culminated with two performances at the Hollywood Palladium that were recorded and edited for their DVD *Bad Religion: Live at the Palladium*. They closed out the year with a trio of shows in South America. At the Radio Cidade festival in Rio de Janeiro, the wheels came off the bus, in a manner of speaking, for Jay.

Since his relapse in 1998, Jay's drinking had steadily gained momentum, and it was taking a toll on his physical health and the well-being of those around him. "There were days when I would drink myself blind," Jay said. "You hear the expression, drink yourself blind, but I actually did it. I would drink so much that the next day I couldn't see. *I don't know what I'm going to do. I guess I'm blind now.* I would be like, 'Brian, man, I need a banana!' He would come and get me and walk me around like a blind man. The weird thing is I would do that, and then I would do it again."

By 2004, Jay's marriage had fallen apart and he'd moved into an apartment in Vancouver so that he could be close to his children, but he wasn't in a good place. He didn't have any furniture and all his stuff was packed away in boxes. All he did was drink. "I was living a double life on the road," Jay said. "The minute I'd get to the hotel I'd walk straight to the bar. It was game on until the tour was over and then I'd go home and dry out. I didn't make it a secret. I wasn't lying to anyone. I just didn't do the same things I did at home that I did on the road. Then eventually I stopped caring and I did it everywhere. At home, on the road, everywhere."

Toward the end of tour, Jay's friends in Vancouver told him not to come back until he got his life straightened out. With reality rearing its ugly head and nothing to come home to, Jay went on a bender. "We played a show with Pennywise at some giant festival in Rio," Jay said, "and I got hammered with Fletcher before the show.

We were drinking Pringles cans of White Russians. Each Pringles can was four White Russians and I probably had eight cans. Just powering those cans. They found me in the bushes before the show and pushed me out onstage. I didn't play one right note. The stage was like twenty feet high, and they had to tie a rope around me because I almost fell off. I don't remember one fucking thing. The next day everybody was really mad at me. I didn't remember any of it, but I knew enough to feel really ashamed. I shouldn't do that to my band."

As bad as he felt, he drank again that night and through the end of the tour, but afterward, instead of going home, he went to L.A. and dried out for a few days. In February 2005, he went to the seventh annual Punk Rock Bowling tournament, an epic weekend of drug taking and debauchery in Las Vegas. "I drank myself to oblivion," Jay said.

Jay returned to Vancouver utterly demoralized by his desire to quit and his inability to stay sober. "One of the saddest parts of my life was when I decided to quit quitting. I was trying to quit, and I couldn't quit, so I said, *Fuck it. I'm not going to stop. I'm just going to double down and drink more.* And I did. That was really bad."

One gruesome hangover morning, he was lying on the floor of his apartment in Vancouver trying to remember a prayer, but he couldn't come up with the words. He knew the prayer was in what is commonly referred to as the Big Book of Alcoholics Anonymous, which he had from his first period of sobriety, but it was buried in his boxes. He kept telling himself, *Just get up and get the book,* but he couldn't summon the energy to dig through all the boxes. This went on all day. "At some point I got up to get the book," Jay said, "and the book was on top of the box. I'd never opened any of the boxes. It was just there."

A few days later, he received a card from a psychotherapist in his mailbox out of the blue. Jay took this as a sign and called the number on the card. He ended up making an appointment where he spilled the beans about his compulsion to drink and inability to quit. The therapist gave him the number to the Alcoholics

Anonymous Vancouver central office, and an hour later he was sitting in a meeting down the street from his apartment. That was February 21, 2005, and he's been sober ever since. "All of those things happened without me trying to do anything. I didn't call someone and say, 'I need help.' It just happened."

Despite these emotional ups and downs and the disappointing result of the presidential election, Bad Religion continued its support of *The Empire Strikes First* with two jaunts across the United States broken up by a trip to Europe. In progressive Southern California, the mood was particularly grim. "It felt like I had been punched in the throat," Brian said of the election, "especially the way it was 'lost.' I was shattered, but my eyes were opened. It had never occurred to me that electoral malfeasance would decide a candidate. It was an eye-opening experience."

In 2006, Bad Religion performed at a number of festivals and clubs that required them to hopscotch around the globe. With the proliferation of fairs and festivals popping up around the country and all over the world, Bad Religion's irregular schedule provided a glimpse of a new way of touring. Instead of going from club to club and city to city, many bands found it was more economical to play to the large crowds of a festival than at several smaller venues, despite the logistical challenges of moving the band greater distances in shorter periods of time.

This also represented the band's lightest touring schedule since 2001. The band had been working virtually nonstop since they started recording *The Empire Strikes First* in late 2003, and they promoted the album for nearly two years. Bad Religion needed a break.

Greg, however, stayed busy. In 2006, Greg released his second solo album, *Cold as the Clay*. Although the record is a continuation of Greg's love of old-time American music, unlike *American Lesion*, most of the tracks are traditional classics that Greg didn't write, and the record was made with a full complement of musicians, including Jolie Holland, members of the Weakerthans, and David Bragger, Greg's neighbor from Canoga Park who is a virtuoso fiddle player and a frequent collaborator on old-time music projects. Brett produced the album, which was recorded and mixed in a little over a week and released through Anti- in July 2006. A pair of songs from the album, "Don't Be Afraid to Run" and "Talk About Suffering," were made available for download on the Epitaph website.

If fans wanted to see Bad Religion in 2006, they could do so by picking up a copy of the DVD *Bad Religion: Live at the Palladium.* The DVD featured the live performance of thirty-one songs from albums between *How Could Hell Be Any Worse?* and *The Empire Strikes First.* The only albums that weren't represented were *Into the Unknown, No Substance,* and *The New America.* The DVD also included both of their appearances on *New Wave Theatre,* six music videos, a photo gallery, and footage from various interviews.

Rumors had been circulating about the next Bad Religion album for over a year. With the advent of social media sites like MySpace, fans could share articles, updates, and rumors about their favorite bands with a few keystrokes. If a member of Bad Religion made a casual remark on a message board or joked in an interview on the radio, those comments were circulated on various platforms and read as official announcements. Greg, Brett, Jay, Brian, Hetson, and Brooks were bombarded with requests from zines, magazines, and music websites to confirm or corroborate something that someone in the band had said. Whoever was asked the question would have to check in with the band to see if there was a new development he hadn't been made aware of. Sometimes band members would have fun with this by intentionally putting less than accurate information out there. Then the process would start all over again as fans scrambled to keep up with the latest "news." It was entertaining but exhausting, and it would only get worse.

24

EVOLUTION OF REVOLUTION

I N 1982 BAD RELIGION POSED A QUESTION WITH the title of their debut album, *How Could Hell Be Any Worse?* Twenty-five years later, Bad Religion provided an answer—albeit a pessimistic one—with *New Maps of Hell.*

The difference between the 1980s and the 2000s was that in the eighties the moral outrage propagated by the conservative right was sincere. In some respects, punk rockers and religious zealots were critiquing the same hedonistic decay. "Punk was both a musical and cultural movement," Brett explained. "It was a reaction to disco. It was a reaction to the crappy music and fashion that was in the zeitgeist. 'Fuck my hippie parents and their fucking coked-out disco parties!' It was a youth movement, but there was also a sense of community with shared values."

But on the twenty-fifth anniversary of "Fuck Armageddon . . . This Is Hell," the war criminals in the White House could no longer lay claim to any moral high ground as they funneled tax dollars into a campaign of endless war in the Middle East and conned their base into voting against its own interests with an agenda that pandered to Christian fundamentalism. Progressive issues like a woman's right to choose, gay marriage, and climate science went out the window as right-wing Republicans strove to hold on to power by any means necessary. Their hypocrisy was out in the open and Bad Religion was having none of it.

"I've always loved science," Brett explained. "I was a punk rocker and a miscreant and a rebellious kid, but a big part of who I am is I've always had my nose in sci-fi novels. I've always believed that progress was possible and desirable, from reading Jules Verne when I was nine years old, to Arthur C. Clarke when I was twelve, and William Gibson when I was sixteen. I've also been interested in hard science and philosophy since I was a kid. I've always been very positive about science and natural philosophy, and against dogma, religion, and authoritarianism. These have been fruitful themes for Bad Religion. 'New Dark Ages' is about the anti-rational, anti-science view that the Republican majority espouses."

For *New Maps of Hell,* Bad Religion went outside the band for a producer. Joe Barresi, however, wasn't a total unknown. The Florida native was an experienced producer, mixer, and engineer who'd worked at some of the best music studios in Hollywood, had earned a reputation for being open-minded and willing to experiment, and had been nominated for a Grammy.

Barresi had produced the Melvins, who recommended him to Pennywise when they were looking for someone to produce *Land of the Free?* After working as an engineer for the High Desert rockers Kyuss for many years, Barresi was brought in by Queens of the Stone Age to produce their groundbreaking first album. Most importantly, Barresi was the engineer and mixer for Bad Religion's previous record.

"*The Empire Strikes First* was the first one that we did with Joe Barresi," Brett said, "and he's a metal producer. *Process of Belief* sounded great, but a lot of bands have a comeback record and then they get wimpier. I wanted to get heavier. Joe's records are heavy. That was the thought behind bringing in Joe, and that started a relationship with him." Brett promoted Barresi from engineer/mixer to co-producer for the record.

Greg and Brett had been working on the album since 2005. They had generated so much material that rumors circulated on the Internet that Bad Religion's follow-up to *The Empire Strikes First* would be a double album. This ended up not being the case. Another erroneous report that made the rounds was that the new record would be called *The Ultra Tyranny*.

Prior to recording, Brooks went to Australia to tour with Tenacious D, and Jay, Brian, and Hetson participated in the ninth annual Punk Rock Bowling tournament, which was held at Sam's Town Casino in Las Vegas, Nevada. Recording started at Grandmaster Recorders in Hollywood in February 2007 and continued into April.

As with the previous album, *New Maps of Hell* had a more aggressive sound than the skate shredders of the late eighties and early nineties, as if the songs were written not for a basement or a club, but for the massive stages of the festival circuit. This is certainly true of the song "New Dark Ages" with its driving bass line, explosive drumming, ferocious pick slides, and layered harmonies. The song takes the temperature of the times and delivers an indictment of the human project:

> *Because we're animals with golden rules*
> *Who can't be moved by rational views, yeah*

The intelligence failures of 9/11, the mishandled elections, and an epically misguided war may have diminished the band's optimism for the future, but they stoked their outrage at a system of government that consistently manipulated its citizens in bad faith. Although Bad Religion's catalog was already full of anthems, in "New Dark Ages" they delivered a perfect strike.

"That was a pretty big hit for us," Brett said. "It got a lot of airplay. I like how surfy it is. I like the vibe. That might be my favorite song from that album. It means a lot to me."

Bad Religion played material from *New Maps of Hell* for the first time during an encore at Santa Monica Civic for a Heal the Bay benefit. Bad Religion released two singles from the album. The first, "Honest Goodbye," came out in May, a few days after they'd played the KROQ Weenie Roast in Irvine, California. "Honest Goodbye" was inspired by Truman Capote's 1965 international bestseller, *In Cold Blood,* an account of a quadruple murder in Kansas by a pair of ex-cons. Although Capote came under fire for manufacturing scenes to fit his version of the story and crafting a sympathetic portrait of the killers, *In Cold Blood* launched the true crime genre.

Bad Religion's short set at the Weenie Roast included the first single as well as the second track on the album, "Heroes & Martyrs." The show served as a warm-up for the 2007 Vans Warped Tour. Although they were limited to playing nine or ten songs a night, by early July, the band was rotating new songs off the album into their set. "New Dark Ages" quickly became a fan favorite and was released as the second single in October.

The Warped Tour lasted from late June until the end of August, and for many band members it was a welcome break. Many fans assume that when their favorite band goes out on the road, they hang out with the musicians they're playing with, and in this manner form lasting friendships that get rejuvenated each time their paths cross. That's not how it works.

But the Warped Tour was different. The sets were short and everyone had the same travel schedule. "Warped Tour is the same story every time," Brian recalled. "We'd wake up, shake off whatever we'd done the night before, and set up camp. The experience of being on the tour left a much bigger impression than the actual concerts. I met so many people because we were basically hanging out in a parking lot with a hundred musicians every day. It was a traveling circus, but no animals were harmed."

Bad Religion released a deluxe version of *New Maps of Hell* the following year. This version included two discs: a CD with all of the material from the original release, plus acoustic versions of seven Bad Religion songs and a DVD packed with videos and bonus material. The acoustic versions included some old and new favorites, such as "God Song" from *Against the Grain,* "Skyscraper" from *Recipe for Hate,* "Sorrow" from *The Process of Belief,* and "Dearly Beloved" from *New Maps of Hell.* Two of the songs, "Adam's Atoms" and "Chronophobia," were exclusive to the deluxe edition, and "Won't Somebody" was a sneak peek of a song that would eventually appear on their next album, *The Dissent of Man.*

The DVD featured videos for "New Dark Ages" and "Honest Goodbye," a free all-ages show presented by MySpace at the House of Blues in Las Vegas that had been recorded the previous summer, and two behind-the-scenes videos about the making of the album and the acoustic EP. With the twenty-fifth anniversary of their first album and the thirtieth anniversary of the band's formation looming in the not-too-distant future, Bad Religion was focused on their fans. By mixing nostalgia over their long career with emerging technology, Bad Religion continued to surprise and delight fans with innovative features, engaging reissues, and arresting shows.

In 2009 Bad Religion went on the Warped Tour in the United States for the fifth—and final—time. The band wrapped up its touring for the year with a return to Australia. The light schedule—if playing the Warped Tour can be considered light—was consistent with their years in between albums, and 2010 was shaping up to be a huge year for the band.

In the late eighties and early nineties, Bad Religion released a new album every year. As they became more popular, this moved to every other year so that they could take advantage of opportunities to play all over the world. After their return to Epitaph, they shifted to releasing an album every three years. The band would spend two years promoting a new release and a year getting ready for the next one.

Bad Religion celebrated their thirtieth anniversary as a band by playing a series of club shows at the House of Blues in Anaheim, San Diego, West Hollywood, and Las Vegas. Each night the band performed a new set list of thirty songs from across the spectrum of their thirty-year career. These shows were recorded, and the best performances were handpicked for inclusion in Bad Religion's second live album, *30 Years Live,* which was distributed on May 18, 2010, as a free download to fans who'd signed up for the band's mailing list.

When *30 Years Live* came out, Bad Religion was in the studio working on their new album, *The Dissent of Man.* The title fuses Greg's ongoing interest in evolutionary biology—Greg was now teaching a course in evolution at UCLA during the winter quarter—and the band's politics of protest. "One of Charles Darwin's most famous books is called *The Descent of Man,*" Greg explained. "*The Dissent of Man* is a play on words."

The band was poised to leave for an eight-week 30th Anniversary European Tour in early June, which left less than a month to make the record. They hadn't planned on being so busy. "Offers came out of the woodwork to tour because it was our thirtieth anniversary," Greg said.

The Dissent of Man is less frenetic than the two preceding albums and picks up where the acoustic EP leaves off, with folksier-sounding songs such as "Won't Somebody," "Turn Your Back on Me," and "I Won't Say Anything," but it keeps the spirit of punk protest alive with rippers like "The Resist Stance" and "Someone to Believe." The goal of the album was to show the evolution of Bad Religion's sound over the course of thirty years. "The most insightful dissent is usually satire," Brett said. "That's what I try to do and that's really the difference between Greg's style and my style. Greg's more of a documentarian. He has an idea and he puts it forth. I tend to be a little more political, but also more ironic and sarcastic."

The Dissent of Man is one of Bad Religion's longer records: fifteen songs in just under forty-three minutes, with six songs longer than three minutes and only one under two: "The Day the Earth Stalled," which opens the album. Bad Religion typically selected one of their faster, shorter songs for the opening track as a way of reassuring the band's oldest and most loyal fans that, no matter how much they'd evolved, they would always remain true to their roots as a hardcore band.

The first single, "The Devil in Stitches," was released in July while the band toured Europe. The album came out at the end of September and was followed by a six-week tour of North America that coincided with the release of their second single, "Cyanide," which once again features Mike Campbell on guitar. Fans who pre-ordered the album received a free digital download of four live tracks that were recorded during the band's thirtieth anniversary club tour but not selected for *30 Years Live*. These included "Generator" and three songs from *Suffer:* "Best for You," "Pessimistic Lines," and "What Can You Do?" The download also featured "Finite," one of Greg's songs that had not appeared anywhere else.[11]

Bad Religion celebrated its thirtieth birthday with a bang: the release of the 30 Years LP Box Set. This massive vinyl reissue of all fifteen studio albums the band had released between 1980 and 2010 included *Into the Unknown*—much to the astonishment of hardcore Bad Religion fans. This was the first time in twenty-seven years the record was made available. The box set was limited to three thousand editions and the records were pressed on red vinyl. The first five hundred fans to order the set also received a free Bad Religion flag. The box set was a huge hit and quickly sold out, despite an asking price of $224.99.

Even after thirty years, the band was still crossing new thresholds and achieving new milestones with the Southern Continents Tour, which included Bad Religion's first show in Jakarta, Indonesia.

It was a time of new accomplishments for Greg as well. The Milwaukee Brewers baseball team invited Greg to sing the national anthem at Miller Park—a thrilling moment for the Wisconsin

---

11. The third and final single from *The Dissent of Man*, "Wrong Way Kids," wouldn't be released until the following year.

native and a highlight of Greg's musical career that didn't involve Bad Religion. Greg also published his first book, *Anarchy Evolution: Faith, Science, and Bad Religion in a World Without God,* in October of 2011. Cowritten with science writer Steve Olson, *Anarchy Evolution* explores many of the same themes Greg had addressed in his songwriting, but through the lens of evolutionary theory. Through a mixture of memoir and science, Greg draws comparisons between punk rock and evolution and makes connections between the two. *Anarchy Evolution* reads like a fusion of class lectures and tour stories told over the course of a long road trip. Unlike his dissertation, which Greg made available to fans through his website, *Anarchy Evolution* was published by Harper Perennial.

Bad Religion had settled into a comfortable three-year album cycle and had proven to record stores, radio stations, and festival organizers that they were still in high demand. Being on Epitaph allowed them to call their own shots and tour if they wanted, when they wanted, for as long as they wanted. The band had outlasted most of their peers in the scene and they had moved into the elder statesman phase of their careers.

As punk rock veterans, the members of Bad Religion could be forgiven for thinking they knew the drill and had a good idea what the future held in store for them. But unbeknownst to the band, storm clouds were gathering on the horizon that would shake up Bad Religion.

25

HERE WE GO AGAIN

BAD RELIGION'S EXTENSIVE CATALOG CONTAINS a wide range of styles and reflects continuous growth and experimentation. It is helpful to think of their work as an extended family. Just as siblings share traits that are characteristic of their gene pool, melodic hardcore is wired into Bad Religion's DNA. It can be heard in everything they do, and it makes their music instantly recognizable. If *Suffer, No Control,* and *Against the Grain* are the rowdy triplets, then *Into the Unknown* is the moody black sheep of the family. Using this analogy, *True North* is the upstart, angry kid who wants to be like her older siblings.

The band started recording their sixteenth studio album in July 2012. The record was co-produced by Brett Gurewitz and Joe Barresi at Joe's House of Compression. A photo of the band in the recording studio was posted to the Bad Religion Facebook page in late July with the caption "Here we go again." All of the members of the band were featured—except Greg Hetson—and his absence would prove to be prescient.

To Brett's way of thinking, *True North* was a reset. "I wasn't happy with the way *The Dissent of Man* came out. Our mission [with *True North*] was to go back to basics and write a bunch of short, straight-forward songs." According to Jay, part of the inspiration for this approach came from Brett's relationship with singer-songwriter Tom Waits, who had recently put out an album of brilliantly concise songs. "We were playing these two-minute punk rock songs and having the greatest time," Jay said.

Of the sixteen songs on the record, ten were written by Greg, including both of the singles, "Fuck You" and "True North." This was something of an anomaly as Brett's songs were usually selected for the singles. "On *True North*," Brett said, "I feel like Greg was the stronger writer, and my stuff was just okay."

One reason why Greg did most of the heavy lifting on *True North* had to do with how personal the project was for him. "I didn't talk about it much at the time," Greg admitted, "because I was going through it, but it was based on a letter that my son wrote to me when he ran away from home. He basically said, 'I'm going to follow my true north.' A lot of those songs have to do with my son and I."

That includes the first single, "Fuck You," which was directly inspired by Greg's eldest son, though "inspired" doesn't really capture the emotion. "You never think your son is going to say, 'Fuck you' to you," Greg said, "but it was shocking when I first heard it! After he said it, it took a while to sink in, but I had a 'Cat's in the Cradle' realization. When you teach your kids to have a healthy punk attitude, you really can't be that angry at them for putting it to good use and spitting it back at you now and again."

These rites of passage—the son's rejection of the father's authority and the forging of his own identity—struck a chord with a lot of fans. In recent years, Bad Religion's records had been driven by the band's anger at the government's imperialist adventures in the Middle East, but for many punk rockers, protest begins at home. What's more punk rock than saying, "Fuck you!" to your parents?

"That's why I wrote the song," Greg said. "I think it reso-nated with a lot of young kids because it's a classic expression of disharmony."

While Brett may not have written as many songs for *True North,* he contributed in other, unexpected ways, like singing on the song "Dharma and the Bomb." "I sang all the verses and Greg sang the chorus," Brett said, "and I don't think anyone even noticed. I'm like the Dee Dee Ramone of Bad Religion. Sometimes I come in and sing a line, but not a whole song. Greg is one of the great punk singers of all time so it doesn't make sense for me to sing."

While *True North* was a rebirth of sorts for the band, on a per-sonal level, Brian was struggling. He was staying at Brett's house in Pasadena, and trying to manage his drinking. During the mak-ing of *True North,* Brian would record from noon to six every day and then leave the studio. He'd get a bottle of scotch and hole up in his room at Brett's house while his bandmates continued without him.

"I had the guitar part of being in Bad Religion dialed in," Brian said, "but I was a mess. I was at the end of my ride, and the sadness of it all was profound. I was no longer able to interact with the people I cared about most." That fall, a few months after Bad Reli-gion finished recording *True North,* Brian went to rehab at Kolmac Outpatient Recovery Center in Silver Spring, Maryland.

Two singles from *True North* were released in advance of the album at the end of 2012. With a song like "Fuck You," they weren't expecting major airplay. Nevertheless, when the album came out in January 2013, *True North* had the highest placement on *Billboard* of any previous Bad Religion record.

Despite its provocative title, or perhaps because of it, "Fuck You" proved to be extremely popular and remains so. On any given day it's typically one of Bad Religion's top five songs on streaming services like Spotify.

Bad Religion began 2013 with a club show at the Echo in L.A. Brett, who frequently played local gigs, joined the band onstage for a rousing set. The band began its North American tour at

Musink Tattoo & Music Festival at the Orange County Fair and Event Center on March 8. The tour lasted six weeks and featured another performance by Brett, who played the tour's penultimate show at the Palladium on April 18. The band had one more show to play on April 20 in Mesa, Arizona, but Hetson didn't make the trip. What happened?

Bad Religion had a long-standing practice of not commenting on changes to their lineup, especially when members left the band, because the band felt it was up to the individual to tell his own story. But to fans paying attention, Hetson's absence felt different, and they were right.

Within the band, concern had been growing for some time over Hetson's erratic play. In rock and roll, a good soundman can hide a bad show from the crowd, but there's no hiding it from your bandmates. It's fairly easy to disguise an off night with music that's loud and fast and generates a great deal of energy, but it puts more pressure on the rest of the band when one member isn't locked in.

The band believed that Hetson's off nights were occurring with greater frequency. While Hetson was able to compensate for his lapses, to some degree, with his energetic stage presence, the band had to make adjustments for the quality of his performance. For the soundman, Ronnie, this meant turning down Hetson's levels and featuring other band members. But things came to a head at the Hollywood Palladium. "He was just having one of those nights," Brooks said.

While most of the band members had, to varying degrees, become accustomed to dealing with Hetson's up-and-down level of play, it came as a shock to Brett, who was understandably upset.

After the show at the Palladium, the band held an emergency meeting and discussed Hetson's immediate future with the band. They weighed the pros and cons of leaving Hetson at home for the True North Tour. They took into consideration Hetson's contribution to Bad Religion over the years, which was significant. Though he wasn't one of the founding members he'd been there virtually from the beginning, playing in "Part III" on *How Could Hell Be Any Worse?* He helped keep Bad Religion going after the failure of *Into the Unknown*, bolstered the band with his celebrity status during their comeback on the Suffer Tour, and brought energy and excitement to their shows with his stage presence.

This wasn't the first time the band had met to discuss Hetson's performance, and they felt the situation was getting worse. With several festivals in the spring, including Coachella, and a long European tour in the summer already on the books, the band believed that bringing Hetson along constituted a liability, and they told Hetson to take some time off.

Hetson's departure bothered Greg a great deal. The two had formed a strong bond during the years between *Into the Unknown* and *Suffer* that no one else in the band shared. Even though he ultimately voted to dismiss Hetson from the True North Tour, Greg did it for the harmony of the band. "I didn't want the unit to be dysfunctional," Greg said, "but he was always one of my best friends."

"There was obviously a lot of pain involved," Brooks said. "When you think of Bad Religion you think of Greg Hetson. He was a staple of the band. For that to be taken away from him had to be heartbreaking. Not only for him, but for the fans."

Hetson's departure created a vacancy that Bad Religion needed to fill in a hurry. While they were reluctant to take a quick-fix approach that would disrupt the continuity of the band, they had to consider the possibility that whomever they brought in would be a temporary hire. "There was a sense," Brian said, "that we needed to go outside our circle of friends who would have loved a shot at the gig."

Brian had someone in mind: an old bandmate from his early days in L.A. named Mike Dimkich. Mike had a punk rock pedigree, knew how to tour, and was a talented guitar player. He'd spent the last six years playing rhythm guitar with the Cult. "He plays like Steve Jones, and dresses like Mick Jones," Brian said of

Mike. "A very old-school punk rock guitar player whose talent was being wasted in the Cult."

Mike was born in St. John's Hospital in Santa Monica. He lived in Memphis and Houston, but after his parents split up, he moved back to L.A. with his mother and they lived in a series of apartments on the Westside.

Mike loved the Sex Pistols and obsessed over the Professionals, which featured ex-members of the Sex Pistols Steve Jones and Paul Cook. "I got into *Rodney on the ROQ*," Mike said. "Saturday and Sunday from eight until midnight, I'd have my yellow Panasonic recorder and just stay by the radio." When the Professionals came to town, they appeared on Rodney's show. Mike called in and peppered Steve Jones with questions about his gear. "It was fucking Steve Jones! I was fucking beside myself!"

Mike joined a number of bands that never went far enough to have a name, but he played in a few talent shows and at high school parties. He was more interested in watching bands play than getting wasted at parties. One of those bands was Chequered Past, Steve Jones and Michael Des Barres's band with Nigel Harrison and Clem Burke of Blondie.

"I would see Chequered Past any chance I got," Mike said. "So amazing. Super loud. Seeing Steve Jones play live blew my fucking mind. It was unbelievable how good he was. He'd see me all the time and I'd bug him and talk to him and get his autograph. I was a punisher because I'd already have his autograph and then I'd go get it again."

Out of this fandom, an unlikely friendship developed after Chequered Past broke up. Jones put another band together that played blues rock at the Central, which would later become the Viper Room.

"Steve would borrow my Fender Blackface Twin amp and my Gibson Les Paul Goldtop, and I would drive him around and roadie for him because he was my hero. I'd buy him burritos because he had nothing. He didn't use me, but he didn't turn down rides or free burritos or the use of my guitars. It was Steve Jones! Perfectly fair trade. I was on the winning end as far as I was concerned."

What Mike didn't know was that Jones's struggles to stay afloat were due to his drug use, but Mike would find out soon enough. Steve was doing session work on a project produced by the infamous Kim Fowley—"who was just as creepy as you could imagine," Mike said. Mike had lent Jones his gear and was giving him a ride back to Jones's apartment, but they kept making stops along the way. "Finally," Mike recalled, "we went someplace in East Hollywood and he came running out and I realized, *He just scored dope.* I was driving around with narcotics. *If we get pulled over,* I thought, *my mom will kill me!*"

Mike was seventeen years old and still in high school. Watching Jones disappear into the bathroom to shoot up was both sad and scary. When Izzy Stradlin came by, Mike knew it was time to go. Although Izzy would go on to be a part of the biggest rock and roll band of the eighties, Guns N' Roses, he was just a junkie then. "It was all so real," Mike said. "It was like a *Scared Straight!* thing or an after-school special." Mike left without his gear only to find out a week later that Jones had hocked his guitar. Mike was able to recover his Les Paul from the pawnshop, but he learned a valuable lesson about drugs and rock and roll.

After high school, Mike went to college at California State University, Northridge, where he continued to get good grades. During his first semester of school, he auditioned to play bass with Channel 3 and went on a short tour of the Midwest, where the band played a lot of gigs in and around Chicago and Detroit. The last show was at the Metro, where they opened for Naked Raygun. Back in Southern California, they played a steakhouse in Pasadena where Jane's Addiction opened for them, but the band fizzled out.

After he left Channel 3, Mike got a spot playing with his on-again, off-again idol in the Steve Jones Band. They opened up for the Hunter Ronson Band with Ian Hunter and Mick Ronson and then did some shows with the Cult, where he got to know

Ian Astbury and Billy Duffy. After the Steve Jones Band broke up, Mike went back to school and started a band with his friend Tim Mosher called High City Miles. Tim was from Washington, D.C., and had introduced Mike to Brian Baker. In fact, when Brian left Junkyard, Tim was his replacement. Tim subsequently recruited Brian to join High City Miles. "We did two gigs with Brian," Mike recalled. "I remember the first one Brian took mushrooms and did the gig."

Mike felt disenchanted with the music industry, and part of the reason was the pressure at home. He'd moved into his mother's house to go back to college, but she became seriously ill and died within a matter of months. Mike was heartbroken, the bills were stacking up, and he had no idea what he was going to do with his life.

High City Miles rehearsed at Cole Studios, where Brian worked and, as luck would have it, the Cult was also rehearsing. Billy Duffy invited Mike to go on the road with them as a second guitar player while they opened for Metallica in Europe. Mike didn't want to leave his friends in the lurch, but the creditors were calling, so he accepted the offer to go on tour with the Cult. It was exactly what he needed.

"I was twenty-four," Mike said. "My mom had just died. I was getting paid. In retrospect, it wasn't much money, but at the time it seemed like a lot. I was touring and playing soccer stadiums. The Cult was still quite big in Europe."

Mike came home and the Cult didn't ask him back for its next tour, which was just as well as they broke up in the middle of it. Mike went through a period where he alternated between joining bands and giving up on music, an experience he compared to what people go through when they quit drugs or alcohol. "I've had some great times, but you've done nothing good for me, and I'm sick of you. Fuck you, I'm done!" At one point, he didn't play his guitar for two years and put all his energy into running marathons and training for endurance events. "Whatever side of my mind that dug music," Mike said, "I put into my running."

The Cult re-formed in 2006 and invited Mike back into the fold. He was playing with another band called Jacked, and for a while he played in both bands, until Jacked faded away. The Cult had gotten another big record deal and the label provided extensive tour support. Over the years, the album sales dropped off, the venues got smaller, and three tour buses were downsized to one. Mike could see the writing on the wall, and that's when he received a call from his old friend Brian Baker.

"I was finishing a bike ride in Malibu when I got a voice mail message. 'Hey, Mike, it's Baker. I'm in between flights. Give me a call. I want to talk to you about something.' Baker and I have been friends for thirty years, but we never talked on the phone. Ever. We would text or I would see him at a party with Tim Mosher and we'd catch up, but Baker doesn't call me. My first thought was, *Maybe Baker's going to rehab.*"

Eventually, Mike got Brian on the phone, and Brian explained the situation with Hetson. Bad Religion was going to Germany and Belgium that weekend to play a pair of festivals, and then the band had a week off before playing a radio show in Tucson, Arizona. Could Mike learn fifty minutes of material by then?

"I said, 'I'll give it my best shot.' I had no idea what was in store. The Cult was easy because every rock club I went to I heard that shit night after night. With Bad Religion I knew the radio hits, like 'Infected' and 'Sorrow.' I knew the slow stuff, but I had no idea what was coming."

With the band en route to Europe, Mike was on his own. He had less than two weeks to prepare and he didn't have any of Bad Religion's music, so Mike rushed out to a used record store to see what he could find. As soon as he started listening to the albums, he knew he was in trouble. The songs were shorter than the Cult's, sometimes much shorter, but more complicated and a hell of a lot faster. "With the Cult," Mike explained, "the songs were mid-tempo, really laid-back. I knew their patterns. I knew how things went. I could learn the new album while driving to the first rehearsal in the car."

The learning curve with Bad Religion was much, much steeper. Mike went to Mates in North Hollywood and rehearsed with Jay and Brooks. They blasted through the songs a few times and that was it. "All right," Jay said, and Mike hoped that it would be, but his first show in Tucson was much more challenging.

"I went up there and was just hacking," Mike said. "They were like, 'Don't worry, you're going to get it.' I wasn't used to going on-stage and not being dialed in. I was just barely hanging in there."

Slowly but surely, Mike started to get the swing of things, but at the fifteenth annual Punk Rock Bowling tournament, the inevitable finally happened. Mike went onstage, and the song "You" was on the set list. A frantic conversation with Jay ensued.

MIKE: I don't know that song.

JAY: What? You don't remember it?

MIKE: No, I've never heard it before. Can we please not play it?

"It was like the nightmare when you show up for a final and realize you've never been to that class before," Mike said.

Once Mike was able to rehearse with the band, he became much more comfortable with the catalog. Bad Religion set out on a six-week European Tour with their new guitar player, came back for a few shows, and then returned to Europe for another six weeks.

In Europe, a strange thing kept happening: people were sharing photos of Mike playing with Bad Religion and tagging him as either Greg Hetson or Brett Gurewitz. While a fan of the band would never mistake Mike for Brett or Hetson, to casual observers Mike blended right in. Bad Religion felt the same way.

Toward the end of the year, Bad Religion announced they would be releasing a new compilation of holiday classics called *Christmas Songs*. The announcement was met with skepticism and surprise. The punk band whose very existence was an affront to Christianity was celebrating the most important day on the Christian calendar?

Actually, the idea wasn't as far-fetched as it sounded. Singing Christmas songs was an integral part of Greg's training and tradition, but Brett also had a deep appreciation for Christmas music. "The heartfelt yearning of religious music has always been very poignant for me," Brett said. "Far more poignant than their literal interpretation. *Christmas Songs* might be our most subversive album because it sneaks a humanist message in through the side door. It says, 'Hey, listener, Bad Religion loves these religious songs not because we believe in god or religion, but because we're human and music is a universal of human nature.' It's our common evolutionary heritage."

It also didn't hurt that Bad Religion had a fund of punked-out Christmas songs to draw from. The band had been a frequent guest at KROQ's Almost Acoustic Christmas. In fact, it was because of Bad Religion that KROQ had to change the name of the event from "Acoustic" to "Almost Acoustic."

"They invited us to play," Brett explained. "We said, 'Yeah, but we don't wanna play acoustic, can we play electric?' They said, 'Sure,' and that opened the door and they changed the name. It was fun. We got to be the big loud band that year and from then on everyone did it. I don't think anybody plays acoustic anymore. Everyone's up there playing with their regular gear."

Each time the band was invited to KROQ's Almost Acoustic Christmas, it performed a Christmas tune like "Little Drummer Boy." But the band didn't stick to popular carols for their album. *Christmas Songs* opens with Greg, an outspoken atheist, belting out "Hark! The Herald Angels Sing," a hymn that has been sung in churches and cathedrals since the early eighteenth century.

Christmas Songs was released at the end of October so that punk rockers could stuff their stockings with a jolly new Bad Religion record. They had good reason to be merry. The band had put out not one, but two albums in 2013. However, fans would have to wait a long time for the next one.

26

THE WORLD AND ELSEWHERE

BEFORE EMBARKING ON THE TRUE NORTH TOUR, Bad Religion released a new group photo with Mike Dimkich. Although the band didn't make a formal announcement, fans correctly assumed that the new photo meant that Hetson was officially out and Mike was officially in. This was confirmed with tweets from both Hetson and the band. After nearly three decades, Greg Hetson was officially no longer a member of Bad Religion and a new era was underway.[12]

As the Bad Religion ship sailed into uncharted territory, so to speak, Mike got his sea legs while he learned Bad Religion's massive catalog. He kept all of his notes and charts with him at all times so that he was ready for whatever the band threw at him. "When we went to South America, I still had a three-ring binder with all my notes in it," Mike recalled. "In Chile, some kids stormed the stage and my notebook was down by my monitor. I

---

12. Although Greg Hetson was contacted numerous times, he declined to be interviewed for this book.

stood over that thing like it was Custer's Last Stand. *If someone takes that book, I'm ruined!*"

Bad Religion was conscious of the fact that their most hardcore fans would come see them play multiple times in a touring cycle, and they took great pride in changing the set list every night so that if someone saw two shows back-to-back, even in different cities, they'd get a different experience. This was great for fans, but not so great for Mike, who was trying to get a handle on all of the material.

To add to the degree of difficulty, the new set list was created the day of the show. During sound check, the band would discuss what they wanted to do differently that night and work on the set list. But sometimes Greg, who would often arrive well after sound check, would have different ideas about that particular show. The band would even consult set lists from the last time they'd played that venue to ensure they gave their loyal fans something new and different. As a result of all these considerations, the creation of the set list could take hours, and sometimes the band wouldn't see the list until a few minutes before they went onstage.

"Watching Greg and Jay try to figure out the set list," Brooks recalled, "even if you weren't involved and were just watching, you would feel anxiety about what those two were trying to achieve. But there's something to be said for putting so much effort and care into creating something for rabid Bad Religion fans going to multiple shows. They're stoked they're going to get a different set list every night."

Jay insisted coming up with a new set list each night wasn't as painful as it appeared. Time-consuming and inefficient? Yes. Stressful? No. "I always say I hate it, but as long as I'm fairly unfettered, I enjoy the challenge. I really do."

Although Bad Religion had a lighting technician, Dave Gibney, a longtime veteran of the punk scene, their light show wasn't so large and cumbersome that it had to be preprogrammed. The bigger the light show, the more static the set, and Bad Religion was determined to keep things flexible. Their willingness to change up their set list and pull from different parts of their catalog on any given night set Bad Religion apart from its peers. The focus of the live performances was almost always on the fans.

"I care about the aesthetic about the band," Brian said. "Not that no one else does, but I like to curate the presentation. When you come see the band, what is the experience like? What does the stage look like? What's the backdrop? I want to make sure we're doing the best we can with that. I'm very protective of the legacy because I think that besides the amazing songs that Greg and Brett have written over the years, we have credibility that cannot be compromised. The credibility that we've earned over forty years isn't something you can buy. You need to nurture that. You can't do stupid shit. I'm sort of a cop about that."

In the spring of 2015, Bad Religion brought their music to a new audience with an old friend. Both Bad Religion and Keith Morris's new band OFF! had been invited to play the Coachella Valley Music and Arts Festival, so they put together a West Coast tour before, in between, and after the festival dates.[13] The members of OFF! piled into their van and followed Bad Religion. "We were basically chasing their bus," Keith recalled.

Bad Religion played back-to-back nights in Denver, Las Vegas, and San Francisco, a schedule they dubbed the Battle of the Centuries. On the first night, the band played Bad Religion songs from the twentieth century, and on the second night they performed material recorded in the twenty-first century. Same band, two wildly different set lists.

As for Coachella, neither Bad Religion nor OFF! knew why they had been invited to the annual gathering of hipsters in the desert. There weren't tons of punk rockers at the festival, but the band made the most of the experience. Bobby Schayer was also at Coachella, but he was working for Jack White as a drum tech and didn't get to spend much time with the band.

After Coachella, Greg added another feather to his cap with the publication of his second book—third if you count his dissertation.

---

13. Coachella runs on consecutive weekends every April.

In *Population Wars: A New Perspective on Competition and Coexistence,* Greg challenges a critical misunderstanding of one of the major platforms of evolutionary theory. In Greg's view, the oversimplification of natural selection as "survival of the fittest" excuses humankind's worst impulses and encourages binary thinking.

For example, a system of thought that views wars as having winners and losers will deem conflict as beneficial to the conquerors. Using examples from the bacterial, viral, and human experience, Greg demonstrates how war is unwinnable and competition is untenable. He argues we'd be better off as a species if we learned to stop killing each other and worked together. This was familiar territory for fans of *The Gray Race,* which pushes back against kneejerk either/or thinking and calls for a more nuanced view of coexistence.

Unlike with his previous book, *Anarchy Evolution,* Greg wrote *Population Wars* himself, and while it provides plenty of insight into the life he has made with his wife, Allison, in Ithaca, New York, it contains fewer anecdotes about the band.

When Bad Religion went on the road that fall, most of the members of the band had no idea that the makeup of its own population was about to change. In Vancouver, on the final stop of their North American tour, Brooks stunned the band when he told them that he had decided to leave.

"They were the hardest phone calls I've ever had to make," Brooks said. "I called one member and finished the conversation and was speed-dialing the next guy because I didn't want anyone to learn via text. I wanted to talk to everyone in person. They were shocked because there was no lead-up. Everyone was supportive, but it wasn't easy."

Brooks had been approached by Avenged Sevenfold, a heavy metal act from Huntington Beach, California, about joining their band. After careful consideration, Brooks decided to accept the offer. "I felt like it was time for a change," Brooks said. "It wasn't anything more or less than that. As a musician, I wanted to explore some different territories and go there. It was difficult. I dwelled on it for some time. It wasn't like I was on the phone the following morning, 'This is my last tour.'"

Even though Brooks had decided to leave, he stayed with the band for the rest of the touring season and went to Europe with Bad Religion that fall. He played his final show on October 10, 2015, at the It's Not Dead Festival at San Manuel Amphitheater in San Bernardino, California. The Brooks Wackerman era, which lasted fifteen years, longer than any other Bad Religion drummer, had come to an end.

Bad Religion returned to California in the familiar position of needing a new drummer. They found one in Jamie Miller, whose route to becoming the band's eighth drummer was perhaps the most circuitous.

Like his future bandmate Brian Baker, Jamie was born in Baltimore, Maryland, where his first exposure to punk rock was listening to D.C. hardcore legends Minor Threat long after they'd broken up. "When I learned about Minor Threat," Jamie said, "that kind of opened my eyes and led me down the road that I'm on now."

Jamie was exposed to music at an early age and grew up in a family of musicians. "I've been a musician my whole life," he said. "Allegedly, I started playing drums at three. I have no recollection of starting to play drums. Apparently, I always played. My earliest memory is playing drums."

Jamie would go to this grandparents' house, where he had a drum kit in the attic, and bang on the drums for hours and hours. His grandparents didn't discourage him and, incredibly, the neighbors never complained. Occasionally, he would play with his dad and his uncle during school talent shows and local gigs. "They'd sneak me into the bar, and we'd play a couple songs," Jamie recalled, "and mom would sneak me out before they got in trouble."

A talented drummer is always in demand, and Jamie played in a number of bands before achieving some success with Mary Suicide ("We were big Jane's Addiction fans," Jamie said about their name), who often played with the veteran heavy metal act

Wrathchild America. When the drummer for Wrathchild America left to play for Ugly Kid Joe, Jamie was invited to take his place. But with heavy metal on the wane, Wrathchild America morphed into Souls at Zero.

In 1996, Jamie joined the nu metal band Snot, which brought him to Santa Barbara, California. The band signed a deal with Geffen, released the album *Get Some,* and toured extensively. They hit the road with Suicidal Tendencies, whose drummer was none other than Brooks Wackerman.

While the band was preparing its second album, the lead singer, Lynn Strait, was killed in a car accident, and Snot disbanded. Jamie immersed himself in session work in L.A. and married the musician Aimee Echo. Together they formed a post-punk band called theSTART. Aimee sang and Jamie played guitar and synthesizer. "I found it easier to find a capable drummer than a guitar player I didn't want to kill," Jamie said. In 2002, theSTART was invited to play Warped Tour when Bad Religion was one of the headliners.

"We were on one of the side stages," Jamie recalled, "and every day Hetson would come watch us. He'd heard of us in the scene in L.A., and liked our band, so he would come and hang out. He would bring other people and invite us to these infamous barbecues that Bad Religion would have. Other people on the tour were like, 'Do not go to the barbecue or Jay Bentley will shoot you with a fire hose!' We'd heard the stories, so we didn't go anywhere near the Bad Religion camp."

In early February 2011, Jamie joined the Austin indie rock band . . . And You Will Know Us By the Trail of Dead, where he could put his skills as a drummer, guitar player, and songwriter to use. In 2015, Trail of Dead went on a break, and he received a strange email from Cathy Mason, who asked if he'd like to try out for "BR."

"A couple years ago," Jamie explained, "I did some session work for Billy Ray Cyrus. People refer to him as BR. I didn't know Cathy, so I assumed it was Billy Ray." Jamie was mildly put out by the request. He'd recorded with Billy Ray and his band. They knew what he could do and what he was like, so why were they making him audition? Instead of firing off a querulous email, he replied, "Absolutely!"

He quickly learned that "BR" stood for Bad Religion and Cathy Mason was their tour manager. Jamie first heard about Bad Religion when he was thirteen years old. "There was a guy in my high school, the one punker at my school, that had the crossbuster painted on his leather jacket. 'What's that?' I asked. 'Bad Religion from L.A. Check it out!' He gave me a bootleg cassette of *Suffer*. The quality was terrible, but it was pretty cool."

Twenty-seven years later, Jamie auditioned with Jay and Brian while Brett took notes on his computer. While he was familiar with the band and its legacy, Jamie didn't realize that Hetson had left the band until he asked Brett, "Where's Hetson?"

Three drummers tried out on the day of Jamie's audition, and Jamie was third. Because it was around the holidays, he didn't hear back from the band for a month, and they requested a second audition at Mates. This time everyone except Mike was there. Jamie felt it went well but suspected he played some of the tunes too fast. As he was pulling out of the parking lot, Brett banged on his window and said, "I didn't want you to leave before telling you that you're at the top of my list. You're my guy!"

While that was gratifying to hear, it didn't make Jamie feel any better about his chances. On all the auditions he'd been on, the only time he didn't get the gig was when he was told he was the lead candidate for the position. That anxious feeling intensified when weeks passed and he didn't hear back from the band. He'd heard through the grapevine the names of some of the other people who'd tried out, and he felt certain that one of them had made the cut. Then he had a strange text exchange with his friend Zach Blair of Rise Against:

ZACH: You got the gig!
JAMIE: What are you talking about?
ZACH: You got the Bad Religion gig.

JAMIE: I haven't heard from anybody.
ZACH: Oh shit!

An entire day went by with Jamie wondering if he had indeed gotten the gig. Finally, the next day, he got a call from Jay Bentley welcoming him to the band, and Jamie had to pretend he hadn't already heard.

Now that he was officially a member of Bad Religion, all he had to do was learn sixteen albums' worth of material. Jay had put Jamie's mind at ease by telling him that out of the four hundred or so songs in the Bad Religion catalog, they would never play half of them. While this turned out not to be the case, it narrowed down the field somewhat. Jamie went online and found photos of set lists from recent shows to figure out which songs he needed to learn and went to work.

Jamie's first gig was at Lollapalooza in Bogotá, Colombia, on March 10, 2016. A few days prior to the show, the band got together to rehearse, and Greg showed up with ten songs he wanted to play that hadn't been on any of the set lists that Jamie had used to prepare. But with a little help from his fellow Baltimorean, Jamie got through the show. "We were onstage in Bogotá," Jamie said, "and I looked at Brian and he gave me a riff. That happened two or three times during the first show. Just give me the first two or three notes and I'll be good!"

Fans noticed the difference in Jamie's style right away. Some complained that Jamie wasn't as technical as Brooks, which was something of an oversimplification. Like Brooks, Jamie came from a musical family, had a heavy metal pedigree, and was an accomplished session musician who could play in a wide range of styles. But when Jamie joined Bad Religion, he was asked to do two things: slow it down and keep it simple. The band wanted to get back to performing songs, particularly their older material, at album speed, and Jamie was happy to oblige.

Although Jamie was aware of the criticism, it didn't bother him. "I've played with so many musicians," Jamie said. "I've played with people with amazing personalities, and I've dealt with unreasonable people with ridiculous egos. I'm not going to add to the muckety-muck. How can I help to make this work? That's been my thing since I was nineteen or twenty. Whatever you need, I'm here to help."

That attitude helped Jamie as he learned the personalities of his new bandmates. All bands have baggage, especially bands that have been around for nearly forty years, and Jamie's likable demeanor and can-do approach made the transition a smooth one.

He quickly won over fans with his energetic style of play. "I have a long swing," Jamie said. "I think it comes from keeping the sticks out of my face. I took a shot when I was young, right in the eye—I've got a scar—so I made a point to keep them away from my face. My swing is an extension of 'I don't want to injure myself ever again,' and it just got bigger. Plus, there's nothing worse than a guy hunched over his drums like it's the hardest thing in the world, because it's not. It's really fun and easy for me, so I'm just back there having fun."

Jamie joined Bad Religion at an unusual time. The band was neither promoting a record nor making a new one, but the extended Bad Religion family had grown. Greg, Brett, and Jay had all remarried and once again had young children at home. Greg and Allison welcomed a new addition to their family on March 10, 2014. Brett and Gina had Nico Moon on July 4, 2009, and Emiko Belle on December 25, 2012. Jay and Natalia Fabia brought Peribeau into the world on April 22, 2012.

The band discussed scaling back their touring operation, only to receive more opportunities to perform. "The minute we say we don't feel like touring much this year," Greg said, "the offers go up and we get more of them."

In spite of the added responsibilities at home, the show went on and Bad Religion remained in high demand. The proliferation of music festivals in Europe and North America made the notion of a conventional tour something of an outdated concept. The new tour manager, their old friend Rick Marino, helped the band manage the logistics of all the clubs and festivals that wanted a piece of Bad Religion.

In the summer of 2016, the band traveled to Europe and then went on the Vox Populi Tour with Against Me! in the fall. Bad Religion's first show of 2017 was at the House of Blues in San Diego the day after St. Patrick's Day, but Greg was already hard at work promoting and supporting his third solo album, *Millport*. Like his previous records, *Millport* was put out by Anti- and features Greg in singer-songwriter mode exploring American roots music like country, bluegrass, and even gospel, but sung with an edge.

Bad Religion fans were well aware of Greg's passion for politics, and his readers knew of his erudition in evolutionary theory, but the songs in *Millport* reveal an interest in local and national history. From the lore of the Finger Lakes in the song "Millport" to the national spectacle of "Lincoln's Funeral Train," Greg's restless imagination is on full display. In interviews, Greg linked *Millport* and *Population Wars,* calling them different expressions of the same theme of persistence in the face of overwhelming change. These projects also served as a reminder that while Bad Religion took time off throughout the year, its front man rarely did. Whether he was composing songs, writing books, teaching classes, or conducting research, Greg remained one of the hardest-working people in the music industry.

That fall Bad Religion played four dates at Fat Mike's Punk in Drublic Craft Beer & Music Festival, which celebrated a somewhat redundant combination of punk and beer. Sponsors pulled the plug on the festival after an incident in Las Vegas, but Punk in Drublic shifted its operations overseas, where it continues to thrive.

The following year marked the thirtieth anniversary of the release of *Suffer,* and the band planned something special for their fans: a series of shows where they played the entire album as an encore. After a set that lasted anywhere from thirty to sixty minutes, depending on the venue, the band walked offstage. The crossbuster backdrop was lowered to reveal the album art for *Suffer,* and Bad Religion returned and blew the crowd away with fifteen scorching songs from 1988.

For Greg and Jay, it was a blast from the past, but for Brian, Mike, and Jamie, it meant learning the "new" material and rehearsing relentlessly. Bands don't write, record, or perform songs in album sequence, but this is how fans experience the music. When a band plays an entire album in the order the songs appear on the record, they are re-creating the moment when their fans fell in love with that album. But *Suffer* wasn't just another album in the band's extensive catalog; it was the album that literally changed everything.

The first *Suffer* anniversary show was held at the Troubadour in West Hollywood in May 2018, and performances of the *Suffer* set continued throughout the year in Europe and North America. The *Suffer* shows were immensely popular with fans and begged the question: would the band do something similar for the thirtieth anniversary of *No Control* in 2019 or *Against the Grain* in 2020?

Bad Religion had something bigger and better in mind.

27

THE END OF HISTORY

THE SIX YEARS, THREE MONTHS, AND SEVEN DAYS that passed between the release of *True North* and *Age of Unreason* represent the longest period of time that fans had to wait for a new studio album from Bad Religion.

The band began recording in October 2018, and the songwriting had been underway for some time before that, but the album effectively got its start on November 8, 2016, when Donald Trump was elected the forty-fifth president of the United States. After the election, members of Bad Religion voiced their dismay on Twitter, with Brett, Jay, and Brian being the most consistent in their critiques.

The first indication that the new Bad Religion record would be about the Trump administration arrived with the release of "The Kids Are Alt-Right," a scathing rebuke of the conman's takeover of the executive branch and its grassroots support from white nationalists and white supremacy groups around the country. The song lambasts right-wing youth for their xenophobic worldview and lack of historical perspective. Some dullards on the extreme right felt the song's lyrics celebrated their cause.

"We put out 'The Kids Are Alt-Right,'" Brett lamented, "and were hit by a tsunami of conservative trolls pretending they don't understand irony and that it's a pro-alt-right song. These people were saying the alt-right is the new punk, which is bullshit. This made me realize how prevalent irony is in my songwriting. For me, the song is a way to say, 'Look how far we've come from the revolutionary youth culture of the Who's *The Kids Are Alright* when today it's uncontroversial for a gang of disgruntled conservatives to claim they're the authentic revolutionaries.'"

Despite the controversy it created, some fans weren't thrilled with the song because they felt like it strayed too far from Bad Religion's format in order to make a point. The band quickly followed up "The Kids Are Alt-Right" with "The Profane Rights of Man," which has a classic Bad Religion structure and sound. Like "The Kids Are Alt-Right," Greg's song has a political message, but to decipher its meaning you have to go back to an eighteenth-century book called *Rights of Man* written by Thomas Paine, one of the country's founding fathers and an important American thinker.

The point of the song is to illustrate that the inalienable rights of man are not divine but secular in origin. The dollar bill may say we are "one nation under God," but our freedoms depend on reason and rational thinking. In other words, we're all equal not as the result of some divine decree but because we are each in our own way worthy, regardless of race, religion, color of skin, or country of origin. The song is a beautiful expression of our founding fathers' best ideals.

For fans, the song, which is just a little over two minutes long, served as a timely reminder that Bad Religion could still deliver old-school muscular music and potent political lyrics. Both songs were recorded in the spring of 2018 at Sunset Sound in Studio 3, the same room where Jim Morrison recorded "The End." Brett and Greg co-produced the songs, but they were victims of the band's high standards and neither made the final cut on *Age of Unreason*. This was nothing new. Greg estimated that while he was getting ready for the new album he had written approximately thirty songs, of which only a handful were "any good."

Although the president had given them plenty of inspiration, the songwriters recognized that Trump was a product of a broken political system. When Trump eventually went away, they reasoned, the problems would remain. So Greg and Brett strove to address the sickness, not the symptoms.

"We called it *Age of Unreason*," Brett explained, "because the songs are about the values of the Enlightenment—humanism and the scientific worldview. That's really what Bad Religion has been about all along, and precisely what's been under attack. It's the closest thing we've ever done to a concept album."

The band reconvened at Sunset Sound for three weeks in October 2018 to record the new material. This time a new figure sat at the board. Carlos de la Garza had produced Teenage Wrist's *Chrome Neon Jesus* for Epitaph, and Brett was so impressed he brought Carlos in to record *Age of Unreason*. While Brett and Greg helped get the sounds they wanted for their respective songs, Carlos provided a fresh new perspective.

Carlos wasn't the only new face in the studio. Two of the band's members—Mike and Jamie—had not made a record with Bad Religion before. Though Mike and Jamie were the "new guys," they both had a deep fund of experience to draw from. Plus, Mike was hardly new. He had been in the band for five years by then and knew the ins and outs of Bad Religion's song structures. "It's not terribly stressful," Mike said.

Nor did Greg and Brett's unique method of songwriting strike Jamie as unusual. He and his wife had taken a similar approach in their band, theSTART. But there were a few surprises in store when he was summoned to lay down the drum tracks for *Age of Unreason*. "The funny thing is Brett's a little more picky," Jamie said. "He hates drum programming, but he likes his beats. So he was the one who was a little more, 'Keep it close to what I've got, but do your thing.' Greg was like, 'Go nuts, and I'll let you know if I don't like it.' You would think it would be the other way around based on their personalities."

As was his habit, Jay tried to be in the studio whenever the band was recording, regardless of what instrument was being tracked that particular day. When asked why he came to the studio on days he didn't have to be there, Jay quipped, "The one time I wasn't around when we made a record, *Into the Unknown* happened." Joking aside, Jay's diligence came from a desire to make something great. "I just want it to be the best thing we've ever done," he said.

Despite the long layoff, a new producer, and new players in the mix, the band demonstrated a high level of communication that seemed borderline telepathic at times. "I have a pretty good idea of what Brett wants," Brian clarified, "because we've worked together for so long and I'm so familiar with Bad Religion. It comes from years and years of experience. Also, we share a lot of arcane musical knowledge. We're fans of the same kind of guitar players. When he asks for something, I know what he's talking about right off the bat. I know what he wants to hear. Also, what he wants to hear is kind of what I would want to hear, too. To me it seems completely natural and intuitive. There's a very good chance I know exactly what he's talking about because I know exactly what he's talking about."

The first single for the album, "My Sanity," was released in November 2018 and received heavy airplay on KROQ. When the band played the song at KROQ's Almost Acoustic Christmas show, kids in the front row already knew all the words. As the old adage goes, the more things change, the more they stay the same.

On the day Bad Religion announced the release date for their new record, they dropped "Chaos from Within," an up-tempo, hard-charging shredder. The song explores Trump's xenophobic obsession with building a wall along America's southern border, but Greg's lyrics suggest the real enemy is a lot closer to home.

Threat is urgent! Existential!
Omnipresent like a skin
But the danger's purely mental
It's chaos from within

"Chaos from Within" echoes the role of personal responsibility that the band first articulated with their theme song, "Bad Religion." The lyrics revisit Brett's explanation of the band's name on *New Wave Theatre*: If you give up your sense of independent thought and you're not thinking for yourself, that's a bad religion. You'd be hard-pressed to find a better explanation for the hyper-partisan tribalism among American voters in the 2016 election.

But even the songs that seem like a direct attack on Trump-era politics are more subtle than their titles suggest. "Do the Paranoid Style," which was released on March 26, 2019, addresses a culture cluttered with conspiracies. The lyrics reference an essay by the twentieth-century historian Richard Hofstadter called "The Paranoid Style in American Politics." This essay, which was published in 1964, discusses the historical precedent for our country's long love affair with conspiracy theories. "The paranoid style is an old and recurrent phenomenon in our public life," Hofstadter writes, "which has been frequently linked with movements of suspicious discontent." The essay goes on to cite examples dating back to before the Civil War.

This is classic Bad Religion. By putting the problem of InfoWars-era conspiracy mongering in a historical context, Bad Religion reminds us that we're not dealing with a new and intractable problem, but old tricks delivered in a new way. By pushing back and thinking for ourselves we can see these "movements of suspicious discontent" for what they really are: a bad religion.

The video for "Do the Paranoid Style" features a hypnotic montage of black-and-white dance footage that emphasizes both the breakneck pace of the song and our propensity for fads that in retrospect seem foolish. That these dancers look ridiculous, and in some cases crazed, underscores the point of the song. Just as these dancers had deluded themselves into thinking that what they were doing was cool, those that slavishly accept a warped and unsubstantiated view of politics, science, or history are destined to look like fools. In other words, history is not going to be kind to us, so stop being led by your emotions and think.

That's a lot for a song that's a little over one hundred seconds long, but it demonstrates how much thought has gone into every track on *Age of Unreason*. Some of the songs are more direct without being too on the nose. For instance, Brett wrote "End of History" while on a family vacation in Iceland. Reading the news reports from home while he was so far away provided the perspective he needed to synthesize the values of the Enlightenment, the philosophy of Karl Popper, and the crisis surrounding asylum seekers fleeing from political turmoil in a catchy, clever song:

Sweet children, Locke's burden
Why did mother draw the curtains?
Free will is your dilemma
What will the dust remember
Tell me where do you really want to be
At the end of history?

Musically, "End of History" is a throwback to the early days of punk that Brett loved as a kid. "It's got a little bit of a Dead Boys vibe," Brett said. Whereas "Faces of Grief," a song Brian wrote, is much more in your face and reflects his hardcore roots.

Age of Unreason represents a new way to look forward, not by scowling at the world and saying how shitty things are, but by having the courage to stick to bedrock principles and beliefs that are worth believing in, even if those ideas are three hundred years old. To paraphrase what the poet Allen Ginsberg said about LSD, it's not the trip, but what you do with it. After all these years, Bad Religion still demands its listeners to ask themselves "What Can You Do?"

Age of Unreason hit the streets at a dark time in America's history. The release of the heavily redacted Mueller report, and all the political spin that preceded it, underscored the partisan politics that had hijacked the will of the people since Hillary Clinton lost to Donald Trump in the 2016 presidential election despite receiving three million more votes. With each nonsensical proclamation Trump made on Twitter, a platform that helped get him elected through influence campaigns orchestrated by WikiLeaks and the Russian government, Trump gave Christian fundamentalists, Second Amendment advocates, climate deniers, and white nationalists something to cheer about. As backward as things seemed, it would have been easy to conclude that it must have been an awfully depressing time to be Bad Religion. After all, weren't Brett and Greg writing songs about all this stuff four decades ago?

In spite of the darkness out of which *Age of Unreason* emerged, there was considerable optimism in the Bad Religion camp about their new album as they prepared to go out on tour. "We've been doing this for a really long time," Jay said, "and not much has changed. Maybe that's just human nature. All I know is the older you get the more focused your anger gets."

Bad Religion wasn't the first punk rock band to respond to the Trump presidency. Protests from the punk community emerged while he was still a candidate. Some music critics naively stated that Trump would be good for punk rock. While the notion that an administration that goes out of its way to disenfranchise the country's most vulnerable citizens could be "good" for anything was problematic, it prompted critics to think about Bad Religion's new record in terms of their legacy.

Yes, the band had been singing about these things for a really long time, but who else who was around back then was still doing it? A lot of popular punk bands have reunited to play shows, but who else was still writing and releasing music? Who else from the earliest generation of punk was still inspiring the next generation by taking on the issues that matter most *right now*?

While Greg felt that it was too early to discuss the merits of individual songs on *Age of Unreason,* he was extremely pleased with the final product. "I'm an overly sensitive artist," Greg confided.

"I don't like hearing criticism. If it's not constructive, I beat myself up over it, and feel like I've let people down. That's shielded me from being too optimistic early on. I can speak more confidently about *True North* than *Age of Unreason*. But as a mature artist, I've never felt more satisfied than I do now."

That's a telling statement from someone who has been at the front of Bad Religion for the last forty years. Through the course of the band's many highs and lows, only one person has been onstage every time Bad Religion has performed, and that's Greg Graffin. From the very beginning when Greg declared, "This isn't art, this is suicide," to the dissolution of the L.A. punk scene, to the rebirth and revitalization of the genre after *Suffer*, through the Atlantic years between Brett's departure and return, to the latest chapter in this improbable punk rock saga, Greg's voice has been the one constant.

Greg has recorded on every album, sung every song, and performed at every show. He's witnessed every phase of the band's evolution. No one else in Bad Religion can say that. So, not only is his optimism remarkable for someone who has been in the game for so long, it masks his drive and determination. "There is a belief within the band that we still haven't achieved what we set out to do," Greg said, "and if you don't believe you can achieve greater things, you might as well retire."

Bad Religion doesn't put out records to put out records. They aren't a nostalgia act, nor are they beholden to a major label. Bad Religion is the captain of its own destiny. They do what they want and no one can tell them otherwise. Unlike many of their peers, Bad Religion has been touring steadily since 1988, so they have experience and momentum on their side.

Their touring operation isn't a stop-start affair, but an ongoing enterprise headed by their friend and tour manager, Rick Marino. The crew is led by longtime soundman Ronnie Kimball, who has been working with the band since 1994. Lighting director Dave Gibney was the soundman for the Circle Jerks and was in the band Fear Factory prior to working for Bad Religion. Even the techs have long tenures with the band. Greg "Shakes" Stocks signed on as the drum tech back in 2009, when Brooks was still the drummer. The Orange County native was in the band Hellbound Hayride and collaborated with Steve Soto before working as a drum tech for the Adolescents, Manic Hispanic, and Lagwagon. Since 2010, Gavin Caswell has been working as a guitar tech for Bad Religion whenever his own band, Senses Fail, isn't recording or on the road. Tess Herrera joined the crew in 2013 as a shiatsu massage therapist. She started with the Warped Tour in 1998 and went back every year until Bad Religion hired her. The fans might not notice them or know their names, but they make the show go.

Even more important than the crew are the fans, who will come out and support Bad Religion wherever they go, whenever they come. Bad Religion doesn't need a new album to tour. Whether it's Jacksonville, Florida, or Oulu, Finland, there are Bad Religion fans eager to see them.

And those numbers are growing. As strange as it may seem, Bad Religion has never been more popular than they are right now. People are finally appreciating the role Bad Religion played in the history of rock and roll. In the seventies and eighties punk was declared dead more times than a villain in a horror movie, only for its shambling corpse to come to life so it could be killed again and again. After punk went mainstream in the mid-nineties, music critics needed to find a way to connect the dots between its "death" after the Ramones, the Sex Pistols, and Black Flag, and its "rebirth" when the Offspring, Green Day, and Blink-182 became superstars. Their solution to this conundrum was to anoint Nirvana as the bridge between the old and the new, which was convenient since Kurt Cobain was venerably dead and in no position to protest.

Fans of Bad Religion know there's more to this story. They don't have to be reminded of the impact *Suffer* had on the punk rock scene, how it single-handedly rejuvenated a style of music that was hard, fast, and fun to listen to. That it was distinctly Southern

California in both its DNA and its aesthetic. That it became the soundtrack for every bored suburban kid with a skateboard who'd been waiting their whole life for someone, anyone, to say "Do What You Want."

Their former manager, Michele Ceazan-Fleischli, believes that "because of Bad Religion's longevity, people take them for granted." But that's starting to change. The public is beginning to understand what Bad Religion's fans have known since 1988: *Suffer* was the spark, the catalyst, the game changer. Just as fans were beginning to accept that punk really was dead, Bad Religion's furious fusion of melodies, harmonies, and intelligent lyrics reignited the genre. Without *Suffer*, Epitaph would have never gotten off the ground. Without Epitaph there's no Pennywise, no NOFX, no Rancid, and no Offspring. And without those bands there's no punk explosion in '94, no Vans Warped Tour in '95, and no Hot Topic (perhaps not a bad thing). Moreover, without the mainstreaming of punk, all the bands that split up the punk rock pie into different subgenres, from Good Charlotte to New Found Glory, Fall Out Boy to My Chemical Romance, would have had very different careers. In other words, without Bad Religion the rock and roll landscape would look very different today.

"People are finally filling in the chapter between 1983 and 1991," Greg said. "What happened? Two words: Bad Religion."

Another reason for the band's long-standing success is its tradition of writing songs that maintain Bad Religion's signature sound, but exceed expectations. "I want to fight the idea that we're just a punk rock band," Jay said. "I want to prove that we're outside of everything. I don't mind being lumped in with people. But the truth of Bad Religion is we're not like anyone. We never have been. We've never been part of anything. We came from a place that was ostracized. People thought we were assholes for what we were saying. We were outside of every box possible. We were okay with that. Now, since punk rock has become mainstream we're part of that bigger box, but we're not really like these people. We're not like anybody."

One way the band flouts the perception that they play a particular style of punk is with their set list. Fans come to Bad Religion knowing what to expect, but have no idea what they're going to get. Bad Religion can put together a set of mid-tempo songs that are over three minutes long that perfectly fit the pop format. If you saw this set and had never heard Bad Religion before you might say to yourself, *That's not a punk band.*

Or, Bad Religion can put together a set that's nothing but barn burners under two minutes long and leaves fans walking away thinking, *Holy shit! That was the most intense show I've seen in decades!* Brett and Greg have crafted heartfelt anthems and superfast hardcore songs during every phase of their career, but they've also written plenty of material that doesn't fit either mold.

Bad Religion is its own subgenre. It doesn't fit into easy Aristotelian binaries. Bad Religion isn't this or that, but both at once, and it's always been that way. The disaster that was *Into the Unknown* taught Greg and Brett how to experiment with their sound without disenfranchising the fans who support what they do. They figured out they had a shot at getting their music on the radio if they packaged it a certain way. It had to be melodic, it couldn't be too fast, and it had to fit a pop formula. Bad Religion could do all of those things, but it wasn't *all* they could do, nor did they let it limit what they set out to accomplish.

"When I look at our catalog," Jay said, "I think of bands who are considered our peers that have never done anything like we've done and never will." For example, when the band kicked off the Age of Unreason Tour at the Roxy on the Sunset Strip, the encore featured all of *No Control* to celebrate its thirtieth anniversary. But the biggest surprise of the night came when the band played "Dichotomy" from *Into the Unknown.*

"I was going through songs," Jay said of his decision to add "Dichotomy" to the set list, "and thought, *If this song ended right here before the two-minute keyboard solo, it would be a pretty good song. I'm going to put it on the set list. See what happens.*" Just as "Dichotomy" surprised fans, the selection caught his bandmates off guard. After all, this was the album that broke up the band, and Jay was the first defector.

"I brought that song to the band when we were in rehearsal," Jay said. "We put the tape on and we learned it. Got it down pretty well. When Greg came in he said, 'Really?' I said, 'Yeah. Let's try this. If we're all aware of the power this song has, I think we can deliver it.'"

And deliver they did. What's so remarkable about the inclusion of a song from an album that came out in 1983 and that no one in the band knew how to play was that "Dichotomy" was sandwiched between the new material from *Age of Unreason* and songs from *No Control* they rarely, if ever, played. Didn't they have enough on their plate?

"Some bands do the same thing night after night," Jay explained. "They don't care that it's boring because it's *all* boring to them. They don't want to be there. They want to play and leave. We're not like that. We want to mix it up every night and keep it exciting and invigorating. Rock and roll is supposed to be dangerous and mixing up the set list is as dangerous as it gets."

The ugly truth of most rock and roll bands that achieve a degree of popularity is that eventually they become businesses that play just to make money. Not only do the members of these bands often despise one another, but they stop creating music together. Once that happens, in Brett's view, they are "not artistically credible." They become human jukeboxes: put some money in and out come their greatest hits. Bad Religion could never do that.

Jay may have told Jamie when he joined the band that there were songs that Bad Religion would never play, but this is no longer the case. Bad Religion has written approximately four hundred songs and none of them are off the table. With the release of *Age of Unreason*, the band wanted to pull songs from their catalog that fit the theme of the new album. When the band kicked off its 2019 tour, the set list included songs they didn't typically play, like "Flat Earth Society" from *Against the Grain*, "Struck a Nerve" from *Recipe for Hate*, and "Them and Us" from *The Gray Race*.

If there's something about the Bad Religion experience that fans are nostalgic for, they will most likely hear it when they go see the band play (even if the band doesn't play their favorite song from their favorite album). And those fans will leave with something else: a glimmering recognition that Bad Religion is not the band they thought they were. Sometimes the surprise comes from new material, and sometimes it comes from their catalog.

An example from 2018 was the inclusion of "Streets of America" from *The Gray Race*. "I don't think anybody thought that song was worthy of coming back," Jay said. It had been twenty-two years since the album was released, and Bad Religion no longer played the song with any kind of frequency. But the band believed that true fans would love it and casual fans would scratch their heads over the inclusion of a song that was only nominally punk. For Bad Religion it was a way to go back and revisit moments in time that were truly special to them. "The downside of having all of this material," Jay said, "is that eventually you have to put it back in the closet. Even if you love them you have to say, 'Bye, it's been fun, but now you gotta go and get replaced with something else.'"

The replacements from *Age of Unreason* are exceptional in their timeliness and timelessness. Not only are they precisely what the world needs to hear right now, they serve as an inspiration to keep going, whether you're a fifty-year-old doing your part, or a fifteen-year-old freaking out about your place on this ball of confusion. For example, the bridge from "Lose Your Head" provides words to live by no matter how old you are:

And when your life endeavor evades your clever meddling
It's only headphone weather, so get your head together

"Get your head together" is something each member has striven for and struggled with throughout the course of the band's convoluted history. If being in a band is hard, being in a successful band is next to impossible. The demands come from all over the place: family members, fans, managers, bandmates, booking agents, business partners, publicists, promoters, and on and on it goes. It becomes so overwhelming that sometimes something as simple as responding to a guest list request from a close friend—or resolving an argument over one—feels insurmountable.

"Most bands never find the balance," Brett said, and balance is what makes the engine go. Bad Religion has achieved that balance, but it wouldn't have survived this long without sacrifice and effort from each member of the band. "We've tried to kill this band so many times," Brian confessed. "But it just won't die." Brian's tongue-in-cheek response belies a larger truth that each member of the band had to go through prolonged periods of darkness, sometimes more than once, in order to reach the light. Along the way, as various members battled their addictions, their bandmates often bore the brunt of these skirmishes, but none more so than Greg, who has never been tempted by the pleasures and perils of intoxication. But here they are in their fortieth year with their seventeenth studio album in the books. It took a lifetime of labor to get to this moment, and the band makes no apologies for making the most of it.

Bad Religion is exactly where it wants to be. The band isn't in competition with anyone else. They don't care about what the industry deems a success. They leave that to those whose job it is to track album sales and song streams to determine which artists are making the most money for their label. Bad Religion's story is not a story of perseverance, although that's certainly part of it; they persevered because they had something to say. The conversation they started in the Hell Hole forty summers ago about what they wanted to do as a band continues to this day.

They are in it for one another and for their fans. When the band embarked on their 2019 tour, they were genuinely excited to be sharing their new album with the world. "We're gonna go out on the road, and we're gonna play, and we're gonna talk to people," Jay said. "We'll ride this wave [of *Age of Unreason*] for a few years and then we'll see what happens. People always ask, 'How far out do you plan?' I try to be a year ahead. But if you're saying what's going to happen next week? I can't tell you. We're playing a show. It might be our last."

Will there be more albums from Bad Religion? Or will *Age of Unreason* be their epitaph?

For Bad Religion, the future remains to be written, but the thing that worked against them in the beginning—their youth—is squarely on their side now. Because they were teenagers when they started the band, they are all relatively young to be playing the role of elder statesmen.

But if *Age of Unreason* is Bad Religion's swan song, the kids from the Valley will have gone out on a high note. "With *Age of Unreason* we achieved our objective," Greg said, "and it's an objective we have stood for all along. Get people to think, and reject the falsities of pseudo-science and superstition. Punk is the last place you would think to look for these truths. Who would think to consult a punk album about objective truth and the enlightenment? It's a paradox, but this speaks to one of the enduring truths about punk: You can't tell by looking at a punker with a Mohawk if you're looking at a philosopher."

While it's reasonable to expect the band to slow down, it would be shocking if these philosophers of punk suddenly stopped making music. Whether they go out on one final tour and call it quits or play for another decade, they will leave behind an enduring legacy as one of the most influential punk bands in the world. Bad Religion represents nothing less than the marriage of punk rock protest and intellectual inquiry. Theirs is not a legacy of mindless fury, nor of self-effacing debasement, but one that champions questioning authority, challenging dogma, and resisting easy answers. For the last forty years, Bad Religion has urged its audience to think for themselves, and by doing so has made the world a more intelligent place, one lyric, one listener, at a time.

ACKNOWLEDGMENTS

BAD RELIGION would like to thank the following people for their various contributions to our health, happiness, and sanity over the years: Julie Anastasio, Ian Astbury, Kelly Bakst, Steven Barlevi, Joe Barresi, Rick and Sherry Bragger, Andrew Buscher, Gavin Caswell, Arnel Celestial, Tom Clement, Katy Corsmeier, Mike de la Cruz, Greta Dewey, Susan Donner, Roger Dorresteijn, Billy Duffy, Paul du Gre, Aimee Echo, Willy Ehmann, Darryl Eaton, Pete Finestone, Michele Ceazan-Fleischli, Tim Gallegos, Jens Geiger, Michelle Gerien, Dave Gibney, Mike Gitter, Danny Goldberg, Lisa Graffin, Eric Greenspan, Danny Heaps, Tess Herrera, Greg Hetson, Greg and Bonnie Husebye, Steve Jones, Peter Katsis, Ronnie Kimball, Diane Kirchner, Heike Kramer, The Kleinheinz Family, Lucky Lehrer, Treva Levine, Jon Luini, Kevin Lyman, Rick Marino, Cathy Mason, Tim McDuffy, Howard Menzies, Jim Miller, Chantal Neeten, Frank Nuti, Steve Olson, Ric Ocasek, Alex Perialas, Jay Phelan, David Pollack, Jack Price, Jack Rabid, Elliott Roberts, Todd Rundgren, Debby Sander, Jodi Sax, Bobby Schayer, Konrad Schraml, Megan Shull, Gary Soltys, Donnie Spada, Greg Stocks, Taylor Thompson, Paul Tollett, Gary Tovar, Brooks Wackerman,

Andy Wallace, Christina White, Ian Winwood, Angry Andy Wright, and Jay Ziskrout.

Extra-special thanks . . .

GREG GRAFFIN: I would like to thank those who helped shape my musical identity before Bad Religion existed: Mom (Marcella) Graffin and Dad (Walter) Graffin, Grant Graffin, Uncle Stanley Carpenter, Wryebo Martin, Jeff Shimeta, Art Shannon, Frank Mejia, Tommy and Danny George, Dave George, Jon Murer, David Bragger, and Mrs. Perkins. Later came treasures for which I feel most grateful, Allison, Ella, Graham, and Stanley, without whom most of this journey would be meaningless.

BRETT GUREWITZ: Richard and Lorrie Gurewitz, Gina Gurewitz, Max Gurewitz, Frida Gurewitz, Nico Moon Gurewitz, Emiko Belle Gurewitz, Sue Lucarelli, Jeff Abarta, Donnell Cameron, John Albert, Peter Robbins, the Ramones, the Germs, and the Adolescents.

JAY BENTLEY: Brett, Greg, JZ, Pete, Hetson, Bobby, Brian, Brooks, Dim, and Jamie. ♥ Steve Soto.

BRIAN BAKER: Victoria Reis and Ian MacKaye.

JIM: When I was in the Navy, a skinhead with a fondness for hardcore turned me on to Bad Religion. We made a mixtape from his record collection that included the *Back to the Known* EP. I played that tape all over the Western Pacific and it became the soundtrack to a lot of great memories. I can still recall racing across a highway in Yokosuka, Japan, while singing "Frogger" like a loon. After I got out of the Navy, I took that tape to college in ultraconservative southwest Virginia, where it helped keep me sane, and then I brought it back to Southern California when I returned for good. There are only five songs on *Back to the Known*, a fraction of Bad Religion's output, but I've been carrying them with me for over thirty years. Without that tape, I never would have had the courage to write Bad Religion's history. But I couldn't have done it without early readers Todd Taylor and Michael Fournier (*Razorcake* por vida!) or the incomparable Amanda Johnston for her impeccable editorial assistance. The Bad Religion Page was my go-to resource for information about the band's enormous output and impact. (If you're a fan, you owe it to yourself to check it out at www.thebrpage.net.) I also owe a debt of gratitude to Jack Rabid of *The Big Takeover*, who has been chronicling the band since the beginning. Thanks to everyone who shared their story with me, including former and current members of Bad Religion. Sincere thanks to Tod Goldberg and Maggie Downs for keeping an old sailor rat in their thoughts, and to Rick Marino, Ben Schafer, and Peter McGuigan for making the magic happen. I am especially grateful to Bad Religion's talented and hardworking crew, whose humor and camaraderie brought a great deal of joy to the enterprise. Lastly, a huge thank you to Greg, Brett, Jay, and Brian for trusting me with their stories and welcoming me into their homes / offices / green rooms / tour buses / lives. My deepest gratitude goes to my wife, Nuvia, and daughter, Annie, who have listened to a lifetime's worth of Bad Religion songs over the last few years.

DISCOGRAPHY

Bad Religion (EP)

1. *How Could Hell Be Any Worse?*

2. *Into the Unknown*

   Back to the Known (EP)

3. *Suffer*

4. *No Control*

5. *Against the Grain*

6. *Generator*

   80–85 (compilation)

7. *Recipe for Hate*

8. *Stranger Than Fiction*

9. *The Gray Race*

   All Ages (compilation)

   Tested (live album)

10. *No Substance*

11. *The New America*

12. *The Process of Belief*

    Punk Rock Songs (Sony release)

13. *The Empire Strikes First*

14. *New Maps of Hell*

15. *The Dissent of Man*

    30 Years Live (live album)

16. *True North*

    Christmas Songs

17. *Age of Unreason*

INDEX

"21st Century (Digital Boy),"
    120–122, 163, 183
30 Years Live (album), 264–266
30th Anniversary European Tour,
    265
80–85 (album), 146–147, 149
120 Minutes (TV show), 138
"1000 Memories," 228

Abarta, Jeff, 139–140
Adams, Jay, 52–53, 55
"Adam's Atoms," 264
the Adolescents, x, 22, 26, 35, 47,
    55, 63, 76, 147, 298
The Adventures of Hersham Boys
    (album), 39
AFI, 227
"Against the Grain," 119
Against the Grain (album), 82, 119,
    122–126, 129–130, 146, 148,
    160, 163, 264, 268, 289, 301

Against the Grain Tour, 129, 141
Against Me!, 288
Age of Unreason (album), 290–292,
    295–297, 300–304
Agnew, Dennis, 52–53
Agnew, Rikk, 47
Ain't Life a Mystery Tour, 183, 190,
    197
Albert, John, 76–77, 209
albums, list of, 308. *See also specific*
    albums
All Ages (album), 196–197
Alley Cats, 36
Allman, Duane, 230–231
the Allman Brothers, 153, 230–231
"Along the Way," 74–75
Along the Way (video), 114
"American Jesus," 150–151, 162
American Lesion (album), 202, 206,
    214–215, 222, 258–259
"American Society," 121

Anarchy Evolution: Faith, Science, and Bad Religion in a World Without God (book), 91, 267, 282
And Out Come the Wolves (album), 208
. . . And You Will Know Us By the Trail of Dead, 284
"Anesthesia," 120
Anthrax, 204
Anti- (record label), 245, 252, 259, 288
Armstrong, Tim, 159, 163, 173
Astbury, Ian, 275
Atlantic Records, 127, 152–156, 160–164, 168–173, 183, 190, 197–201, 206, 221–223, 228, 231–233, 240, 246–247
"Atomic Garden," 137–138
Aukerman, Milo, 65
"Automatic Man," 108
Avenged Sevenfold, 282

Baby . . . You're Bummin' My Life out in a Supreme Fashion (album), 82
Back to the Known (album), 75, 79, 93–94, 121, 146
Bad Brains, 59, 148, 192
Bad Religion
  awards for, 213–214
  beginnings of, ix–xi, 1–13
  booking agent, 106, 112, 115, 125
  challenges for, xi, 69–77, 97–98, 104–130, 302–303
  changing course for, 92–103
  changing demographics of, 165–166
  changing music of, 64–70
  changing record labels, 152–156
  Christmas songs and, 162, 277–278
  conflict within, 142–144, 166–175
  crew for, 216–217, 297–298
  critics of, 37, 149–154, 246, 296–298
  at crossroads, 231–233
  debut album by, 40, 43–47
  demo tapes by, 11, 26, 222
  discography, 308
  DVDs by, 256, 259, 264
  early years of, ix–xi, 1–70
  fans of, 48–68, 141–142, 197–198, 279–281, 298–304
  first recordings by, ix–xi, 1–13, 28–40, 43–47
  first shows for, 21–23
  fortieth year of, 303
  founding members of, ix–xi, 1–23
  future of, 303–304
  influences on, 23–25, 61–63
  intelligent lyrics by, x–xi, 28–34, 63, 95–99, 105–132, 149–150, 156–161, 165–166, 196–207, 246–247, 299–304
  logo of, xi, 6–7, 37, 75, 98, 113, 187, 285, 288
  longevity of, 298–300
  marketing/promoting, 34–35, 99–100, 111, 197–200
  media reviews of, 37, 149–154, 246
  music videos by, 137–138, 151, 183, 259
  origins of, 1–13
  popularity of, x–xi, 26–30, 47–57, 92–130, 140–156, 186–219, 260–278, 298–304
  pressure on, 116–130, 143–144
  reflecting on, 296–304
  regrouping, 72–77
  reuniting with, 85–87, 92–98

rumors about, 72, 145–146, 208, 259, 262

thirtieth anniversary of, 264–267

tours of, 86–87, 100–102, 111–115, 124–129, 140–142, 148–152, 156, 181–190, 197–202, 214–221, 229–236, 248–249, 255–259, 263–267, 270–272, 276–289, 297–301

Bad Religion: Live at the Palladium (DVD), 256, 259

Bad Religion Research Fund, 215

"Bad Religion" theme song, 8, 27, 74, 93, 146

The Bad Times (newsletter), 185

Bad4Good, 237

the Bags, x

Baker, Brian

audition of, 181–182

background of, 147, 176–179, 275–276

bowling tournament and, 262

collaborating on material, 190–194

early years of, 147, 176–179

former bands and, 147, 176–181, 186

new albums and, 240–241

new material for, 289, 293

personal issues for, 270

in recording studio, 179–180, 204, 225–226

reflections of, 303

replacing Gurewitz, 176, 180–183, 186

tours and, 181–187, 221, 234–235, 263, 281, 289

Bakker, Jim, 8

Bakker, Tammy Faye, 8

"Bang the Drum All Day," 223

Barker, Travis, 229, 238

Barresi, Joe, 261–262, 268

Barrett, K. K., 83

Bash & Pop, 180

Bat Out of Hell (album), 223

Bators, Stiv, 83

Bauhaus, ix

the Beach Boys, 1, 73, 235

Beat, Nickey, 135

the Beatles, 2, 17, 129, 138

"Believe It," 233–234

Benatar, Pat, 242

Beneath the Shadows (album), 60, 64, 66

Bentley, Hunter, 164

Bentley, Jay

children of, 164, 287

conflicts and, 143–144, 166–175

at crossroads, 232–235

divorce and, 256

early years of, 2–5, 18–23, 27–57, 62–70

first shows for, 21–23

as founding member, 2–5, 18–23

Hetson and, 84–85, 115

hockey and, 214

in hospital, 76–77

influences on, 62–63

leaving Bad Religion, 73, 84

marriage of, 142, 164, 287

personal issues for, 141–143, 218–219, 256–258

popularity and, 92–130

in recording studio, 137–139, 162, 222, 226, 292–293

reflections of, 296, 299–303

returning to Epitaph, 233–235, 240

reuniting with, 85–87, 92–98

as roadie, 55

sales goals of, 199–200

tours and, 86–87, 100–102, 113–115, 124–126, 141–142, 148–152, 216–219, 231–233, 256–257, 280–289

Bentley, Miles, 164
Bentley, Peribeau, 287
"Best for You," 100, 266
"Beyond Electric Dreams," 254
The Big Takeover (fanzine), 75, 206
"The Biggest Killer in American History," 222
Billboard (magazine), 206, 231, 246, 270
"Billy Gnosis," 62
bin Laden, Osama, 250
Bingenheimer, Rodney, 25–27, 59, 73, 156, 273
Biohazard, 152, 202
Black, Frank, 254
Black Flag, x, 1–2, 21–22, 31, 40, 50, 63, 73, 109, 113, 121, 134, 147, 181, 298
"Black Magic Woman," 221
Black Sabbath, 19, 62, 230
Blair, Zach, 285
Blink-182, 229–231, 236–238, 248, 298
Blondie, 35, 273
Blue (album), 149
Blue Hawaii (film), 131
Blue Stingrays, 253
Bomp! Records, 25, 70, 79, 82
"Boot Stamping on a Human Face Forever," 252
Born to Run (album), 208
Bowie, David, 18, 63
"The Boxer," 246
Bradbury, Dan, 53–54
Bragger, David, 258–259
Braun, Alison, 133
"Broken," 245
Burke, Clem, 236, 273
Burroughs, William S., 160
Bursting Out tour, 42
Bush, George H. W., 150

Bush, George W., 249–256
the Buzzcocks, 23, 116, 248

Cameron, Donnell, 87
Campbell, Mike, 139, 253, 266
Campino, 215
"Can't Stop It," 241
Careless, 179
Caron, Doug, 106
the Cars, 192
Cathedral of Tears, 85
Cat's Cradle (book), 160
"Cease," 202, 248
Ceazan-Fleischli, Michele, 217, 220–222, 299
Celestial, Arnel, 42
"Centerfold," 46
"Change of Ideas," 248
Channel 3, 274
"Chaos from Within," 293–294
"Chasing the Wild Goose," 63
Cheap Trick, 177
Cheech and Chong, 73, 131–132
the Cheifs, 35
Cheney, Dick, 251
Chequered Past, 273
Cherry Poppin' Daddies, 216
China White, 35, 40, 43
Christian Death, 47, 63, 76, 134
Christmas Songs (album), 162, 277–278
Chrome Neon Jesus (album), 292
"Chronophobia," 264
the Circle Jerks, 22–28, 31, 40, 45, 47, 51, 61, 63, 71, 74, 83–87, 92, 100–101, 113, 119, 131–134, 164, 174, 181, 190, 194–195, 297
Clark, Keith, 85
Clarke, Arthur C., 261
the Clash, ix, 42, 68, 193, 260
Clearmountain, Bob, 223, 228

Clement, Tom, 2–3, 22, 75, 98
Clinton, Hillary, 296
Cobain, Kurt, 146, 161, 298
Coffin Break, 147
Cold as the Clay (album), 258–259
Cole Rehearsal Studios, 179–181,
    238, 275
Colver, Edward, 40, 146
Concrete Blonde, 12, 151
Cook, Paul, 273
Cooper, Alice, 121
Copeland, Stewart, 242
Costello, Elvis, 63, 118, 120, 137
"Cowgirl in the Sand," 94
the Cramps, 177
Crash, Darby, 23–25, 28, 36, 49, 73,
    118
crossbuster logo, xi, 6–7, 37, 75, 98,
    113, 187, 285, 288
the Cult, 162, 274–276
the Cure, ix, 138
"Cyanide," 266
Cyrus, Billy Ray, 284–285

Dag Nasty, 134, 147, 176, 179, 181,
    190
the Damned, ix, 35, 55
"Damned to Be Free," 45–46
Dance with Me (album), 63
Danzig, Glenn, 179
The Dark Side of the Moon (album),
    135
Darwin, Charles, 265
"The Day the Earth Stalled,"
    265–266
the Dead Boys, 63, 83, 223, 228,
    295
"Dearly Beloved," 264
Death Row Records, 207–208
The Decline of Western Civilization
    (film), 24
Dedona, Paul, 64

"The Defense," 245
DeFranco, Tony, 214
Deftones, 216
DeLonge, Tom, 229
demo tapes, 11, 26, 222
Denney, Dix, 1, 83
Denney, John, 1
Des Barres, Michael, 273
the Descendents, 65, 109
The Descent of Man (book), 265
Desperate Teenage Lovedolls (film), 72
Details (magazine), 201
"The Devil in Stitches," 266
Devo, 35
"Dharma and the Bomb," 270
"Dichotomy," 61, 300–301
the Dickies, 1, 36, 135
Die Toten Hosen, 215
the Dils, 73
Dimkich, Mike
    background of, 272–276
    early years of, 272–276
    new material for, 289, 292–293
    replacing Hetson, 276–280
    tours and, 276–289
Dirksen, Dirk, 35
Dirty (album), 162
Discharge, 63
Dischord, 145, 166–167, 178
disco music, 45, 68, 260
discography, 308. *See also specific*
    albums
The Dissent of Man (album),
    264–266, 269
"Do the Paranoid Style," 294–295
"Do What You Want," 99, 196, 299
D.O.A., 76, 99, 123
"Dogs," 61
Don Kirshner's Rock Concert (TV
    show), 132
"Don't Be Afraid to Run," 259
Dookie (album), 152, 157, 166, 200

Down by Law, 140, 147, 149, 167
Downe, Taime, 214
Dragge, Fletcher, 210, 238, 256
"Drastic Actions," 8, 120–121, 146
Dream 6, 12
"Dream of Unity," 198
drugs, 67–68, 77, 80–83, 87–89,
    208–213
Duffy, Billy, 275
DVDs, 256, 259, 264
Dylan, Bob, 118

Echo, Aimee, 284
Eddie and the Subtitles, 121
Electric (album), 162
Electric Lady Studios, 193, 195
Emerson, Lake & Palmer, 62
EMI Studios, 162
"The Empire Strikes First," 252
The Empire Strikes First (album),
    251–262
The Empire Strikes First Tour, 255
"Empty Causes," 192
"The End," 291
"End of History," 295
End of the Century (album), 12, 132
Enema of the State (album), 229
"Epiphany," 242
Epitaph Records
    conflict within, 143, 166–174
    first employees of, 139–140
    growth of, 139–174, 196–200,
        207–213, 232–234, 299
    marketing/promoting, 99–100,
        158–160
    recording at, 79, 82, 88, 104,
        114–115, 126, 136–140,
        143–153
    releasing Bad Religion, 155
    relocating, 136–137
    responsibility for, 70, 114–115,
        126–127, 143, 148–149

returning to, 233–235, 240–241,
    246–247
signing bands with, 93–94,
    104–105, 136, 147–153,
    157–158
starting, 13, 33, 66, 70, 88
Escalante, Joe, 237
*Evolution, Monism, Atheism, and
    the Naturalist World-view*
    (dissertation), 248
the Exploited, 76

Fabia, Natalia, 287
"Faces of Grief," 295
the Faith, 177, 178
"Faith in God," 46
Falwell, Jerry, 8
Faster Pussycat, 214
Fat Mike, 104, 232, 256, 288
Faye, Kerry, 121
Fear, 1, 43, 134
Fear Factory, 297
Finch, Jennifer, 100–101
Finestone, Pete
    early years of, 35–45, 52–55,
        64–67, 73
    Grohl and, 105–106
    leaving Bad Religion, 127–130
    Lehrer and, 133
    reuniting with, 86, 97
    as roadie, 35–36, 41
    role of, 127–130, 175
    support from, 206
    tours and, 112–115
"Finite," 266
Fishbone, 83
Fishell, Steve, 88
the Fishermen, 127, 129
"Flat Earth Society," 301
Fleetwood Mac, 135
Flipside (fanzine), 102
Four, Bobby Fuller, 210

Four on the Floor (album), 181
Fowley, Kim, 274
Frampton, Peter, 62
Francis, Sage, 252
"Free Fallin'," 139
Freese, Josh, 238
"Frogger," 74, 96
"Fuck Armageddon . . . This Is
    Hell," 36, 39, 43–46, 93, 196,
    260
"Fuck You," 269–270
Fugazi, 144–145
Full Moon Fever (album), 139
Fun Lovin' Criminals, 227

Gallegos, Tim, 73–74, 85, 132
Gang Green, 86
Gardner, Suzi, 100
Garza, Carlos de la, 292
Geffen (record label), 179, 284
Generation X, 144
"Generator," 218, 221, 254, 266
Generator (album), 82, 136–139,
    147–148, 152, 160
Genesis, 63
George, Tommy, 75
Gerdler, John, 79–80, 87
the Germs, x, 8, 23–26, 35–36, 49,
    63, 73, 133, 166
Get Some (album), 284
Geza X, 73
Gibney, Dave, 280, 297
Gibson, William, 261
Ginn, Greg, 147
Ginsberg, Allen, 295
"Give Punk a Chance," 129
"Give You Nothing," 94
Glackin, Paul, 213–214
"God Song," 119, 206, 264
Gold Star Studios, 12
Goldberg, Danny, 152–154, 199
Goldenvoice, 111, 116, 128

Goldman, Davy, 19, 64
Government Issue, 178
Graffin, Allison, 282, 287
Graffin, Grant, 3, 15
Graffin, Greg
    books by, 91, 267, 281–282, 288
    children of, 269–270, 287
    Christmas songs and, 162,
        277–278
    college and, 56–59, 65, 69–74,
        78–80, 89–90, 115, 149, 165,
        215, 247–248
    conflicts and, 142–144, 165–175
    dissertation by, 248
    divorce and, 201–202
    early years of, ix, 2–23, 27–70
    evolutionary biology and, 248,
        265
    expedition and, 89–91
    as founding member, ix–xi, 1–23
    Hetson and, 71–73, 119,
        174–175, 180, 194–195
    hockey and, 214
    in home studio, 165, 190, 198,
        204–205
    influences on, 61–63, 118–120
    marriage of, 102, 287
    paleontology and, 58–59, 65,
        89–91, 115, 165
    popularity and, 26–30, 47–57,
        92–130, 140–156, 186–219,
        260–278
    in recording studio, 137–139,
        164–165, 222–226
    reflections of, 296–297, 299–301,
        303–304
    returning to Epitaph, 233–235,
        240
    reuniting with, 85–87, 92–98
    Rundgren and, 222–232
    singing national anthem,
        266–267

Graffin, Greg (*continued*)
  solo albums by, 201–206,
    214–215, 222, 258–259, 288
  tours and, 86–87, 100–102,
    111–115, 124–129, 140–142,
    148–152, 156, 181–190,
    197–202, 214–221, 229–236,
    248–249, 255–259, 263–267,
    270–272, 276–289, 297–301
  Vedder and, 116, 151, 189–190
  writing lyrics, 105–132, 190–207,
    227, 232, 241–247, 252,
    258–259, 265–269, 290–292
Graffin, Marcella, 7–9, 15–17
Graffin, Walter, 16
Grand Funk Railroad, 223
Grandmaster Recorders, 262
"The Gray Race," 191
The Gray Race (album), 190–194,
    197–199, 202–204, 248, 282,
    301–302
The Gray Race Tour, 198
"The Greatest Killer in History,"
    205
Green Day, 152, 157, 165–166, 172,
    183, 188, 199–200, 298
Greene, Ryan, 162
Greenspan, Eric, 154–155
Grisham, Jack, 31, 44, 85
Grohl, Dave, 105–106, 144
Group Sex (album), 47, 133
grunge music, 144, 161, 179
Guns N' Roses, 274
Gurewitz, Brett
  business savvy of, 157–160,
    170–173, 232–236, 253–254,
    261–263
  changing record labels, 152–156
  children of, 208, 242, 287
  Christmas songs and, 278
  college and, 78–79

conflicts and, 143–144, 166–175
divorce and, 208
drugs and, 77, 80–81, 83, 87–89,
    208–213
early years of, ix, 2–13, 17–70
first shows for, 21–23
as founding member, ix, 2–13,
    17–23
influences on, 23–25, 61–63,
    118–120, 160–162
leaving Bad Religion, 167–176,
    194, 196, 199
marriage of, 115, 287
offers for, 207–208
personal issues for, 207–213
popularity and, 92–116, 140–141
as recording engineer, 79–83,
    87–89, 93–97, 104–116,
    135–136
in recording studio, 137–139,
    162–163
reflections of, 301, 303
in rehab, 210–212
replacing, 174–176, 180–183,
    186
responsibilities of, 70, 114–115,
    126–127, 143, 148–149
reuniting with, 92–98, 233–248
tours and, 86–87, 100–102,
    112–115, 124–126, 148–152,
    156, 234, 248, 270–271
writing lyrics, 117–130, 160–162,
    196, 234–247, 251–252,
    265–269, 290–292, 295–297
Gurewitz, Emiko Belle, 287
Gurewitz, Frida, 208
Gurewitz, Gina, 287
Gurewitz, Max, 208, 242
Gurewitz, Nico Moon, 287
Gurewitz, Richard, 33–34, 69, 80,
    82

Hameron, 177

Hampton, Michael, 176

"The Handshake," 164

Harris, Emmylou, 88

Harrison, Nigel, 273

Hatfield, Juliana, 180

Hawk, Tommy, 53

Hawk, Tony, 111

Heaps, Danny, 167, 217

heavy metal music, 19, 282–284, 286

Hell Hole, 8–13, 42, 96, 229, 303

Hellbound Hayride, 298

"Hello It's Me," 223

Hendrix, Jimi, 193, 230, 237

Herrera, Tess, 298

Hesse, Herman, 5

Hetson, Greg
    Bentley and, 84–85, 115
    early years of, 22, 26, 45, 59–60
    Graffin and, 71–73, 119, 174–175, 180, 194–195
    hockey and, 214
    leaving Bad Religion, 268, 271–272, 276–277, 279, 285
    with other bands, 45, 84–85, 119, 174–175, 181, 190, 194–195
    personal issues for, 271–272
    in recording studio, 194–195
    replacing, 92–93, 276–280
    role of, 115, 129, 134–137, 180–181
    tours and, 100–101, 164, 234, 271–272
    writing lyrics, 146–147, 194–195, 204

High City Miles, 275

"The Hippy Killers," 206

Hofstadter, Richard, 294

Holland, Jolie, 258

"Honest Goodbye," 264

"Hooray For Me," 160

Hoppus, Mark, 229

Hot Water Music, 254

How Could Hell Be Any Worse?
    (album), 40, 43–47, 59, 65, 71, 81, 86, 94, 98–99, 107, 120, 146–147, 181, 196, 199, 203, 229, 259, 260, 272

H.R., 148

Hunter, Ian, 274

Hunter Ronson Band, 274

Hüsker Dü, 97

"I Fought the Law," 210

"I Love My Computer," 227

"I Saw the Light," 223

"I Want to Conquer the World," 108

"I Won't Say Anything," 265

Iggy Pop, 144

Ignition (album), 149

"Imagine," 244

"Incomplete," 163

"Individual," 164

"Infected," 160–163, 253, 276

Insted, 129

Interscope Records, 207–208

Into the Unknown (album), 64–70, 72–76, 96, 107–109, 118, 130, 146–147, 259, 266–268, 289, 301

Iovine, Jimmy, 207–208

Iraq invasion, 150, 250–251, 255

"Iron Man," 19

"It's Only Over When . . . ," 61, 64

"It's Reciprocal," 198

Ivers, Peter, 27, 59

Jacked, 276

Jackson, Michael, 80

the Jam, 35, 63

Jane's Addiction, 274, 283
jazz music, 45, 64, 237
Jealous Again (album), 181
Jethro Tull, 42, 62–63, 77
Jobs, Steve, 68
John, Elton, 63
Jones, Mick, 272
Jones, Steve, 272–275
Joseph, Lee, 139
Joy Division, 60, 61
Jughead's Revenge, 140
Junkyard, 147, 179, 186

Kaulkin, Andy, 245
Kerouac, Jack, 160
The Kids Are Alright (album), 291
"The Kids Are Alt-Right," 290–291
Kimball, Ronnie, 185, 198, 205, 271, 297
King Crimson, 13, 62
KISS, 62, 177
Knight, Suge, 207
Kramer, Wayne, 163, 213
Kraut, 76
Kuehn, Greg, 60
Kyuss, 261

L7, 93, 100–101
Lagwagon, 255, 298
"Land of Competition," 94
Land of the Free? (album), 261
the Last, 121, 134
"Latch Key Kids," 36
Late Night with Conan O'Brien (TV show), 156
Lavette, Darren, 151
Leave It to Beaver (TV show), 134
"Leave Mine to Me," 164, 248
Led Zeppelin, 18, 62, 153, 193
Lee, Bruce, 73
"The Legendary Starbolt," 82
Lehrer, Chett, 73

Lehrer, Keith "Lucky," 22–23, 26, 64, 73, 86–87, 133–134, 213
Lennon, John, 25, 138, 244, 247
Leonard, Gary, 23, 35
"Let Them Eat War," 252
Let's Go (album), 157, 159, 164, 200, 247
Liberal Animation (album), 104
Life Won't Wait (album), 208
Lindberg, Jim, 163
"Lint," 163
Litt, Scott, 180
Little Kings, 88, 138
Look Homeward, Angel (book), 160–161
Lord-Alge, Chris, 205
Lord-Alge, Tom, 205
Lords of the New Church, 83
"Los Angeles Is Burning," 252–253
"Lose Your Head," 302
L.O.S.T., 129
Love Canal, 76
Lyman, Kevin, 215

MacKaye, Alec, 177
MacKaye, Ian, 145, 177–178, 180
Mad Society, 51
Madonna, 173
Mahoney, Jerry, 98
The Making of the Atomic Bomb (book), 217
"Man with a Mission," 152, 253
Manic Hispanic, 298
Mankey, Earle, 12
Mankey, Jim, 12, 39
Marginal Man, 178
Marino, Rick, 217, 287–288, 297
Mark, Tom and Travis Show Tour, 229–230
"Marked," 163
Markey, David, 72
Martin, Wrye, 74

Mary Suicide, 283

Mason, Cathy, 284–285

the Masque, 76

Maurer, Greta, 72, 94, 102

Maximum Rocknroll (fanzine), 49, 66, 102, 145

MC5, 163, 213

McCartney, Paul, 138, 247

McDonald, Steve, 72

Meat Loaf, 223

Meatmen, 179

the Melvins, 148, 261

Metallica, 105, 275

Miller, Jamie
  audition of, 285–286
  background of, 283–284
  early years of, 283–284
  marriage of, 284
  new material for, 289, 292–293
  replacing Wackerman, 283–287
  style of, 286–287
  tours and, 284–289

"Millport," 288

Millport (album), 288

Ministry, 138

Minor Threat, 147, 176, 178, 180–182, 283

Minutemen, 97

Mr. Smith Goes to Washington (film), 131

"Modern Man," 119

Mommy's Little Monster (album), 147

the Monkees, 230

Moore, Angelo, 83

the Morlocks, 82

Morris, Keith, 21–25, 82–85, 100, 119, 133, 222, 281

Morrison, Jim, 291

Mosher, Tim, 275, 276

Muir, Mike, 52, 54–55

Mullen, Brendan, 76

music videos, 110, 137–138, 151, 183, 259

"My Sanity," 293

"My War," 147

Naked Raygun, 274

Napolitano, Johnette, 12–13, 151, 163

Nazz, 222

Nelson, Jeff, 177–178

Nelson, Ricky, 23

Nevermind (album), 147, 152, 162

The New America (album), 226–233, 240–241, 259

The New America Tour, 231–235, 259

"New Dark Ages," 261, 262, 264

"New Leaf," 36, 75

New Maps of Hell (album), 260–264

New Wave music, 2, 27, 120

New Wave Theatre (TV show), 27, 59, 259, 294

New York Dolls, 223

Nicolai, Lena Sharon, 215

Nietzsche, Friedrich, 99

Nirvana, 144–147, 152–153, 162–163, 172, 200, 298

Nixon, Dale, 147

"No Control," 107–108

No Control (album), 82, 106–111, 114–119, 120–122, 129–130, 248, 268, 289, 300–301

No Control Tour, 125

"No Substance," 206

No Substance (album), 204–205, 213, 215, 222, 259

No Substance Tour, 214

"Nobody Listens," 192

NOFX, 104–105, 127, 149, 162, 167, 200, 216, 232, 247, 255, 299

Nugent, Ted, 177

Oakley, Berry, 230–231
Ocasek, Ric, 3, 192–195
Oddities, Abnormalities and Curiosities
    (album), 190
OFF!, 281
the Offspring, 149, 157–160,
    164–168, 171–173, 183,
    199–200, 208, 227, 298–299
Oki-Dog, 36, 50–55, 100
"Oligarchy," 27, 31, 45
Olson, Everett C., 89
Olson, Steve, 267
the Omega Band, 2
On Golden Pond (film), 46
Only Theatre of Pain (album), 47, 63
Operation Ivy, 163, 166
"Operation Rescue," 119
Oppenheimer, Robert, 205
Orwell, George, 252
Overkill, 204
Oz Factor (album), 204

Pacifica Studios, 75, 80–81
Paine, Thomas, 291
"The Paranoid Style in American
    Politics," 294
"Part II (The Numbers Game),"
    98–100
"Part III," 36, 45, 59–60, 99, 272
"Part IV (The Index Fossil)," 99
the Patti Smith Group, 223
Pearl Jam, 123, 151, 189–190
Pennywise, 127, 136, 163, 167, 210,
    238, 255–256, 261, 299
Perialas, Alex, 204, 205
Perkins, Jayne, 16
Perspective Sound, 64
"Pessimistic Lines," 97, 266
Petty, Tom, 105, 139, 253
Pietasters, 208
Pink Floyd, 61, 135, 185
Pirates of the Caribbean (film), 138

"Pity," 46
the Plugz, x
"Poison," 121
"Politics," 3, 26, 31
Polypterus Studios, 190, 204
Popper, Karl, 295
*Population Wars: A New Perspective
    on Competition and Coexistence*
    (book), 282, 288
Preslar, Lyle, 177–178
Presley, Elvis, 73, 131
the Primates, 82
Prince, 230
Priority Records, 207–208
The Process of Belief (album), 241,
    244–247, 251, 261, 264
The Process of Belief Tour, 248
"The Profane Rights of Man," 291
the Professionals, 273
prog rock music, 61–63, 68–69, 237
"Prove It," 241
Public Image Limited, 60, 68
Public Service (album), 146
Punk in Drublic (album), 247
Punk Planet (fanzine), 230
punk rock
    altering future of, 92–103
    changing demographics of,
        165–166
    early punk rock, ix–xi, 1–2
    mainstreaming of, 144, 153–157,
        207, 298–299
    popularity of, ix–xi
    reaching plateau, 203
"Punk Rock Song," 192, 206, 248
Punk Rock Songs (album), 248
Pyramid Sound, 204

the Quarks, 2, 18
Queens of the Stone Age, 261
"The Quickening," 254
Quiet Riot, 19

Rabid, Jack, 75, 206
Rachtman, Riki, 214
Rage Against the Machine, 162, 163
"Raise Your Voice!," 215, 222
Raitt, Bonnie, 153
Ramone, Dee Dee, 132, 193, 270
Ramone, Joey, 3
Ramone, Tommy, 236
the Ramones, ix, 3, 12, 18, 23, 34–35, 62, 107, 111, 132, 230, 232, 237, 298
Rancid, 157, 159–160, 164–167, 173, 200, 208, 216, 247, 253, 299
Raw Power (fanzine), 19
Reagan, Ronald, 46
"Recipe for Hate," 151, 156, 184
Recipe for Hate (album), 149–152, 155, 196, 239, 264, 301
Red Hot Chili Peppers, 115, 138
Redd Kross/Red Cross, 71, 72, 144, 146
reggae-style music, 237, 242
Reign in Blood (album), 162
religion, 5–9, 15
R.E.M., 180–181
REO Speedwagon, 76
the Replacements, 180
Repo Man (film), 134
"The Resist Stance," 265
Reverend Horton Heat, 216
Rhoads, Randy, 19
Rhodes, Richard, 217
Ribbed (album), 105
"Ridin' the Storm Out," 76
Rights of Man (book), 291
Rise Against, 285
Rissmiller, Jim, 105
Robinson, John Talbot, 65
Robo, 134
Rock Against Bush (album), 256

Rodney on the ROQ (radio show), 25, 26, 273
Rogerson, Roger, 22–23
Rolling Stone (magazine), 228
the Rolling Stones, 230
Rollins, Henry, 176
Ronson, Mick, 274
Rove, Karl, 251
Rude, Dick, 134
Rumbo Recorders, 162
Rumours (album), 135
Rundgren, Todd, 222–232
"Runnin' Fast," 72

S&M Airlines (album), 105
Saccharine Trust, 35
"Salvation," 164
Samhain, 179
"Sanity," 121
Santana, Carlos, 177, 221
Sax, Doug, 135
Saxon, Sky, 82
Say, Bob, 38
Scarface (film), 209
Schayer, Bobby
    audition of, 134–136
    background of, 131–134
    collaborating on material, 190, 194
    conflicts and, 167–168
    as drum tech, 281
    leaving Bad Religion, 235–236
    Lehrer and, 133–134
    in recording studio, 137–139, 162–163, 204, 226
    replacing, 236–238
    shoulder injury of, 235–236
    tours and, 140, 230–231
Schayer, Steve, 132–133
Schloss, Zander, 134
Scream, 105–106, 144
the Screamers, x, 61, 83

Sears, Colin, 134
the Seeds, 82
Semaphore, 106
Senses Fail, 298
"Sensory Overload," ix, x, 3
the Sex Pistols, ix, 23, 34, 42, 166, 237, 248, 273, 298
Sham 69, 21–23, 206
Shaw, Greg, 25, 79, 82
Shaw, Suzy, 79, 82, 83, 89
"Shut Down," 8
Siddhartha (book), 6
Silent Thunder, 177
Simon & Garfunkel, 246
"Sinister Rouge," 254
Siouxsie and the Banshees, ix
Skateboard (film), 18
skateboarding videos, 111, 117
"Skyscraper," 264
Slater, Kelly, 110–111
Slaughterhouse Five (book), 62
"Slaves," 8, 27, 146
Slayer, 162
Slovak, Hillel, 115
"Slumber," 248
Smalley, Dave, 147
Smash (album), 157, 160, 164, 171, 200
Smear, Pat, 23, 73
"Smells Like Teen Spirit," 144
Smith, Patti, 223
SNFU, 188, 214
Snot, 284
Snot Recording Studios, 80
Social Distortion, 21–22, 28, 35, 47, 100, 147
"Someone to Believe," 265
"Sonic Reducer," 228
Sonic Youth, 97, 153, 162
Sony Music, 154–156, 197–199, 248
"Sorrow," 241–246, 264, 276
Soto, Steve, 22, 76, 298

Soul Asylum, 183
Souls at Zero, 284
Sound City, 251
Sounds Good Imports, 79–81, 88, 93
the Source Family, 82
Southern Continents Tour, 266
Sparks, 12
Sparks, Donita, 100
the Specials, 216
Spector, Phil, 12
Spit Stix, 134
theSTART, 284, 292
State of Alert, 176
"The State of the End of the Millennium Address," 205–206
Stern, Adam, 43
Stern, Mark, 43
Stern, Shawn, 43
Steve Jones Band, 274–275
Stevens, Cat, 17
Stevenson, Bill, 109
Stiff Little Fingers, 206
Stinson, Tommy, 180
Stipe, Michael, 180
Stocks, Greg "Shakes," 298
Stradlin, Izzy, 274
Strait, Lynn, 284
"Stranger Than Fiction," 160, 162, 166, 183
Stranger Than Fiction (album), 157, 160–164, 170, 173, 183, 186, 196, 199, 208, 213, 218, 224, 237–238, 248
Stranger Than Fiction Tour, 188
"A Streetkid Named Desire," 227
"Streets of America," 302
"Struck a Nerve," 151, 156, 206, 301
Strummer, Joe, 118
Studio 3, 291
Studio 9, 10–12, 42, 82

Sublime, 46
"Suffer," 94, 138, 161
Suffer (album), 82, 94, 97–107,
    114–119, 122, 124, 129–130,
    142, 151, 200, 203, 241, 254,
    266, 268, 272, 285, 288–289,
    297–299
Suffer Tour, 100–101, 272
Suicidal Tendencies, 40, 52, 238,
    255, 284
Sunset Sound, 291–292
"Supersonic," 241
Swaggart, Jimmy, 8

"Talk About Suffering," 259
Taupin, Bernie, 118
Teen Idles, 177
Teenage Wrist, 292
"Television," 163
Teller, Edward, 205
Tenacious D, 262
terrorist attacks, 244–247,
    250–251, 262
Testament, 204
"Tested," 198
Tested (album), 198
Thelonious Monster, 82
"Them and Us," 192, 301
the Things, 82
Thoreau, Henry David, 5
Thrasher (magazine), 99–100
"Time and Disregard," 62
"Tiny Voices," 164
"To Another Abyss," 252
Tom Petty and the Heartbreakers,
    253
Tony Hawk's Pro Skater 2
    (video game), 111
Too Free Stooges, 134
Tovar, Gary, 111
Track Record, 39, 43
"True North," 269

True North (album), 268–272, 290,
    297
True North Tour, 271–272
Trump, Donald, 290–296
T.S.O.L., 31, 35, 40, 44, 60–63, 66,
    84–85, 129
Tuch, Maggie, 100, 115, 208
"Turn Your Back on Me," 265
Turner, Bryan, 207

U2, 105, 193
Ugly Kid Joe, 284
Uncle Rehearsal Studio, 93–95,
    115, 134–137
University of Sound Arts, 79
Unwritten Law, 204
Up in Smoke (film), 73, 132

Vai, Steve, 237
"Valley Girl," 1
the Vandals, 106, 227, 237–238
Vans Warped Tour, 215–218,
    263–264, 299
Vassos, Michaela, 142, 164
Vaughn, Peter, 89
Vedder, Eddie, 116, 151, 189–190
Verbinski, Gore, 88, 137–138, 151,
    183
Verne, Jules, 261
video games, 111, 117
Ving, Lee, 1
Vitalogy Tour, 189–190
"The Voice of God Is
    Government," 39, 45,
    205–206
Void, 178
Vonnegut, Kurt, 62, 160
Vox Populi Tour, 288

Wackerman, Brooks
    audition of, 236, 238
    background of, 237–239

Wackerman, Brooks (*continued*)
  collaborating on material,
    242–243, 253–254
  early years of, 236–237
  leaving Bad Religion, 282
  in recording studio, 253–254
  replacing, 283–287
  replacing Schayer, 236–238
  tours and, 248, 255–256, 262,
    280–283
Wackerman, Chad, 237
The Wall (album), 135
Wall of Sound, 12
Wallace, Andy, 162–163, 170
Waltrip, Darrell, 188
Warped Tour, 215–218, 248, 255,
  263–264, 284, 298–299
Wasted Youth, 73, 84, 100
"Watch It Die," 151
"Watching the Detectives," 120
Wave (album), 223
We Got Power (fanzine), 72
the Weakerthans, 258
Weathered Statues (album), 60
Weezer, 179, 192, 194
the Weirdos, x, 1, 34, 61, 83, 135
We're an American Band (album),
  223
"We're Only Gonna Die," 36, 39,
  45–46, 93, 181
Westbeach Recorders, 80–88,
  95–96, 104–105, 109–110, 122,
  135–139, 149, 162, 239, 247
Westlake Recorders, 80–81
"What Can You Do?," 266
White, Jack, 281
White Frogs, 220, 221

White Trash, Two Heebs and a Bean
  (album), 149, 247
the Who, 291
Wild in the Streets (album), 47
Wilson, Brian, 235
Wilson, Thom, 63–64, 80
Wolf, Steve, 105
Wolfe, Thomas, 160–161
Wollard, Chris, 254
Wonder, Stevie, 18
"Won't Somebody," 264, 265
"World War III," 8
Wrathchild America, 284
"Wrong Way Kids," 266

X, x, 29, 61, 63, 133

Yard Trauma, 139
Yellow Submarine (album), 17
Yes, 62, 77
"Yesterday," 74
Yohannan, Tim, 49
"You," 111, 277
"You Are the Government," 154
Young, Neil, 94
Youth Brigade, 43

Zappa, Frank, 1, 237
Zerr, Edward M., 15
Ziskrout, Jay
  early years of, 2–12, 19–23,
    26–41, 44–45
  as founding member, 2–12,
    19–23
  leaving Bad Religion, 40–41
  in marketing/promotions,
    158–159